The Seven Fruits of the Land of Israel

with their Mystical & Medicinal Properties

The Wholesome Spirited Cookbook Nutrition & Health Series
with Torah Teachings & Recipes

MENORAH BOOKS

HONG KONG · JERUSALEM · USA

The Seven Fruits of the Land of Israel
with their Mystical & Medicinal Properties
The Wholesome Spirited Cookbook Nutrition & Health Series with Torah Teachings & Recipes

שבעת המנים של ארץ ישראל
עם סגולותיהם המקובלות והרפואיות

Published by MENORAH BOOKS

Copyright © September 2014

EDITING: Chaim Natan Firszt, Ashirah Yosefah, Ariela Kaplan Mendlowitz

ART WORK: Jessica Vaiselberg

COVER DESIGN: Ruth Simchi and Gal Narunsky based on art work by Jessica Vaiselberg

TYPESETTING: Chana Wax

GRAPHIC ART: Ruth Simchi

TYPOGRAPHICAL ADJUSTMENTS: Gal Narunsky

ISBN: 978-1-940516-03-5

First Edition: Printed in Jerusalem

FOR ORDERS:

Internet: www.menorah-books.com
Email: orders@menorah-books.com

MENORAH BOOKS

The Seven Fruits of the Land of Israel
with their Mystical & Medicinal Properties

Midreshet B'erot Bat Ayin:
Holistic Torah for Women on the Land
www.berotbatayin.org

Translation of Sources

English translations of Hebrew Bible verses are based on
The Jerusalem Bible, with the author's adaptions.
English translations of Talmud is based on *Contents of the Soncino
Babylonian Talmud,* Translated into English with
notes, glossary and indices under the editorship of
Rabbi Dr. I. Epstein B.a,, Ph.d., D. Lit.
The Soncino Press, London, with the author's adaptions.
English Translations of other Hebrew texts are the author's.

Please Protect the Sanctity of this Book

This book contains quotations from the Torah. Please treat it with
respect and do not take this book into places that are impure, such as
a bathroom.

Table of Contents

Vitality • Stimulate Blood Circulation • Highly Restorative • Strengthen the Bones • Rambam on the Health Benefits of Figs • Remove Warts • Alleviate Coughs • The Eternity of the Torah – Compared to Figs • Figs –The Cause of Downfall and Rectification • Table of Correspondence between Fruits, Soul Part and Character • Health benefits of Fig leaves • Purifying from Death • Figs before Grapes • A Taste of Kabbalah – Light, Shells, Souls and Fruit • Dreaming of a Fig Tree

POMEGRANATES ~ רִמּוֹן *Punica Granatum*
HOD ~ הוֹד (SPLENDOR/MAJESTY) 228

The Song of Pomegranates • Nutrition Facts and Information about Pomegranates • Pomegranates correspond to Hod • Easily Adaptive to Various Conditions • Hod and the Immune System • Separating Sweet from Bitter • The Pomegranate and the Star of David • Pomegranates Boost the Immune System • A Natural Skin Treatment • Balancing the Hormones • Rambam on the Health Benefits of Pomegranates • Ancient Symbol of Healing • Preventing and Treating Heart Ailments • Preventing and Curing Cancer • The Pomegranate in Judaica • The Pomegranate's Mitzvah Seeds • The Prayers of the Sinners • The Good Deeds of the Wicked Compared to Pomegranates • The Pomegranate's Silent Torah • Pure Pleasure of Pomegranate Seeds • A Taste of Kabbalah – Outer Garment for Eternal Life • Dreaming of Pomegranates

OLIVE OIL ~ זַיִת שֶׁמֶן *Olea Europaea*
YESOD ~ יְסוֹד (FOUNDATION)

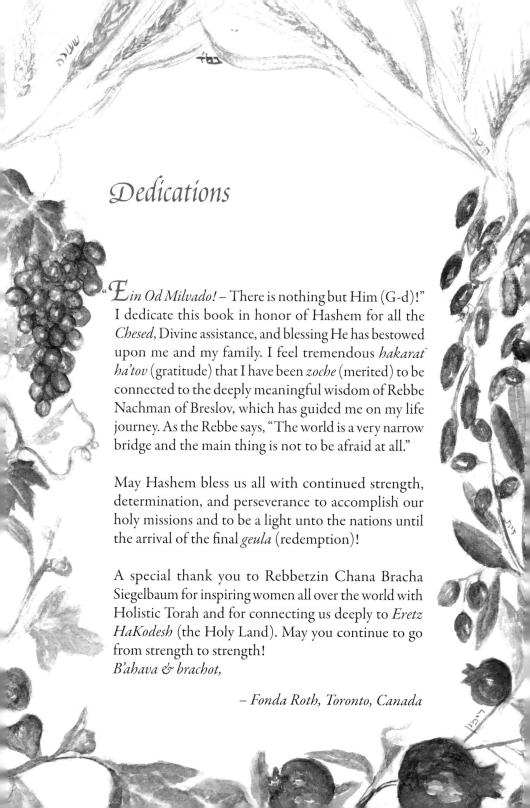

Dedications

"*Ein Od Milvado!* – There is nothing but Him (G-d)!" I dedicate this book in honor of Hashem for all the *Chesed*, Divine assistance, and blessing He has bestowed upon me and my family. I feel tremendous *hakarat ha'tov* (gratitude) that I have been *zoche* (merited) to be connected to the deeply meaningful wisdom of Rebbe Nachman of Breslov, which has guided me on my life journey. As the Rebbe says, "The world is a very narrow bridge and the main thing is not to be afraid at all."

May Hashem bless us all with continued strength, determination, and perseverance to accomplish our holy missions and to be a light unto the nations until the arrival of the final *geula* (redemption)!

A special thank you to Rebbetzin Chana Bracha Siegelbaum for inspiring women all over the world with Holistic Torah and for connecting us deeply to *Eretz HaKodesh* (the Holy Land). May you continue to go from strength to strength!
B'ahava & brachot,

— *Fonda Roth, Toronto, Canada*

'In loving memory of our parents and in-laws Mario (Meir) and Trudi Erteschick, who truly treasured the Land of Israel and her fruits.'

– *Mirjam and Sally Vainer*
Holte, Denmark (Parents of the Author)

'To our healthy happy Israeli family.'

– *Jack and Noreen Siegelbaum,*
Montvale, New Jersey (Parents-in-law of the Author)

'In honor of my dear friend Rebbetzin Chana Bracha Siegelbaum; I treasure the time I have spent at her Holistic Midrasha soaking up her Torah with that special Land of Israel flavor. "Give her of the fruit of her hands; and let her deeds praise her in the gates."'

– *Yehudis Schamroth, Ramat Beit Shemesh, Israel*

'For continued *hatzlacha* for B'erot; may we all be *zoche* to see the fruits of our labor and see Moshiach now!'

– *Best wishes, The Meshchaninov Family*
Spring Valley, New York

'Dedicated to the memory of my parents. S. Lawerence and Rose Atkins.'

– *Yehudit Chaya Atkins, Atlanta, Georgia*

'In beloved memory of my parents Label ben Gadolia and Tsvia bat Menachem.'

– *Karen K. Moss, Memphis, Tennessee*

'In honor of my parents Zeev and Vivian Kazmirik.'

– *Ester Karaguilla, Highland Lakes, Florida*

'*I*n loving memory of my parents, Yechiel ben Yitzchak HaCohen and Genesia bat Moshe, Dr. Eli and Grace Katz, and their generous spirit.'

– Karen Katz, Toronto, Canada

'*L*'*iluy Nishmas* Dov Beryl (C. Fishel) ben Yaakov Kletter.'

– Fraidel Leah Kletter, North Milford, Pennsylvania

'*L*'*iluy Nishmas* Eli ben Zvi *z"l*, may his memory be for a blessing.'

– Susan Zilberman, Manhattan, New York

'*I*n memory of Rivka bat Chaim, and for the fulfillment of our higher selves.'

– Leah Morris, Hollywood, Florida

'*I*n memory of my great grandmother Ava M. Goode.'

– Elizabeth D. Dickerson, Dallas Texas

'*I*n honor of Ziporah Farber, תְּהֵא נִשְׁמָתָהּ צְרוּרָה בִּצְרוֹר הַחַיִּים – May her soul be bound in the bond of Life!'

– Alona Sadovski Zibell, Montreal, Canada

'*D*edicated to Shays & Sorah Chasha Greenberg, in recognition of their Tu b'Shevat Engagement.'

– Naomi Greenberg, West Hempstead, New York

'*I*n honor of the marriage of my daughter, Julia to Daniel.'

– Esther Bortnick, Toronto, Canada

'*F*or the complete *refuah shelema* of Solange Soulika bat Fany.'

– Rabbi Shimon and Caroline Lea Elkeslassy Montreal, Canada

בע"ה

הרב דניאל כהן

רב היישוב

בת עין

October 14, 2013 / יום שני י' חשון תשע"ד

I have known Rebbetzin Chana Bracha Siegelbaum for many years to be a true woman of valour, with *yir'at shamayim* and dedication to Torah. She has built a very special place of deep Torah learning for women with true *mesirut nefesh*. Now she has also produced her second book – a beautiful and deeply researched work about the Seven Fruits of Israel. I have reviewed the *halachot* written in this book and have found them to be correct and accurately worded. I would like to add that in spite of the special holiness of the Seven Species and their general priority when it comes to blessings, when one prefers to eat one fruit before the other because of health reasons or a preferred order of menu, one may do so. The laws of the priority of the Seven Species only pertain to the case when the fruits are being eaten together.

May the whole Jewish people merit soon to be rooted again in their Land and eat from its fruits together,

Rav Daniel Kohn

Rabbi of the village of Bat Ayin

בת עין ד.נ. צפון יהודה 90913 ✠ טל. 02-9932478. לשכה: 02-9934435

בס"ד

Rabbi Avraham Greenbaum

POB 50037 Jerusalem, 91500 Israel
Tel: (972-2) 5370064 Fax: (972-2) 5000512
E-mail: rebavraham@azamra.org

January 27, 2012 / יום שישי ג' שבט תשע"ב

To Whom It May Concern

The Seven Fruits of the Land of Israel: Mystical & Medicinal Properties with Recipes for the Native Species of the Land of Israel by Rebbetzin Chana Bracha Siegelbaum is a fascinating, informative book based on extensive research and containing many original ideas.

I highly recommend this well-written, innovative interdisciplinary work. The book makes connections between the most diverse modalities of knowledge, from Biblical, Talmudic, Kabbalistic, and Jewish legal scholarship to modern medical research. In addition, the writing is interspersed with original recipes, and practical tips relating to the Seven Fruits of Israel.

The book is filled with the redemptive spirit of the Land of Israel, and will appeal to a wide range of readers, including Jewish educators, those with a special interest in the Land of Israel, nutritionists and health-care professionals, as well as anyone interested in discovering and trying out new recipes. The book is suitable for both Jews and non-Jews.

Avraham Greenbaum

Rabbi Avraham Greenbaum
Director, AZAMRA

בן ציון רבינוביץ
בלאאמו"ר זצוקללה"ה
מביאלא
עיה"ק ירושלים תובב"א

9 Kislev, 5774
Tzefat, Israel

I hereby offer my recommendations for Midreshet B'erot Bat Ayin, which educates women in Torah and fear of Heaven, in the path of our tradition, handed down throughout the generations. I have recently received the manuscript produced therein, *The Seven Fruits of the Land of Israel with their Mystical & Medicinal Properties* which discusses in great detail the importance of the Seven Species for which the Land of Israel is praised. It describes the unique qualities of each of the species, their medicinal value, and how they can be used in the preparation of healthy food suitable for everyone.

The importance of this book can be understood based on Rabbeinu Yonah's *Sha'arei Teshuvah* (3:13), in which he writes, "The mitzvah of *chesed* (loving-kindness) can be fulfilled both through charity and through deed. We are obligated to seek the benefit of others, by applying great effort (soul-labor) to help rectify them." From here we see that a book such as this, well prepared and clearly presented, is an act of chesed. It helps people understand and achieve the full benefit of the Seven Species, with all their healing and nutritional properties.

In the writings of our Sages, and the other holy books that followed them, we see the importance of the Seven Species, and their superiority to other kinds of produce. Their blessing takes precedence to the blessings for other foods, and we recite a unique three-fold blessing after eating them. These are the foods through which the Land of Israel is praised, as is written, "Hashem your G*d is bringing you into a good land... a land of wheat, and barley, and vine, and fig tree, and pomegranate; a land of olive oil and honey." The Land of Israel is praised with the foods that give strength to the people of Israel.

It is a great merit to explain the importance of these species, and the importance and praise of the Land of Israel. This is especially true in our times, when many people unfortunately seek to degrade the Holy Land. How much greater is the merit of those who seek to settle the Land, and involve themselves in the special agricultural mitzvos of the Land of Israel. They are indeed praiseworthy.

May Hashem grant you serenity and peace of mind. May He fulfill all your wishes for good, and may we merit the complete redemption and the coming of our Righteous Redeemer, soon and in our days.

I sign with earnest hopes for your success in all matters, both spiritual and material, and with heartfelt blessings

B.S.M. Ben Tzion Rabinowitz
of Biala

בן ציון רבינוביץ

בלאאמו"ר זצוקללה"ה

מביאלא

עיה"ק ירושלים תובב"א

בס"ד פעיה"ק צפת ת"ו יום ג' בשבת ט' כסלו תשע"ד

באתי בזה להמליץ על **מדרשית בארות בת עין** שמחנכות תלמידות לתורה ויר"ש בדרך המסורה לנו מדור דור, והלום קבלתי הקונטרס שנתחבר ע"י '**שבעת המינים של ארץ ישראל עם סגולותיהם המקובלים והרפואיים**' המבואר בהרחבה חשיבותם של פירות שנשתבחה בהם ארץ ישראל, מעלתם ותכונותיהם המועילות לרפואה והאופנים שאפשר להכין מהם מאכלים ראויים ובריאים לכל אדם.

וביסוד הדברים כתב הרבינו יונה בספרו שערי תשובה [שער ג' יג]: וגמילות חסדים בין בגופו בין בממונו, כי חייב אדם לטרוח בדרישת טוב לעמו ולשקוד בעמל נפשו על תקנת חברו, עכ"ק. והמבואר מדבריו שאפשר לקיים גמילות חסדים בגופו ע"י שמסייע לחברו ונותנים לפניו ספר מסודר כשולחן הערוך לידע תועלת הפירות הללו ואיך לנצל את תכונותיהם הבריאים והמזונים של פירות אלו.

ובחז"ל ובספרים הק' מצינו מעלת וחשיבות פירות אלו באשר שונים הם למעליותא מפירות דעלמא, ואף לגבי ברכה יש להם דין קדימה ואחריהם מברכים ברכת מעין שלוש, והן שבח ארץ ישראל כדכתיב [דברים ח ז]: כי ה"א מביאך אל ארץ טובה וגו' ארץ חיטה ושעורה וגפן ותאנה ורימון ארץ זית שמן ודבש. היינו שארץ ישראל משתבחת בפירות אלו ונותנים כח לישראל.

וזכות גדולה היא לבאר מעלתם ומעלת ושבח ארץ ישראל, ובפרט כאשר ל"ע ישנם המבקשים להוציא דיבת הארץ, ומרובה מידה טובה כשמתעסקים ביישוב ארץ והמצוות התלויות בה ואשרי חלקם.

יעזור השי"ת שתזכו להרחבת הדעת ומנוחת הנפש וימלא השי"ת משאלות לבכם לטובה, ונזכה בקרוב לגאולה השלימה בביאת גואל צדק בב"א.

כ"ד המעתיר ומצפה להצלחתכם בכל הענינים לטובה ברו"ג,

הכו"ח ברחשי ברכה והצלחה,

Acknowledgements

*W*ith the greatest gratitude I joyfully thank our blessed Creator, for having ingathered me to His Holy Land. With an overflowing heart I rejoice in the privilege of having received a piece of the Land of Israel where we can grow her holy fruits. In partnership with my devoted husband, Mechael Chaim, we endeavor to be worthy custodians of our plot in the Judean Hills, and together sprout the seedlings of Messiah. I am grateful to my parents, Drs. Salomon and Mirjam Vainer for their blessings, encouragement and pride in our labor of love. Thank you to my wonderful enthusiastic students throughout the years, who learned, picked and prepared the fruits of the Land with me. I appreciate the awesome oil paintings by Jessica Vaiselberg, the artwork by Michal Glaberson and Carina Rock, the graphic art by Brianne Rina Eliav, the editing by Devora Gila Berkowitz and Sara-Malka Laderman, the type-setting by Chana Wax, the graphic design by Ruth Simchi, the photos by Shoshana Shier and Rivka Levron who also checked scientific references – all dedicated alumnae students. I thank Sarah Alper for helping with the nutritional information. Without the faithful and professional work of all these talented women, this book would not have been possible. Through revealed Divine supervision Hashem led me to Menorah Books whose spirit of *tikun olam* (rectifying the world) made me feel immediately at home. I would like to thank the staff of Menorah Books with respect to final editing, design and layout. I especially thank the director Ashirah Yosefah for her kind and professional guidance, bringing this book to its final actualization. More than anyone, I thank my dear husband Rav Mechael Chaim, MD, for his endless support, last-minute editing, and willingness to make his own dinner because his wife was busy writing a cookbook! Together we are exhilarated to live in the Messianic era and experience the fulfillment of the prophesy of return: "For as the seed of peace, the vine shall give her fruit, the earth shall give her crop, and the heavens shall give their dew; and I will cause the remnant of this people to inherit all these blessings."[1] May we merit witnessing the unfolding of "the seed of peace" to blossom and produce the fruits of the Tree of Life!

Introduction

*B*y Hashem's blessing, I'm excited to present you with *The Seven Fruits of the Land of Israel with their Mystical & Medicinal Properties*. This work has been gradually developed over many years, since I celebrated my first Tu b'Shevat Seder in 1981, based on a compilation by Rav Yehoshua Bergman, z"l. The following years, before Tu b'Shevat Seders had gained popularity in the world, I was privileged to lead my own Tu b'Shevat Seder both in Israel and in North America. The centerpieces of these Seders – the holy fruits of the Land of Israel, with their spiritual energies – have always fascinated me. Perhaps it is because the numerical value of my name, ברכה חנה/Chana Bracha, equals the word for fruit in Hebrew: פְּרִי/*p'ri*. Perhaps it is because I have a sweet tooth. In any case, I have enjoyed the fruits of the Land ever since, while researching their mystical and medicinal properties. For many years, this has been one of my favorite teaching topics.

Not every fruit merits being included in the holy fruits of Israel, even if it grows here, or is native to the Land of Israel. The Bible singles out Seven Species as the selected fruits by which the Land of Israel is particularly praised. These are: wheat, barley, grapes, figs, pomegranates, olives and dates. Wheat was originally a fruit tree,

1

and perhaps barley was as well. However, after the eating from the Tree of Knowledge, wheat fell and its status was lowered to become a mere grain.[2] With Hashem's blessing of abundance, all the seven holy fruits of the Land grow in my garden. I, therefore, have ample opportunity to experience their tastes, textures and spiritual energies.

During the early fall, in the Hebrew month of Elul, I teach a series of workshops based on the seven holy fruits of Israel, in my home and garden in Bat Ayin, Gush Etzion, Israel. Together with my students, I have been exploring, year after year, Bible-verses, Talmudic, Midrashic, Chassidic and Kabbalistic insights on each of the Seven Fruits of Israel respectively, as well as their medicinal properties. I have also experimented with their culinary potential, although to be honest, I like most of the fruits fresh exactly the way Hashem created them.

This book is compiled and expanded from the original material of my yearly workshops. The Torah teachings carry the main weight of the book, as Torah is my passion and training. Because I believe in the eternal truth of the Torah, it is my great desire to 'prove' the medicinal qualities of the fruits of the Land mentioned in the Torah, by means of modern scientific research.

Since I am not a scientist, neither by disposition nor by training, this endeavor proved to complicate my work greatly, especially since my starting point is 'faith' rather than 'reason,' which in itself is anything but scientific. Nevertheless, I have included references of scientific sources (more or less), about the Fruits of the Land, which I believe strengthen our faith by enhancing the credibility of the teachings of our Holy Torah. It is amazing to learn how the mystical and medicinal properties of the holy fruits of Israel go hand in hand.

According to Kabbalah, the Seven Fruits of Israel correspond to the seven lower *sefirot*, (Divine Emanations).[3] I have included an in-depth introduction to the sefirot, so you can clearly understand the mystical correspondence between the Seven Fruits of Israel and the seven lower sefirot. This overview covers the correspondence of the sefirot to emotional attributes, biblical personalities and days of Creation. For those of you who are already familiar with Kabbalistic concepts, I have added 'A Taste of Kabbalah' for each fruit. If you don't have a sound background in the mystical teachings of the Torah, you may not yet grasp this small part of the book. With Hashem's help, the majority of the book will be easily understood and lucid for every reader, regardless of background.

I hope that learning about the holy fruits of Israel will help connect us to the Land of Israel and to the unique Torah emanating from the Holy Land. The metaphor of fruit is often employed for new insights in the Torah (*chidushim*). Each of the fruits of Israel imparts its own vital Torah, raising our consciousness and spirit in preparation for the final redemption when "There shall come forth a shoot from the stem of Yishai, and a branch shall grow forth from its roots."[4]

The Seven Fruits of Israel affirm the threefold rope, braided together from the eternal link connecting the G*d of Israel, the People of Israel and the Land of Israel. Each of the holy fruits of the Land embodies another of the Creator's loving gifts to His beloved People. They are each so different, yet complement one another in texture, color and flavor. Wheat is soft and sweet, barley tough and hard. Grapes are succulent and deliciously juicy, figs plump and fleshy, while pomegranates are tangy, vibrant and crunchy. The bitterness of the olives contrasts the perfect honeyed sweetness of the dates. They host not only an abundance of vitamins and minerals but moreover, their spiritual genetics help us develop *emunah* (faith), strengthening our eternal connection with The Land of Israel and the Master of the Universe.

"*For Hashem your G*d is bringing you into a good land, a land of streams, of wellsprings and underground waters that spring out of valleys and hills; a land of wheat, and barley, and vines, and fig trees, and pomegranates; a land of olive oil and honey... You shall eat and be full, and you shall bless Hashem your G*d for the good land that He has given you*" (*Deuteronomy 8:9–10*).

כִּי הַשֵּׁם אֱלֹקֶיךָ מְבִיאֲךָ אֶל אֶרֶץ טוֹבָה אֶרֶץ נַחֲלֵי מָיִם עֲיָנֹת וּתְהֹמֹת יֹצְאִים
בַּבִּקְעָה וּבָהָר: אֶרֶץ חִטָּה וּשְׂעֹרָה וְגֶפֶן וּתְאֵנָה וְרִמּוֹן אֶרֶץ זֵית שֶׁמֶן וּדְבָשׁ:
...וְאָכַלְתָּ וְשָׂבָעְתָּ וּבֵרַכְתָּ אֶת הַשֵּׁם אֱלֹקֶיךָ עַל הָאָרֶץ הַטֹּבָה אֲשֶׁר נָתַן לָךְ:
(דברים ח, ז-י)

Introducing the Holiness of the Seven Fruits of the Land

The Torah praises the Land of Israel for seven special fruits which are specifically suited to the climate of the Land.[5] These Seven Species were the staple foods consumed by the Jewish people in the Land of Israel during biblical times. They contain special holiness reflected in the unique blessing recited after eating them, thanking Hashem for the goodness of the Land.[6]

The Bible paints the shade of the grapevine and fig tree as a metaphor for the idyllic world peace we await. Our ultimate trust in G*d is expressed through the serene environment where "Yehuda and Israel will sit securely, each person under his vine and fig tree..."[7] As we munch on juicy grapes we are reminded that there is no greater sign of the coming redemption than the Land of Israel producing fruit in abundance.[8]

From My Garden of Holiness

I feel very blessed to live on the land, in the Land of Israel, surrounded by her holy fruits. Around *Pesach* (Passover) time, wild barley stalks appear between the fruit trees and flowers. As we move closer to *Shavuot* (Pentecost), the barley is replaced by wheat blowing in the wind. Each year I'm amazed by these grains in my garden – halfway between the biblical cities of Chevron and Beit Lechem. They could be the great-great-great-great 'grand-grains' of the crops mentioned in the Scroll of Ruth.

The holy grapes of the Land of Israel begin to ripen by the intense summer sun during the Hebrew month of Tamuz (approximately July). This period is usually synchronized with the weekly Torah reading of *Parashat Shalach*, about the spies who needed eight people to carry one cluster of grapes on two poles.[9] Perhaps when the Temple will be rebuilt, the grapes will once again grow to these gigantic proportions. Meanwhile, I enjoy their gentle clusters dangling from the arbor, as their leaves shine in the sun, asking to be picked, pickled and stuffed.

The figs promise a powerhouse of sweetness. When they ripen, I just can't get enough of them. As their honey drips into me – my entire being soaks up their nutrients – both physical and spiritual. I dry some for the winter, but they usually don't last that long in my pantry.

The pomegranates are a feast to the eyes in their tender, feminine beauty. As the bees suck their nectar, their peachy flowers gradually make way for the pinker, delicate, bell-shaped, fine, phenomenal fruit, perfectly ripe in time to crown the High Holidays.

In contrast, the olives are supportive, masculine background trees, with modest green fruit. Did you know that most green olives eventually turn black when they ripen? I only found this out by careful observation. The olives ripen in the Hebrew months of Cheshvan and Kislev, just in time for Chanukah. Hashem created them in sync with the Festival of Lights kindled from olive oil. One year, a neighbor made her own olive oil. We were delighted to contribute our olives and in return receive a small bottle of the purest oil to dip our Shabbat challah!

In front of our home we planted a date palm, which is actually growing in spite of our high mountain climate most unsuitable for the tropical palm that loves the heat of the desert sun. We don't expect it, but what a nice surprise it would be if one day it would produce dates. You never know!

The First Fruits Offerings

"You shall bring the First Fruits of your Land to the House of Hashem your G*d..."[10] In Biblical and Talmudic times, immediately following the holiday of Shavuot, the farmers would rejoice by dedicating the beginning of their fruit harvest to Hashem.

"It shall be, when you enter the Land that Hashem your G*d gives you for an inheritance, and you possess it and settle permanently in it. Then you shall take of the first of all the fruits of the earth, which you shall bring from your land that Hashem your G*d gives you. You shall put it into a basket, and you shall go to the place which Hashem your G*d shall choose for His Name to dwell there."[11]

During Temple times, the Jewish farmers would bring the first and the best of their crops specifically from the seven holy species of Israel as a donation to the *kohanim* (priests), who did not have their own land.[12] When entering the Temple with the fruit basket, facing the *kohen* (priest), they would recite a declaration of gratitude to Hashem for bestowing His blessings upon the Land of Israel.[13]

"Those who lived near Jerusalem would bring figs and grapes (because they would not be spoiled by a short journey); those who lived far from Jerusalem would bring dried figs and raisins. An ox went before them with its horns overlaid with gold, and a crown of olive leaves upon its head. The flute was played before them until they approached Jerusalem. When they came close to Jerusalem, they sent messengers before them, and they would decorate their First Fruits..."[14] "The flute was played before them until they reached the Temple Mount. Once they reached the Temple Mount, even Agrippas the King would carry the [fruit] basket on his shoulder and go in as far as the *azarah* (Temple courtyard). Once they reached the azarah, the Levites would sing, 'I will praise You, O G*d, for You have raised me up, and You have not allowed my enemies to rejoice over me!'"[15]

Today, when we anticipate the return of Temple times, I like to practice the First Fruits Offering by thanking Hashem profusely for the produce and by sharing my shiny fruits with rabbis, teachers and students alike. I also try to sanctify the beginning of my day for holiness, thanksgiving and prayer.

Reaffirming our Faith through the Fruits

On what merit were the Seven Species selected for the First Fruit Offering? The flowering and fruiting of these seven holy species take place during the period between Pesach and Shavuot, a season that depends on the delicate balance between contradictory forces of nature. It is characterized by climatic contrasts between extreme dryness and heat on the one hand and cold rainstorms on the other, which could easily be misconstrued as battles between opposing deities. Therefore, these Seven Species are selected to reaffirm our pure faith in the One and only G*d. We express thanks to Hashem, specifically for these fruits of the Land, through the First Fruits Offering and their additional blessings.[16]

Whenever I feel in need of spiritual recharging, I take a stroll in my garden. The hopeful sight of the ripening fruits infuses me with faith, that even if some fruits may fall off unripe to the ground, those that are meant to will make it to full maturity, for blessing and elevation of all.

Returning to the Diet of Paradise

Originally, human beings were '*fruitivores*,' and perhaps fruits will once again become our main diet in the perfected world.[17] According-ing to Rav Tzadok of Lublin,[18] all the hard work and labor we invest in food preparation stems from Adam's curse: "In the sweat of your brow you shall eat bread."[19] In the future, when we will overcome the negative impulse that resulted from partaking in the forbidden fruit, we will no longer be subject to the curse of having to work for a living and toil in food preparation. We will once again be free to devote ourselves to Torah and the pursuit of holiness, when our food will become like the ready-made fruit of the trees in the Garden of Eden. As the Talmud teaches, wheat used to be a tree, producing ready-made 'bread-cakes,' and in the future the Land of Israel will once again bring forth bread-cakes.[20]

The Holy Fruits Connect us to Hashem and the Holy Land

Even if today it may not be realistic to subsist on fruits alone, they still remain an important part of the human diet, as a vital source of vitamins, minerals, antioxidants and fibers. In addition to their nutritional value, fruits are beautiful, bountiful and delicious. They are created with such exciting colors and textures that burst in our mouth, filling us with delight and pleasure, while reminding us of the goodness of the Creator.

    The Torah's mentioning of the Seven Species is not incidental. Rather, these foods are central to a Jewish spiritual path that endeavors to elevate the physical through intentional living. Eating the Seven Species in a conscious way can promote our wellbeing, help connect us to the Land of Israel, and deepen our relationship with Hashem. Each of the Seven Species contains deep divine lessons for our spiritual lives. Every time we eat them, we have the opportunity to tune into their spiritual messages, eat consciously and bring the world a step closer to its perfected state.

Introducing the Sefirot – The Branches of the Tree of Life

The Seven Fruits of Israel are linked to the sefirot – the Divine Emanations or Radiances, which emanate from the infinite Divine Light into our finite world. Therefore, we are revitalized by connecting with these holy fruits, even by just inhaling their scent or enjoying the sight of them growing in the Land of Israel. Since we will be discussing the qualities of the seven holy fruits based on the sefirot they reflect, it is important to introduce the sefirot, which are the building blocks of Jewish mysticism and Kabbalah. The sefirot (singular: *sefirah*) comprise the Divine manifestations within Creation. Hashem created the world through the Ten Utterances corresponding to the Ten Sefirot,[21] which also correspond to the Ten Commandments – the quintessence of the Torah.[22] The sefirot serve as an interface between Hashem's infinite light and the physical reality we experience. They are G*d's imprint in the world – His attributes for us to emulate in order to reflect having been created in His image. The world comprises 32 pathways consisting of Ten Sefirot, and the 22 letters of the Hebrew alphabet.[23] The pathways function much like the arteries and veins in the human body: receiving and transmitting energy in order to nurture and maintain the system of the sefirot.

The Ten Sefirot – Divided into Three Roots and Seven Branches

The Ten Sefirot are divided into two groups, the upper three and the lower seven. The upper sefirot correspond to the head, whereas the lower sefirot correspond to the body. The array of the sefirot constitute the Tree of Life and branch out into three main branches, the right branch embodies the expansive masculine energies, the left branch reflects the contractive feminine energies, and the middle branch represents the perfect balance between them. According to the nature of trees, the Tree of Life also receives its sustenance through its roots. However, in the Tree of Life the roots are above. The branches of the Tree of Life receive their vitality from the roots of Wisdom (*Chochmah*), Understanding (*Binah*) and Knowledge (*Da'at*).[24] These intellectual sefirot – the 'Three Mothers',[25] are the source and root of the seven branches of the lower sefirot – the seven emotional attributes corresponding to the seven days of Creation.[26]

The Seven Emotional Sefirot – the Midot (Character Traits)

The Seven Species reflect the seven emotional sefirot through which G*d created the world. They are like particular vessels that channel Divine Light through their own distinct shape and color, each have their own individual quality. There is no exact translation of the Hebrew character trait embodied by each of the sefirot. This version, therefore, is only an approximation: *Chesed* (Loving-kindness), *Gevurah* (Might), *Tiferet* (Beauty), *Netzach* (Victory), *Hod* (Acknowledgment), *Yesod* (Foundation), and *Malchut* (Royalty). The following description of the seven emotional sefirot will help clarify their different energies, and show how each of them correspond to the Seven Fruits of Israel respectively.

חֶסֶד ~ *Chesed* – **Loving-kindness** is infinite giving without boundaries. Its energy extends outwardly in ultimate expansion. In order not to go overboard, *Chesed* needs to be channeled into proper receptacles. It is the job of its faithful partner, *Gevurah,* to confine *Chesed* and ensure that it remains within proper bounds.

גְּבוּרָה ~ *Gevurah* – **Power/Restraint** is the focused power of concentrating vital energy into accessible vessels. Its energy is confining and contracts inwardly. *Gevurah* has the power to judge, discriminate and restrain according to the worthiness of the receiver. Therefore, *Gevurah* is also referred to as *din* (judgment).

תִּפְאֶרֶת ~ *Tiferet* — **Harmony/Beauty** is the perfectly balanced middle ground between extremes. It especially harmonizes the lights of *Chesed* with the vessels of *Gevurah*, ensuring that *Chesed* flows freely within the channels of *Gevurah*, and that their contrasting energies are reconciled and balanced in exactly the required way.

נֶצַח ~ *Netzach* — **Victory/Endurance** eternalizes the energy of *Chesed*, through its steadfast power to go against obstacles and endure. It has the ability to conquer and overcome despair. *Netzach* also means to 'conduct' or 'orchestrate,' thus *Netzach* orchestrates the energies of the previous sefirot to ensure their eternity.

הוֹד ~ *Hod* — **Acknowledgement/Splendor** is the reflective energy of applied *Gevurah*, which acknowledges the gifts of others, while filtering the friends from the foes. It ensures that the energy of *Netzach* doesn't overpower the goodness of its opponent, but incorporates it into the greater whole. Humility born from submission and deep inner commitment, together with recognizing the noble characteristics of others, endows *Hod* with its soft glow.

יְסוֹד ~ *Yesod* — **Foundation/Covenant** actualizes potential in its capacity as connector between the upper sefirot and the recipient –*Malchut*, representing the earth below. In addition to harmonizing and balancing *Netzach* and *Hod* the way *Tiferet* harmonizes *Chesed* and *Gevurah*, *Yesod* acts as the channel through which *Malchut* receives its proper measure of light and life force. *Yesod* is also referred to as the *brit* – the holy covenant between G*d and Avraham, the first Jew. Through connecting the inner sefirot with their outer manifestation in *Malchut*, unifying above with below, beginning with end, *Yesod* creates ultimate shalom (peace).

מַלְכוּת ~ *Malchut* – **Royalty/Kingdom** is associated with the earth. It has nothing of its own, yet it is the vessel that manifests the lights of all the other sefirot in the lower physical world.[27] *Malchut* is the perfect feminine receiver, providing the space for actualizing the latent potential of all goodness. It is often referred to as 'the world of speech,' since speech is the medium through which we relate to the outer world by expressing our thoughts and emotions to others. It is through the power of speech that we can exert leadership and exercise authority and kingship.

The Ten Sefirot of Gardening

The concept of the sefirot – being the vessels for Divine Light – is quite abstract. In order to facilitate the understanding of the sefirot in a more tangible way, I use a metaphor of the work and enjoyment associated with gardening. I have included the three upper (intellectual) sefirot – the Three Mothers – so you can get a feeling how all sefirot relate and interact in the creation of a garden.[28]

1. חָכְמָה ~ *Chochmah* – **Wisdom** – Planning the garden. Tuning in to the inspirational vision of how the garden should look and be used.

2. בִּינָה ~ *Binah* – **Analytic Understanding** – Applying the vision in practical terms. Assessing the materials needed such as plants, compost, soil, tools, a watering system etc.

3. דַּעַת ~ *Da'at* – **Knowledge** – Stepping back and looking at the whole picture; visualizing the entire procedure of creating the garden. Deciding the different steps of action, in order to actualize the vision of the garden.

4. חֶסֶד ~ *Chesed* – **Loving-kindness** – Nurturing the garden and giving each plant what it needs to grow; watering, supplying soil and adding compost.

5. גְּבוּרָה ~ *Gevurah* – Power/Restraint – Eliminating anything that impedes the creation and growth of the garden; weeding, getting rid of bugs and insects.

6. תִּפְאֶרֶת ~ *Tiferet* – Harmony/Beauty – Ensuring the proper balance between watering and weeding. Enjoying the beauty and harmony of the garden.

7. נֶצַח ~ *Netzach* – Victory/Endurance – Conquering an area of land by completely transforming it from a stony, thorny dry patch to a lush piece of land filled with healthy selected plants. This includes organizing the weeding, removal of rocks, plowing, sowing, watering and composting in one selected area.

8. הוֹד ~ *Hod* – Acknowledgement/Splendor – Reflecting on the needs of the plants. Transplanting them to a place where their individual needs will be better met.

9. יְסוֹד ~ *Yesod* – Foundation/Covenant – Planting new seeds to sprout forth renewed growth in the reproductive cycle of abundance.

10. מַלְכוּת ~ *Malchut* – Royalty/Kingdom – Through harvesting and eating the fruits of the earth, we materialize their uppermost spiritual potential energies into actualized fruits of the Land. "תְּנוּ לָהּ מִפְּרִי יָדֶיהָ – Give her from the fruits of her hands..."[29]

Malchut channels all other *sefirot* and manifests them in the lower world. Thus the final product of the land incorporates all the preceding work done through each of the *sefirot*. In this holographic system, the highest is embedded within the lowest. Eating the fruits of the Land is therefore the reversal of the process of the spiritual eco-cycle. The fruits are transformed into energy used to perform mitzvot, pray, learn Torah and conceive new Torah *chidushim* (insights).

Scriptural Sources for the Seven Sefirot

The Torah is called "A Tree of Life for those who hold on to it."[30] When introducing the Torah reading in the Synagogue, we pay tribute to the Torah, by praising it for its branches of Divine attributes – the seven emotional sefirot. The song we sing when taking the Torah out of the ark and carrying it to the *bimah* (platform in the synagogue for Torah reading) actually has its source in the Bible:

לְךָ הָשֵׁם הַגְּדֻלָּה וְהַגְּבוּרָה וְהַתִּפְאֶרֶת וְהַנֵּצַח וְהַהוֹד כִּי כֹל בַּשָּׁמַיִם וּבָאָרֶץ לְךָ הָשֵׁם הַמַּמְלָכָה וְהַמִּתְנַשֵּׂא לְכֹל לְרֹאשׁ: (דברי הימים א, כט, יא)

"Yours, Hashem, is the greatness, and the power, and the glory and the victory and the majesty: for all that is in heaven and on earth is Yours. Yours, Hashem, is the kingdom and You are exalted as head above all" (I *Chronicles* 29:11).

This Bible verse is the only scriptural source for all of the emotional sefirot. Four of the seven lower sefirot are easily recognized in this Torah verse: *Gevurah, Tiferet, Netzach* and *Hod*. The first attribute mentioned is *Gedulah* which means greatness or expansiveness. *Chesed* is often called *Gedulah* because it expresses the infinite greatness and benevolence of G*d. The attribute of *Yesod* (Foundation) is called "all that is in heaven and on earth," because *Yesod* is the secret of the unity between heaven and earth. It connects and unifies all of the energies of the upper sefirot with *Malchut* below. "Yours, Hashem, is the kingdom" refers to *Malchut*, which includes all other attributes. It receives and channels their influence to the Jewish congregation on earth.[31]

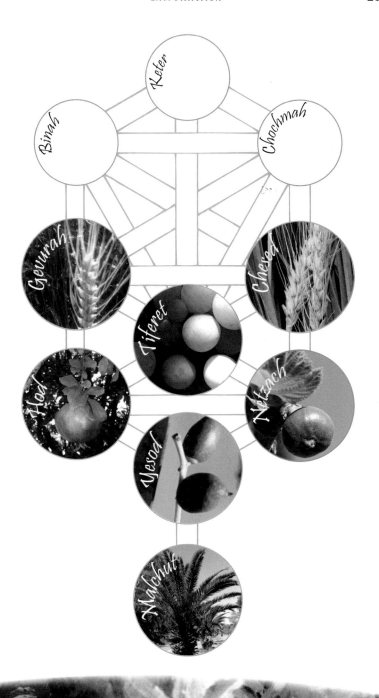

The Seven Days of Creation Reflect the Seven Sefirot

The Creation of the world was established through the seven emotional sefirot. Each day came about through a particular attribute: During the First Day, *Chesed* was dominant; the Second Day, *Gevurah*, and so on, according to the order of the sefirot.[32]

יוֹם רִאשׁוֹן *Yom Rishon* – The First Day of Creation (Sunday) was activated through *Chesed*, for *Chesed* is the beginning of building as it states, "The world is built upon *Chesed*."[33] It was Hashem's desire to give His love and kindness, which created the whole universe on Day One. On this day Infinite Light, the ultimate expression of goodness, was created.[34] This is the light of *Chesed* permeating all of creation and through which all life is built.

יוֹם שֵׁנִי *Yom Sheni* – The Second Day of Creation (Monday) is characterized by the restriction of *Gevurah*. This is the only day about which it does not state "and it was good." Nothing was created on the Second Day; rather, it was a time for separation. On the Second Day of Creation, G*d separated between the upper and the lower waters, which indicates the separation of the infinite *Chesed* called 'the upper waters' from the lower worlds by means of the

רָקִיעַ/*rakia* (firmament).[35] This separation was necessary to limit the giving according to the capacity of the receiver. The world was then blessed with lakes, rivers and oceans without being flooded.

יוֹם שְׁלִישִׁי *Yom Shelishi* – The Third Day of Creation (Tuesday), infused with *Tiferet*, is a day of double goodness. On that day beautiful trees and plants sprouted forth while the separation between water and dry land was completed.[36] As *Tiferet* harmonizes *Chesed* and *Gevurah*, the Third Day sets the proper balance between dry land and water to make perfect forests, deserts, mountains and fields that we experience as beautiful.

יוֹם רְבִיעִי *Yom Revi'i* – The Fourth Day of Creation (Wednesday) is dedicated to the victory of eternity – *Netzach*. On that day the luminaries were created.[37] The sun, moon and stars allow life to endure by their capability to channel the infinite light into usable forms for the finite world. These dependable servants of light guide us from the beginning to the end of the world. As King David praises, "The sun rejoices with power to run his course."[38] The moon represents Israel, the eternal people.

יוֹם חֲמִישִׁי *Yom Chamishi* – The Fifth Day of Creation (Thursday) glows with *Hod* – the humble but necessary life of the sea and air. The fish of the sea and the birds of the sky are humble, as they stay out of the way – below or above our realm of reality. Yet, they are so necessary for the world that life on earth could not be sustained without sea creatures that support the food chain, and birdsong glorifying Hashem. The birds and the fish were the first recipients of Hashem's benevolence and the first to fulfill the commandment to procreate and fill the world.[39]

יוֹם שִׁשִּׁי *Yom Shishi* – The Sixth Day of Creation (Friday) is the foundation (*Yesod*) of the world, when the human beings were created.[40] For the world is created for the sake of mankind.[41] G*d created Adam and Eve in His image to connect intimately with His creation, affect it and plant seeds of mitzvot. Our role as human beings is to connect to the world and each other through the power of *Yesod*, and form strong relationships. Both the animal kingdom  and the first humans were created on the Sixth Day. Humanity was commanded to "be fruitful and multiply,"[42] enacting Divine benevolent kindness by growing and expanding G*d-consciousness. When we were told to rule over the animals it implied transcending the part of ourselves which is similar to the animal world, and actualize our Divine Image – the *Tzadik* (righteous) which is the *Yesod* (foundation) of the world.[43]

יוֹם שַׁבָּת *Yom Shabbat* – The Seventh Day of Creation completes Creation and culminates in *Malchut* (royalty), the ultimate actualization of potential. All the works of Creation lead up to this moment of completion and total fulfillment. Just as *Malchut* has nothing of its own, so is Shabbat a day of rest from work. All the six days of Creation preceding Shabbat do their work so that the culmination of Creation is revealed on Shabbat. When all the weekdays have applied their energies and done their share, then the *Malchut* of Shabbat comes to reap their fruits. Shabbat generates the cycle of receiving and giving. Therefore, all the six days of the week receive their blessing from the Shabbat Queen.

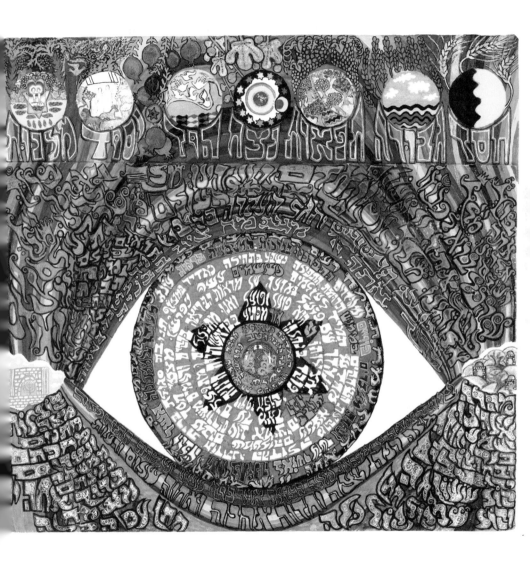

The Sefirot and the Seven Shepherds

There are Seven Patriarchs in the Torah. Each contributes his particular character and energy into forming the Jewish people. These archetypal righteous father figures are also called the Seven Shepherds. Just as a shepherd provides the physical needs of his flock, the Seven Shepherds provide the spiritual needs of the 'flock of Israel,' by drawing life force and G*dliness into their souls.

During each of the seven days of the holiday of Sukkot, one of the Seven Shepherds visits the Sukkah (booth) in spirit, until all Seven Shepherds are gathered together on the last day of the holiday. The seven holy Sukkot guests are called אוּשְׁפִּיזִין/*Ushpizin*, which means 'guests' in Aramaic. Each of these Seven Ushpizin reflects one of the seven lower sefirot.

אַבְרָהָם **AVRAHAM**, our first father, embodies the Sefirah of *Chesed*.[44] The seed of beginning is always connected with the growth of *Chesed*. Just as the world was built through *Chesed*, the Jewish people are built through the *Chesed* of Avraham. Until this day the quality of *Chesed* still characterizes the descendants of Avraham – the Jewish and the Arab peoples. Avraham proactively sought to help others. He expressed his unlimited *Chesed* and love of people in many ways, especially through his kind hospitality for which he is well-known.[45] Avraham actually planted a hospitality tree or inn providing the precedent for today's free soup-kitchens.[46] Avraham's tent opened toward each of the four directions, inviting wayfarers from every corner of the world to partake of his fruits and bless their Creator. Avraham personified the expansive energy of *Chesed*. He was always extending himself in *Chesed* beyond bonds, while actively spreading the knowledge of G*d to the world.[47]

יצְחָק **YITZCHAK**, the son of Avraham, is associated with the Sefirah of *Gevurah* – restriction and concentration of power.[48] Yitzchak was a man of prayer with deep inner conviction. While Avraham, in his *Chesed,* lacked the ability to distinguish between Yitzchak and Yishmael, the seed of Avraham was constricted through Yitzchak to exclude his older brother Yishmael.[49] Yitzchak's journey was inward, to the depths of his soul, the essence within. He persistently re-dug his father's wells through his energy of *Gevurah.* Rather than creating something new, digging wells entails removing the grime, dust and dirt, to allow the quintessential water, the core of self, to well up, fresh and bubbling, of its own accord. Yitzchak did not have to extend himself outwardly, blessings came to him by themselves.[50] Even a wife was brought to him. Yitzchak remained within the boundaries of the Land of Israel, even during the famine. He was a farmer who learned the profound secret of the seed: Growth comes when you allow yourself to disintegrate and become one with the soil from which you stem. Through passive submission while being bound, Yitzchak exhibited the strength of ultimately giving himself over to Hashem in complete surrender.

יַעֲקֹב YA'ACOV, the third patriarch of the Jewish people, son of Yitzchak and Rivkah, and grandson of Avraham, teaches the qualities of beauty and compassion manifested in *Tiferet.* Torah is called *Tiferet.*[51] Beauty is one of the meanings of *Tiferet,* because there is nothing more beautiful than gaining the wisdom of truth. As the Torah scholar of *Tiferet,*[52] Ya'acov imparts the beauty of synthesizing perfectly the expansive energy of his grandfather's *Chesed,* with his father's focused power of *Gevurah,* into the harmony of *Tiferet.* The integration of love with judgment is found in compassion, or mercy, which is Ya'acov's essence, and the inner motivating power of *Tiferet.* It harmonizes and unifies the diversity found on the spectrum between *Chesed* and *Gevurah.* Likewise, Ya'acov bore twelve righteous holy sons, each with his individual qualities and talents. Because compassion is the truly balanced way of life, Ya'acov is known as, 'the select among the forefathers.'[53]

מֹשֶׁה **MOSHE,** our teacher, embodies *Netzach*, being the giver of the eternal, unchangeable Torah. He had the ability to open the gates of heaven and communicate directly with Hashem, while enduring the burning light of the Eternal. Moshe fought many battles and eventually was victorious over Pharaoh and the Egyptians with whom he was raised. He was able to withstand forty days and nights on Mount Sinai without food or water.[54] As a leader of Israel, Moshe conducted all of the energies of his people into a symphony of triumph. Because of his trait of *Netzach*, Moshe was prevented from entering the Land of Israel. Had he entered, the children of Israel could never have been exiled from the Land, and thus would have been unable to fully atone for their sins. Moshe remained eternally youthful, the moisture of life remained within him and his body never deteriorated.[55]

אַהֲרֹן **AHARON,** the holy Kohen *Gadol* (High Priest), who glowed with the soft glow of *Hod*, channeled the natural tendency to strive for victory (*Netzach*) toward attaining spiritual goals. Being in charge of the Temple service, Aharon ensured that his people would only praise and worship that which is truly worthy, and that the splendor of the Holy Temple would remain the vortex point of the world. Just as *Hod* reflects *Netzach* (the two being an inseparable pair), so was Aharon Moshe's faithful partner, reflecting, translating and making Moshe's lofty Torah accessible to the people. Through his humility, he allowed his younger brother, Moshe, and all of the Jewish people to shine through him. Aharon had a precious stone for each of the twelve holy tribes on his breastplate that reflected and channeled the light of each tribe.

יוֹסֵף **YOSEF,** the '*Tzadik Yesod Olam*,' is the righteous foundation of the world.[56] He is moreover called "*Tzafnat Pa'neyach*" – "explainer of hidden things,"[57] or "the person through whom hidden things are revealed."[58] The energy of *Yesod* has the ability to reveal the hidden. It is the bridge that connects the upper sefirot with *Malchut*, the reality of the revealed world. In Egypt, Yosef quickly rose to power and became the distributer of seeds of grain, the foundation of life. Being the source of sustenance for the masses is an expression of *Yesod*.[59] The foundation of life is sexuality. Yosef mastered elevating sexuality when he overcame the most difficult test of temptation with the wife of his master. Yosef's personal purity gave him the ability to draw down a bounty of blessings for Pharaoh's kingdom, in his capacity of *Yesod*, the conduit for *Malchut*. By not giving in to Potifar's wife's seductive overtures,[60] Yosef rectified the *brit* (holy covenant) and anchored himself in righteousness, the moral and healthy foundation for *Malchut* (Kingdom).

דוד DAVID, reflecting *Malchut*, became the first king of the dynasty of the Messianic kingdom. Just as "*Malchut* has nothing of its own,"[61] David mastered ultimate humility and considered himself "a worm and not a man."[62] In total self-nullification, David completely disregarded all consciousness of 'myself' and 'my' accomplishments, relating everything entirely to G*d. Through this powerful sense of G*d's *Malchut* (kingdom), David was able to compose his holy Psalms. These powerful Divine Psalms gave full expression to David's awareness that all of his actions and good deeds were actually reflections of Hashem working through him. *Malchut* is embodied by the mouth, because a king leads his people through speech. David, as a vehicle for the Divine voice, became master of rectified speech and eternal prayer, encapsulated through the composition of his holy Psalms.

The Sefirot and the Seven Prophetesses

The Talmud enumerates seven prophetesses from the Torah: Sarah, Miriam, Devorah, Chana, Avigail, Chuldah and Esther.[63] Although there may have been many other prophetesses (such as all the matriarchs),[64] only those whose prophesy had relevance for both their own time and for all future generations are called 'prophets' in the Torah.[65] Each of the Seven Prophetesses, who lived in different pivotal eras of Jewish history, corresponds to one of the seven emotional sefirot, according to the order of her lifetime.[66]

שָׂרָה SARAH, the first of the Seven Prophetesses, who merited beginning the building of the house of Israel – corresponds to *Chesed*.[67] The seed of beginning essentially grows and expands through *Chesed*. Just as Avraham is known for his *Chesed*, so is Sarah, his faithful partner steeped in deeds of *Chesed*, as she busied herself with the endless task of preparing food for their numerous guests.[68] Moreover, Sarah performed the greatest otherworldly *Chesed* by diminishing herself to allow Avraham to take an additional wife. Sarah was willing to share her husband for the sake of fulfilling the Divine promise that Avraham would sire children.[69]

In relationship with Avraham, Sarah is known for her *Gevurah*, teaching Avraham to separate between Yitzchak and Yishmael. Yet, "the wife shares equally in her husband's accomplishments."[70] Therefore, when viewed as one unified being, together they represent *Chesed*. The holy species of **wheat** connects to Sarah, who assisted Avraham by baking bread and cakes for their countless guests.[71]

מִרְיָם MIRIAM reflects *Gevurah*, for when she was born the bitterness of the servitude began.[72] Everything begins with *Chesed* and moves on to *Gevurah*, where the holy and the unholy are separated. Miriam partnered with her brother, Moshe, in leading the children of Israel out of the decadent Egyptian land.[73]

With her *Gevurah* she knew how to separate between right and wrong. Even as a young girl, Miriam was clear about her father's mistaken outlook, which she didn't hesitate to point out.[74]

She led the women's Song of the Sea,[75] which embodies *Gevurah*. Song enables everyone to rise, for raising oneself up is possible only through the power of *Gevurah*.[76] Therefore, the Levites, whose job it is to play music and sing at the Temple, are connected with *Gevurah*.[77] We, too, can experience how song has tremendous power to raise our spirits and arouse love and desire.

Miriam also brought Israel the well of water in the wilderness. Like her song, the well rose from below to above, as it is written: "Arise, O Well, sing to her."[78] In the merit of Miriam, Israel is aroused to yearn toward the higher realms.[79] The holy species of **barley** connects to Miriam, who was instrumental in bringing about the Exodus, from which we count the *Omer*.[80] During Temple times, the children of Israel offered a daily Omer sacrifice of barley, from the first day of Pesach celebrating the Exodus, until the holiday of Shavuot.

דְּבוֹרָה **DEVORAH**, the only female judge in the Bible, judged the children of Israel once they had established themselves in their full glory in the Land of Israel.[81] She, therefore, embodies *Tiferet*, the beauty of the Land. As a kind judge of her people, she softened the harsh judgments of *Gevurah* with *Chesed*, enabling her litigation to reflect the mercy of *Tiferet*. When Barak (the general appointed by Devorah) refuses to go to war unless Devorah goes with him, her answer is stark: "I will go with you, but there will be no glory (*Tiferet*) for you in the path you are walking, for G*d will deliver Sisera into the hands of a woman."[82] The *Tiferet* will not be Barak's, it belongs to Devorah, Woman of Glory.

Connected to *Tiferet*, Devorah represents the middle pillar of the *sefirot*, a perfect synthesis between opposite qualities refined in their center. All the species associated with the middle pillar are fruits from which we derive a refined inner substance, namely, the date honey of *Malchut*, the olive oil of *Yesod* and the wine of *Tiferet* from grapes. Israel is compared to the holy **grapevine**[83] from which we produce wine for *Kiddush* and other Jewish rituals. Devorah, as a "mother in Israel"[84] was able to mold the Jewish people to become the holy grapevine we were meant to be.

חַנָּה **CHANA** corresponds to *Netzach*, which according to Kabbalah is the source of prophecy (together with *Hod*).[85] She became the mother of prophecy when she bore Shemuel the prophet, who opened the gates of prophecy that had been blocked for Israel until his time. The intensity of Shemuel's prophecy caused others to prophesy in his wake. His prophecy is compared to a great river overflowing into smaller streams.[86] About Chana it is written, "Also the Eternal One (*Netzach*) of Israel, will not lie nor change his mind…"[87] This is because *Netzach* was weakened and blemished until Chana's son Shemuel rectified it.[88]

In Chana's prophetic thanksgiving song, she exclaimed, "My horn is exalted in Hashem."[89] The horn is a stronghold through which one can exert victory (*Netzach*) over the enemies. Moreover, the depth of exaltedness (רוֹם/*rom*), is *Netzach,* according to the Book of Formation.[90] This is because the horn is long-lasting, unlike the flask (פַּךְ/*pach),* which is made from pottery that easily breaks.[91] Chana prophesied about the two kings that her son, Shemuel, would anoint with a horn. She also prayed that G*d would give strength to the kings of Israel to conquer their enemies: "May Hashem give strength to His king, and raise the horn of His anointed one."[92] "His king" refers to Shaul, whereas "His anointed one" refers to David, whose royal dynasty is eternal.[93]

The **fig** may possibly be associated with Chana, because it symbolizes the first fruit offering given to the Temple. "When a person enters his field and sees the first fig beginning to ripen, he ties a string around it,"[94] as a sign that it must be offered in the Temple. Just as the fig represents the first fruit offerings to the Temple, so did Chana offer up her first born son Shemuel to the Temple service.[95]

אֲבִיגַיִל AVIGAIL shines with the light of *Hod* and humility. She fell on her face and bowed down to the ground before David, calling herself "your maidservant" six times in her short speech to David.[96] Although her household was extremely wealthy, she chose to ride down the mountain to meet David on an unpretentious donkey.[97] David and his men were on their way to kill her evil husband, Naval, who refused to support them, while they were guarding his live-stock.[98] Through Avigail's wisdom and intuitive understanding of David's psyche, she carefully chose the precise words which calmed his agitated spirit. With her generosity and utter self-dedication to prevent bloodshed by all means, she was able to raise David to a new level of refinement. Like Aharon, the restorer of peace,[99] with whom she shares the light of *Hod*, Avigail was able to maintain peace and prevent David from shedding blood, convincing him that it would taint his future kingdom.

"She came down the secret of the mountain..."[100] From the extra word "secret" we learn that Avigail revealed her thigh, while David walked three *parsa'ot* (each *parsa* is about four kilometer) by its light.[101] Metaphorically her prophesy emanated from her thigh, which is *Hod*, and the three *parsa'ot* refer to the light of the three prophecies that Avigail revealed to David: 1. "May your enemies be like Naval."[102] Here she informed him that Naval will die. 2. **"This** shall be no stumbling-block unto you,"[103] she warned him. However, David's downfall would eventually happen through Batsheva. 3. "Hashem will certainly make my lord a sure house."[104] She prophesied that David would achieve eternal kingdom, through his descendant, *Mashiach* (the Messiah).[105]

Avigail's appeasement gift to David included, "...two hundred loaves, two bottles of wine, five measures of parched grain, a hundred clusters of raisins, and two hundred cakes of figs..."[106] Most likely the loaves were made from wheat and the parched grain could possible include barley. In this case, Avigail brought a present from all of the species associated with the sefirot preceding hers: wheat bread of

Chesed, parched barley grain of *Gevurah*, wine and clusters of raisins of *Tiferet*, cakes of figs of *Netzach*. These gifts may represent the spiritual qualities already mastered by Avigail as she grew into her own *Sefirah* of *Hod* embodied by the holy **pomegranate**.[107]

חֻלְדָה CHULDAH is connected with *Yesod*, the foundation of the world. She is the only prophetess who lived within the walls of Jerusalem,[108] the foundation of the world.[109] Chuldah means a rat, which mostly lives underground, covered and hidden from the world. Likewise *Yesod* is the most hidden of the sefirot, corresponding to the sexual organ, the most hidden of all the organs in the body.[110] *Yesod* is referred to as the brit, the covenant of peace. About Chuldah it explicitly states that she was the wife of Shalom (Peace), and that she prophesied by means of the righteous of the world, which is the covenant of peace.[111] This covenant entails rectification of sexuality, which brings peace. Likewise, Pinchas who was zealous for the preservation of sexual morality in Israel was given G*d's covenant of peace.[112]

Just as *Yesod* is the link between the upper sefirot and *Malchut*, Chuldah was the interpreter of the upper prophecy for King Yoshiahu, a direct descendant of King David. Through Chuldah's interpretation of the sacred Torah scroll found in the Temple, the King was inspired to repent with all his heart, and renew his covenant with G*d.[113] In this way, Chuldah (*Yesod*) connected with King Yoshiahu (*Malchut*), and by doing so, she helped strengthen Yoshiahu's kingdom in the path of Torah. Just as Chuldah, rooted in *Yesod*, strengthened the kingdom, **olive oil**, the holy species associated with *Yesod*, was used to anoint the kings. This is why any Jewish king is called "Mashiach"[114] meaning, "the anointed one."

אֶסְתֵּר **ESTHER THE QUEEN**, as her title reflects, most completely embodies *Malchut* – feminine royalty. Esther, which means 'hidden,' was the most modest and hidden of all the women in the Bible.[115] Likewise *Malchut*, which has nothing of its own,[116] is the lowest and most humble of all the sefirot. Esther was a poor orphan without a mother or father.[117] Mordechai raised her as his own daughter, just as the role of the 'son' – (represented by the six middle sefirot) is to raise and elevate the 'daughter' (represented by *Malchut*).[118]

Malchut, like the moon, reflects the light of the remaining sefirot. Esther, who manifested Mordechai's light, is compared to the moon, which reflects the light of the sun.[119] At Mordechai's fervent urging, Esther agreed to risk her life by going to the king without being called, in order to plead for her people.[120] Through Mordechai's prodding and building up her *Malchut*, Esther became a full-fledged queen with her own lights of Torah. She, who at first, humbly performed Mordechai's bidding,[121] rose to reveal her hidden *Malchut*, with the authority to command him to suspend Torah law.[122]

When Esther stood in the throne room before the king, the Bible states that she "got dressed up in *Malchut*,"[123] rather than describing her as wearing royal robes. Esther embodied *Malchut*, which rises from a small point until it grows into its full stature.[124] Likewise, the **date palm**, which is tall and stately,[125] is compared to the rising of the *Shechinah* (feminine In-dwelling Presence).[126] Like the date palm, Esther grew into the highest manifestation of her element, *Malchut*. Her decisive royalty was empowered by her ultimate self-sacrifice to save her people from imminent annihilation.

חִטָּה **Wheat**	שְׂעֹרָה **Barley**	גֶּפֶן **Grapes**	תְּאֵנָה **Figs**
חֶסֶד *Chesed* Loving- Kindness	גְּבוּרָה *Gevurah* Might/ Restraint	תִּפְאֶרֶת *Tiferet* Harmony/ Beauty	נֵצַח *Netzach* Victory/ Endurance
אַהֲבָה Love	יִרְאָה Awe	רַחֲמִים Mercy	בִּטָּחוֹן Confidence
Right Arm	Left Arm	Heart	Right Leg
Skeletal System	Circulatory System	Muscular System	Endocrine System
יוֹם רִאשׁוֹן First Day (Sunday)	יוֹם שֵׁנִי Second Day (Monday)	יוֹם שְׁלִישִׁי Third Day (Tuesday)	יוֹם רְבִיעִי Fourth Day (Wednesday)
אַבְרָהָם **Avraham**	יִצְחָק **Yitzchak**	יַעֲקֹב **Ya'acov**	מֹשֶׁה **Moshe**
שָׂרָה **Sarah**	מִרְיָם **Miriam**	דְּבוֹרָה **Devorah**	חַנָּה **Chana**

רִמּוֹן	זֵית שֶׁמֶן	דְּבַשׁ (תְּמָרִים)
Pomegranates	**Olive Oil**	**Date Honey**
הוֹד	יְסוֹד	מַלְכוּת
Hod	*Yesod*	*Malchut*
Acknowledgement/ Splendor	Foundation/ Covenant	Royalty/ Kingdom
תְּמִימוּת	מִימוּשׁ עַצְמִי	שִׁפְלוּת
Sincerity	Self-Fulfillment	Humility
Left Leg	Procreative Organ	Mouth to Feet
Immune System	Reproductive System	Digestive System
יוֹם חֲמִישִׁי	יוֹם שִׁשִּׁי	שַׁבָּת
Fifth Day (Thursday)	Sixth Day (Friday)	Seventh Day (Shabbat)
אַהֲרֹן	יוֹסֵף	דָּוִד
Aharon	**Yosef**	**David**
אֲבִיגַיִל	חֻלְדָּה	אֶסְתֵּר
Avigail	**Chuldah**	**Esther**

The Seven Species Reflecting the Soul of Israel

The Ripening Process Reflecting Self-Improvement

The flowering and fruiting of the Seven Species parallel our own spiritual development during the season between Pesach and Shavuot characterized by self-improvement and preparation for receiving the Torah. Each of these seven weeks corresponds to one of the seven lower sefirot. As we count the Omer during the time period between Pesach and Shavuot, we work on mastering the character traits associated with each of the sefirot respectively, while turning to G*d in repentance and prayer. Since the fruiting of the Seven Species is linked to our own spiritual achievement and merit, it is not surprising that they comprise a wealth of spiritual attributes, nutrients and medicinal properties.

The Spiritual and Medicinal Energies of the Fruits

The special significance of the Seven Species is accentuated by the great Kabbalist, the Holy Arizal, who attributes the spiritual energies of each fruit to one of the seven characteristics of the soul, the seven sefirot that we count each week of the Omer.[127] Their correspondence is according to the order they occur in the Torah verse. Just as every food has particular medicinal properties for the health of the body, likewise its inner dimension (sefirah) vitalizes the soul.[128] It is interesting to note how the medicinal properties of the Seven Species are synchronized with their spiritual energies, as will be demonstrated with Hashem's help.

The Sequence of the Ripening of the Fruits Corresponds to the Spiritual Ripening of Israel

The Seven Fruits of Israel can be divided into three categories: Grains, fruits for eating and fruits for producing derivative products (olives for oil and dates for honey).[129] The ripening period of these Seven Fruits of Israel spans the entire nine months fruiting period in Israel (spring/summer/fall) from the Hebrew month of Nissan to the month of Kislev.[130] This period, which includes most of our holidays, is superior for developing relationships and manifesting spiritual growth.

The two grains, barley and wheat, ripen prior to Shavuot. Barley ripens at the onset of Pesach. The Hebrew word for barley, שְׂעוֹרָה/ *seorah*, is etymologically related to the word שַׁעַר/*sha'ar*, which means 'gate.' Barley opens the gate of spiritual ripening of the Jewish people, as we left Egypt's forty-nine gates of impurity to ascend the spiritual ladder of the forty-nine gates of purity. This process takes place during the forty-nine days following the first day of Pesach, when we count the *Omer* of the barley offering every day, working on our *Gevurah* and ability to 'go against the grain' and overcome the strong negative husk of Egypt that still may be clinging to us.

The forty-nine days of spiritual purification continue until we reach the ripening of the wheat, a more refined grain, on Shavuot, the time for sacrificing the two whole-wheat breads. The *Chesed* – loving-kindness of wheat characterizes the Torah of kindness that we receive on Shavuot.

The grapes, figs and pomegranates begin to ripen in Israel soon after we complete counting the *Omer*, according to the order of their spiritual energies. These fruits ripen one by one from Shavuot until Sukkot. During this time period we integrate the spiritual energies of these fruits. The beautiful grapes of *Tiferet* balance and harmonize us, the endurance of the figs of *Netzach* orchestrate and synchronize our energies, whereas the sheer majesty of the pomegranates of *Hod* teach us humility and acknowledgement, while imbuing us with their glory.

The Torah verse describing the Seven Species separates the last two species from the first five with the repetition of the word אֶרֶץ/ *eretz* – 'land,' to indicate that there is a difference between the first five and the last two species. Whereas the first five species nourish the body, olive oil and date honey also nourish the spirit.[131] Thus, the olives and dates, which ripen between Sukkot and Chanukah, bring us to a new level of body/soul integration. The oil and honey symbolize the spiritual refinement we undergo, while infusing the darker months with the lights of the previous holidays.

Endnotes

1. Zechariah 8:12.

2. *Babylonian Talmud, Shabbat* 30b; Rav Tzadok HaKohen of Lublin, Kreisburg-Lublin, Poland (1823–1900), ספר מחשבות חרוץ/ *Sefer Machshevot Charutz* 15.

3. The *sefirot* (singular *sefirah*) comprise the Divine manifestations within Creation. The sefirot are G*d's imprint within the world, which we are to emulate in order to reflect being created "in the image of G*d" (Genesis 1:27). See the section entitled *Introducing the Sefirot – The Branches of the Tree of Life* for a more detailed explanation about the sefirot.

4. Isaiah 11:1.

5. Deuteronomy 8:8, quoted in full above. The Sages understand the verse's mention of honey to refer to date honey. See Rabbi Yisrael Meir Kagan, Radin, Poland (1838–1933), משנה ברורה/*Mishnah Berurah* 202:45–46: "When it states in the Torah 'honey' it refers to dates, from which the honey flows."

6. We recite the threefold after-blessing *'M'ein Shalosh'* for these fruits, which include wine and grape juice, cake, or any cooked dish made with wheat, barley, or their subspecies – spelt, rye and oats. Rav Yosef Karo, Toledo-Safed (1488–1575), שולחן ערוך/*Shulchan Aruch, Orach Chaim* 208:1–2. This blessing differs from the blessing said after other fruits in its effusive praise of the Land of Israel and its fruits. For the full text of the *'M'ein Shalosh'* after-blessing in Hebrew and English see *Appendix III – The Threefold After-Blessing ('M'ein Shalosh') for the Seven Species*.

7. I Kings, 5:5.

8. *Babylonian Talmud, Sanhedrin* 98a.

9. Rashi, Numbers 13:23.

10. Exodus 23:19.

11. Deuteronomy 26:1–2.

12. The First Fruits Offering applies exclusively to the seven kinds of fruits mentioned in Scripture (Deuteronomy 8:8) for which the Land of Israel is praised (Rashi, Exodus 23:19).

13. This declaration of gratitude is described fully in Deuteronomy 26:5–10.

14. *Mishnah, Tractate Bikurim* 3:3.

15. Psalms 30:2; *Mishnah, Tractate Bikurim* 3:4.

16. Based on Nogah Hareuveni, Founder and Chairman of *Neot Kedumim*, The Biblical Landscape Reserve in Israel, *Nature in Our Biblical Heritage* (Neot Kedumim Ltd., Israel 1980), p. 60.

17. Based on the plethora of books and articles on the subject there seems to be a movement in the world toward returning to the biblical diet. See for example: *Whole Foods & Healing Recipes*, Ron Lagerquist (Foundation to All Freedom, 2003), who holds that a fruit and vegetable diet results in a clear mind.

18. Rav Tzadok HaKohen of Lublin, ספר פרי צדיק/*Sefer P'ri Tzadik*, for *Rosh Chodesh Shevat* 3; *P'ri Tzadik, Parashat B'Chukotai* 10.

19. Genesis 3:19.

20. *Babylonian Talmud, Shabbat* 30b.

21. In the seven days of Creation mentioned in Genesis, chapter 1, it states 10 times "וַיֹּאמֶר אֱלֹקִים – G*d said," see Genesis 1:3, 1:6, 1:9, 1:11, 1:14, 1:20, 1:24, 1:26, 1:28, 1:29. See also *Midrash Numbers Rabbah* 14:11, explaining that the world is created through the Ten Utterances corresponding to the Ten Sefirot.

22. Rabbi Moshe de León, Spain (circa 1250–1305) סוד עשר ספירות/ *The Secret of the Ten Sefirot*.

23. ספר יצירה/*Sefer Yetzirah – The Book of Formation* 1:1–2, the oldest, most mysterious Kabbalah book, attributed to Avraham our Patriarch.

24. It is interesting to note that also the Ten Commandments are divided into three and seven (three positive mitzvot and seven negative mitzvot). Likewise, the Ten Plagues are divided into seven mentioned in *Parashat Va'era* and three in *Parashat Bo*.

25. Although the Seven Fruits of Israel are associated with the seven lower sefirot, wheat is also linked with *Chochmah* (right above *Chesed*), and barley with *Binah* (right above *Gevurah*). Arizal, Rabbi Yitzchak Luria Ashkenazi, Jerusalem (1534–1572), *Sefer HaLikutim, Parashat Ekev* chapter 8.

26. Based on Rabbi Shneur Zalman of Liadi, Russia (1745–1812), לקוטי אמרים תניא/*Likutei Amerim, Tanya* (first part of) chapter 3.

27. "לית לה מגרמה כלום/*leit la mergarma klum* – Kingdom has nothing of her own" (Arizal, ספר הליקוטים/*Sefer HaLikutim, Parashat Terumah*, chapter 26).

28. *The Ten Sefirot of Gardening* has received the *haskama* (approbation) of Rav Yitzchak Ginsburgh.

29. Proverbs 31:31, describing the Woman of Valor.

30. Proverbs 3:18.

31. Based on Rabbi Avraham Yehoshua Heshel of Apta, Poland (1748–1825), אוהב ישראל/*Ohev Yisrael, Parashat B'ha'alotcha.*

32. Rabbi Shneur Zalman of Liadi, *Likutei Amerim, Tanya* chapter 3; Rabbi Shemuel Bornsztain, Poland (1910–1926), שם משמואל/*Shem M'Shemuel, Parashat Tetzaveh,* Year 5673.

33. Psalms 89:3.

34. Genesis 1:3.

35. Genesis 1:6–7.

36. Genesis 1:9–12.

37. Genesis 1:14–15.

38. Psalms 19:6.

39. Genesis 1:22.

40. Genesis 1:27.

41. *Batei Midrashot*, part 1, *Parashat Chayei Sarah* 57.

42. Genesis 1:28.

43. Proverbs 10:25.

44. The Prophets associate Avraham with *Chesed* in the following verses: "Give … *Chesed* to Avraham" (Micah 7:20). "…Avraham, My loving one" (Isaiah 41:8).

45. Genesis 18:1–8 with Rashi's commentary on verse 1. רש״י/Rashi is the acronym for **R**abbi **Sh**lomo ben **Y**itzchak, France (1040–1105).

46. Genesis 21:33 with Rashi's commentary.

47. "These are the generations of the heavens and the earth when they were created…" (Genesis 2:4): The letters of the word בְּהִבָּרְאָם/*behibaram* – "when they were created" permute into בְּאַבְרָהָם/*beAvraham* – 'in Avraham,' suggesting that the heavens and the earth were created in the merit of Avraham's *Chesed* (*Midrash Genesis Rabbah* 12:9).

48. The emotional expression of *Gevurah* is fear. The Torah associates Yitzchak with fear: "The One whom Yitzchak fears…" (Genesis 31:42, 53).

49. "In Yitzchak shall you have offspring that is named after you" (Genesis 21:12).

50. See for example Genesis 26:12, where Hashem blesses Yitzchak with a hundredfold crop.

51. *Yalkut Shimoni* I Chronicles 29:1082.

52. Rashi, Genesis 25:27.

53. See for example Arizal, עץ חיים/*Etz Chaim* 31:2.

54. Deuteronomy 9:9.

55. Deuteronomy 34:7.

56. Proverbs 10:25.

57. Genesis 41:45 with Rashi's commentary.

58. Onkelos, Aquila of Sinope, Israel (circa 35–120), *Targum Onkelos,* Genesis 41:45.

59. Rabbi Moshe Cordovero, Tzefat, Israel (1522–1570), תומר דבורה/*Tomer Devorah* end of chapter 8; Moshe Chaim Luzzatto (The Ramchal), Italy-Israel (1707–1746), עדיר במרום/*Adir BaMarom* pp. 372–374.

60. Genesis 39:12.

61. See the *Introduction* 18, endnote mark 27, Arizal, *Sefer HaLikutim, Parashat Terumah,* chapter 26.

62. Psalms 22:7.

63. *Babylonian Talmud, Megillah* 14a.

64. Genesis 29:34 with Rashi's commentary.

65. *Babylonian Talmud, Megillah* 14a.

66. The Rama of Fano, Menachem Azariah, Italy (1548–1620), ספר עשרה מאמרות/*Sefer Asarah Ma'amarot, Ma'amar Em Kol Chai,* part 2:1.

67. "The world is built through *Chesed...*" (Psalms 89:3).

68. See Genesis 18:6.

69. Genesis 15:4.

70. *Babylonian Talmud, Shavuot* 30b.

71. Genesis 18:6.

72. The first two letters of the name of Miriam spell out the Hebrew word for bitter, מַר/*mar.* See *Yalkut Shimoni* Song of Songs 2:986.

73. Micah 6:4.

74. Exodus 2:1 with Rashi's commentary explains how Miriam as a young girl accused her father Amram of being crueler than Pharaoh, as he had separated from her mother in order to avoid bringing any more children into the terrible world of slavery and child murder. Whereas Pharaoh had decreed 'only' against the boys, Amram's action would not even allow any girls to be born.

75. Exodus 15:20.

76. Arizal, *Etz Chaim* 7:2.

77. The Rama of Fano, *Sefer Asarah Ma'amarot, Ma'amar Em Kol Chai*, part 2:1.

78. Numbers 21:17.

79. Maharal, Rabbi Yehuda Loew ben Betzalel, Prague (1520–1609), נצח ישראל/*Netzach Yisrael*, chapter 54, p. 101.

80. The Counting of the *Omer* is a verbal counting of each of the forty-nine days between Pesach and Shavuot. This mitzvah derives from the Torah commandment to count from the day following Pesach when the Omer (a sacrifice containing an Omer measure of barley), was offered in the Temple, until Shavuot when an offering of wheat breads was brought to the Temple in Jerusalem. Moreover, counting the Omer is a spiritual preparation for the receiving of the Torah on Shavuot.

81. Judges 4:4.

82. Judges 4:9.

83. Hosea 10:1.

84. Judges 5:7.

85. See for example, Rabbi Moshe Cordovero, ספר פרדס רמונים/ *Sefer Pardes Rimonim* 20:12.

86. Malbim, Rabbi Meir Loeb ben Yechiel Michael, Volhynia, Ukraine (1809–1879), I Samuel 3:1.

87. I Samuel 15:29.

88. Rabbi Moshe Cordovero, *Sefer Pardes Rimonim* 23:14.

89. I Samuel 2:1.

90. The Rama of Fano, *Sefer Asarah Ma'amarot, Ma'amar Em Kol Chai*, part 2:1.

91. MaHaRShA, Rabbi Shemuel Edeles (Morenu Harav Shemuel Adel's – Our Teacher Rabbi Shemuel Adel's), Kraków, Poland (1555–1631), *Chidushei MaHaRSHA* on *Babylonian Talmud, Megillah* 14a.

92. I Samuel 2:10.

93. *Metzudat David*, Rabbi David Altschuler, Jaworow, Galicia (18th Century), I Samuel 2:10.

94. Rashi, Exodus 23:19.

95. I Samuel 1:11, 25, 28.

96. I Samuel 25:24–31.

97. I Samuel 25:20.

98. I Samuel 25:5–11.

99. *Ethics of our Fathers* 1:12.

100. I Samuel 25:20.

101. *Babylonian Talmud, Megillah* 14a.

102. I Samuel 25: 26.

103. I Samuel 25:31.

104. I Samuel 25:28.

105. The Rama of Fano, *Sefer Asarah Ma'amarot, Ma'amar Em Kol Chai*, part 2:1.

106. I Samuel 25:18.

107. J. Zohara Meyerhoff Hieronimus, *Kabbalistic Teachings of the Female Prophets: The Seven Holy Women of Ancient Israel* (Inner Traditions Intl., Rochester, VT, 2008), p. 238.

108. II Kings 22:14.

109. Rabbi Yosef Ben Karnitol, (Yosef ben Abraham Gikatilla) Castile (1248 – after 1305) ספר שערי צדק/*Sefer Sha'arei Tzedek*, the second gate.

110. Ben Ish Chai, Rabbi Yosef Chaim, Baghdad, Iraq (1834–1909), *Sefer Ben Yehoyada, Babylonian Talmud, Megillah* 16b.

111. The Rama of Fano, *Sefer Asarah Ma'amarot, Ma'amar Em Kol Chai*, part 2:1,

112. Numbers 25:12.

113. II Kings 23:3.

114. See I Samuel 24:6, 26:16; II Samuel 1:14, 19:22, 23:1.

115. *Babylonian Talmud, Megillah* 13b.

116. See the *Introduction*, p. 18, endnote mark 27 , Arizal, *Sefer HaLikutim, Parashat Terumah*, chapter 26.

117. The Scroll of Esther 2:7.

118. Arizal, ספר מחברת הקודש/*Sefer Machberet Hakodesh, Sha'ar HaShabbat*.

119. *Babylonian Talmud, Megillah* 13a.

120. The Scroll of Esther 4:13–16.

121. The Scroll of Esther 2:10, 2:20.

122. The Scroll of Esther 4:17 with Rashi's commentary, where he explains that the fast that Esther commanded Mordechai to proclaim for all the Jews was on the 14th, 15th and 16th of Nissan. Since the Torah

commands us to eat matzah on the first night of Pesach, the 15th of Nissan, the fast was according to *hora'at sha'ah* – breaking a Torah law in order to save the entire Jewish community from annihilation.

123. The Scroll of Esther 5:1.

124. Rabbi Yitzchak Isaac Chaver, Lithuania (1789–1852), second generation student of the Vilna Gaon. ספר בית עולמים/*Sefer Beit Olamim* 133a.

125. See Song of Songs 7:8, quoted in the beginning of the *Date* section.

126. *Zohar* 3:228b.

127. Arizal, *Sefer HaLikutim, Parashat Ekev*, chapter 8.

128. Rav Tzadok HaKohen of Lublin, *P'ri Tzadik, Et HaOchel* 13.

129. Note that our Torah verse in Deuteronomy 8:8 separates the fruits into two categories by the repetition of the word "land" ("...land of olive oil and honey,") and mentions the products produced from the fruits of the last category rather than the fruits themselves.

130. Approximately from April to November.

131. I heard this from Rav Rachamim Hadani during his lecture in Bat Ayin in year 2,000.

Triticum Vulgare ~ חִטָּה

Wheat

Wheat ~ חִטָה *Triticum Vulgare*
Chesed ~ חֶסֶד (*Loving-Kindness*)

וַיַּאֲכִילֵהוּ מֵחֵלֶב חִטָה וּמִצּוּר דְּבַשׁ אַשְׂבִּיעֶךָ: (תהילים פא, יז)

"He would feed him with the finest of the wheat: and with honey out of the rock I will satisfy you" (Psalms 81:17).

This verse teaches us that when the Israelites walk in the way of Hashem, then the dry places will be transformed to sheer abundance (*Metzudat David*).

לחם חטה בחסד זן בחסדו כל בשר.
(ספר ביאורי אגדות (אפיקי ים) - קידושין לא, ע"ב)

The bread of wheat is in chesed, with chesed He sustains all flesh (*Beurei Agadot, Afikei Yam, Kidushin* 31b).

Attribute: Chesed – Loving-kindness

Character trait: The ability to nourish (expansion)

Holiday: Shavuot, when we offer two wheat *challot* (loaves of bread)

Weekday: יוֹם רִאשׁוֹן/*Yom Rishon* – First day of the week (Sunday)

World: עֲשִׂיָה/*Asiyah* – Action (hard inedible husk)

Body parts: The right shoulder, arm and hand

Shepherd: אַבְרָהָם/Avraham

Prophetess: שָׂרָה/Sarah

Numerical value: 22, equivalent to the word טוֹבָה/*tovah* – 'goodness'[1]

Mentioned in the Bible 29 times[2]

Meaning of Latin Name: A genus of the common cereal grasses including wheat, from the root word 'tritum,' to grind.

פֶּרֶק שִׁירָה
Perek Shirah
The Song of the Universe

שִׁיר הַמַּעֲלוֹת מִמַּעֲמַקִּים קְרָאתִיךָ הַשֵּׁם:
(תהלים קל, א)

The Song of Wheat: "A song of ascents.
Out of the depths I called You, O Hashem"
(Psalms 130:1).

After the wheat is sown, it completely decomposes in the earth before it sprouts forth and grows new sheaves. From wheat we can learn that also when we are in trouble, G*d forbid, and find ourselves in the depths of darkness, we can call out to Hashem and pray from the depths. Just as Hashem allows the wheat to sprout forth, we can trust that He will deliver us from our trouble and sprout us forth to salvation.[3]

Nutrition Facts and Information about Wheat [4]

Mineral Content of Wheat [5]

Wheat is an excellent source of iron, phosphorus, magnesium, manganese, copper and selenium. Wheat berries are particularly rich in selenium. Wheat is a great source of zinc. It also contains potassium and a small amount of calcium.

Vitamin Content of Wheat

Wheat is an excellent source of thiamin and niacin. It is also a good source of riboflavin and vitamin B6, with some folate, and small amounts of vitamin E in whole wheat flour. Wheat germ oil is one of the main sources of vitamin E.

Oriental Medicine

According to Chinese medicine, wheat chaff affects the heart. It is sweet and slightly cold. Its properties are astringent, sedative and tonic. [6]

Wheat Nutritional Facts/100 g

Minerals	Whole Wheat Flour	Soft Red Winter Wheat berries	Recommended Daily Dietary Allowance (RDA)	
Calcium	33 mg	27 mg	3.5%	2.5%
Iron	3.71 mg	3.21 mg	46%	40%
Magnesium	117 mg	126 mg	33.5%	36%
Phosphorus	323 mg	493 mg	48%	73%
Potassium	394 mg	397 mg	8.5%	
Sodium	394 mg	2 mg	<1%	26.5%
Zinc	2.96 mg	2.63 mg	21%	19%
Copper	0.475 mg	0.434 mg	52.5%	48%
Manganese	3.399 mg	3.985 mg	>100%	
Selenium	12.7 µg	70.7 µg	21%	>100%
Vitamins	Whole Wheat Flour	Soft Red Winter Wheat berries	RDA	
C	0 mg	0.0 mg	0%	
B1 (Thiamin)	0.297 mg	0.394 mg	26%	35%
B2 (Riboflavin)	0.188 mg	0.096 mg	13.5%	7%
B3 (Niacin)	5.347 mg	4.800 mg	28.5%	25.5%
B6	0.191 mg	0.272 mg	9%	13%
B9 (Folate)	28 µg	41 µg	7%	10.5%
A	9 IU	0 IU	0.4%	0%
E	0.53 mg	0 mg	3%	0%
K	1.9 µg	0 mg	1.5%	0%

Wheat corresponds to Chesed. The attribute of *Chesed* is expansion: reaching out and extending oneself toward others. Wheat, likewise, has nourishing and expanding qualities. *Chesed*, through which the world is built,[7] corresponds to the skeletal system – the most essential building block of the body.[8] Likewise, wheat is the most essential food, which builds and sustains the body.

Most Nourishing of Foods

Wheat reflects the nourishing food of kindness. Since the times of the ancient Israelites until today, it remains our main sustaining food staple.[9] Wheat bread nourishes the heart.[10] Avraham told the angels, "I will fetch a morsel of bread, and nourish your hearts."[11] Wheat strengthens the body, aids digestion, increases blood volume, and improves circulation. It also increases mother's milk, the ultimate nourishment of *Chesed*.[12] Wheat germ contains significant amounts of vitamin E and folic acid. Vitamin E is an antioxidant, which helps to prevent destruction and waste of nutrients. Folic acid is important for the proper early development of the fetal nervous system.[13]

Protects against Breast-Cancer

I found it interesting that both wheat germ and wheat bran have a protective effect against breast cancer.[14] It is possible that one of the underlying causes for this illness is the expansiveness of *Chesed* going overboard, causing cells to reproduce randomly without proper boundaries. Therefore, in some cases, certain middle-aged women may be prone to cancer, especially breast-cancer, if they can't find a proper outlet for their *Chesed* when their children leave the nest. The breast embodies ultimate giving. Therefore, misplaced *Chesed* or the inability to find a proper recipient for a woman's desire to give, may cause inappropriate growths specifically in her breasts (May Hashem protect us!).

Rambam teaches that one of the healthiest foods to consume on a regular basis is properly prepared sourdough bread made from unrefined un-hulled fully ripened wheat kernels. Nothing else made from wheat is fitting to eat for a health-conscious person.[15] Fine, white wheat flour and anything cooked from wheat products are not proper food.[16] Boiled dough

such as noodles, macaroni, dumplings and fried dough-balls, as well as pancakes and bread soaked in oil, are especially unhealthy. Only a stomach with great power to digest them can derive any nourishment from these wheat products.[17]

Wheat – The Tree of Knowledge

Today, bread produced from wheat represents human technology, since so much human effort is invested into producing bread.[18] There is a rabbinic opinion that the Tree of Knowledge of Good and Evil was a 'wheat tree,' as according to the Talmud a baby only knows to pronounce the initial cognitive words such as 'Mommy' and 'Daddy' after having tasted wheat.[19] In addition, the numerical value of the word חִטָּה/*chitah* – 'wheat' is 22, corresponding to the 22 letters of the Hebrew alphabet, through which we express knowledge. Therefore, in order to imbue within the Jewish people that the Divine Torah (The Tree of Life) takes precedence over scientific knowledge (The Tree of Knowledge), the Torah restricts eating wheat products throughout the week of Pesach. During this holiday, the most pivotal time when the Jewish nation was born and its foundation laid, we may not eat חָמֵץ/*chametz* – (leavened bread), which is most often made from wheat.

The Limitations of Health Consciousness

The restriction against eating regular bread, which is naturally healthier than the dry unleavened matzah, teaches us the principle to choose *halacha* (Jewish law) over health. Keeping Hashem's commandments overrides the importance of healthy lifestyles. Ultimately, human health is determined by Hashem's continual creation and providence, rather than by what we eat. The spiritual nourishment of keeping Hashem's mitzvot enhances our physical health even more than the most wholesome nutritious super-food. We do not take care of our body for its own sake, but rather in order to keep Hashem's directives to "take very good care of yourselves."[20] This mitzvah teaches us that we must do our outmost to treat our body respectfully, and eat only wholesome foods that promote physical health whenever possible. However, sometimes, in order to better serve Hashem, we need to bend our health standards, and trust that He will bless even the white wheat flour to provide us with the nutrients that our body needs. The concept of eating matzah on Pesach signifies that we must avoid worshipping the knowledge of scientific research – including New Age alternative organic wisdom – and realize that the Jewish person is beyond the natural.[21]

In Judaism, bread is the mainstay of every meal. At all seudot-mitzvah (religious celebrations) including circumcisions, bar mitzvahs and wedding celebrations, wheat bread is served. We are encouraged to partake in the bread and join together in the Grace after Meals.

With the increasing wheat allergies and the fact that bread is no longer considered such a healthy food, whether to eat or not to eat bread becomes a serious dilemma, for health conscious, observant Jews. The mitzvah to take care of our health alongside the importance to partake of the mitzvah bread may pull us in opposite directions. Each person must endeavor to make the right decision, depending on the particular circumstances.

Wheat Allergies

Today, allergy to wheat has become very common, and not everyone is able to partake in the bread of mitzvah meals. During the last decade, a growing percentage of people have become gluten intolerant. Perhaps there is a spiritual underlying reason for the prevalent allergies to Biblical grains.

I believe there are physical, emotional and especially spiritual reasons for the increasing wheat/gluten allergies we experience in recent times. On the physical plane, wheat and other gluten-containing grains today are not what they were in the past. In our industrialized world, mass-produced wheat is hybridized to produce a larger, fatter and sweeter grain, to make it more sellable. Dr. William Davis explains that the kind of wheat available today is detrimental to human health. The reason for this is that "genetic differences generated via thousands of human-engineered hybridizations make for substantial variation in composition, appearance and quantities."[22]

On the emotional level, perhaps one reason for the prevalent wheat allergy is that wheat represents the power of food to nourish. Many people today have been force-fed, or required to finish their plate by parents of the post-holocaust generation. Since they were not allowed to be in control over their eating as children, their body may react, attempting to regain control by rejecting specifically wheat, which represents food in general.

In the spiritual sense, the Talmud teaches us that the Tree of Knowledge was a wheat tree.[23] In the Garden of Eden, wheat was a fruit tree producing ready-to-eat fruits in the form of rich cakes or muffins. At the End of Days, "the land of Israel will [once again] produce muffin trees."[24] As a result of eating from the Tree of Knowledge, Adam was cursed: "By the sweat of your brow you shall eat (wheat) bread."[25] Since then, wheat bread became the ultimate 'hard-work-food.' It must be planted, plowed, ground, harvested, bundled, trampled, winnowed, separated from pebbles, sifted, kneaded and baked. Bread became a symbol of all the toil we do in order to make

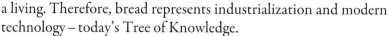

a living. Therefore, bread represents industrialization and modern technology – today's Tree of Knowledge.

Although the Tree of Knowledge, represented by bread, caused the great downfall and expulsion from Eden, it nevertheless can be redeemed. Adam's curse can be redefined as the rectification for eating from the Tree of Knowledge. "The sweat of your brow" entails not only hard physical work, but also emotional and spiritual refinement. Bread, thus, is a manifestation of what it means to be refined and transformed over and over, until we become what we are meant to be. The main rectification is to learn to recognize that even when we apply our ultimate effort to produce our most refined product, nevertheless Hashem is still the Creator of all. He is the One who gives us the wheat and the ability to plough, sow, harvest, winnow, grind, sift, knead and bake it. The more our own effort goes into producing a certain product, and the more the technology of the Western World evolves, the temptation is greater to be misled into thinking that we are the creators and masters of the world: "It is my power and the strength of my hand that made all these."[26] This was the original temptation of the serpent that lured Eve to eat from the Tree in order to become "like G*d."[27]

Today in our industrialized Western World, we have succumbed big time to the temptation of the Tree of Knowledge, the source of our knowledge, science and technology, to think we are "like G*d." This may be a spiritual reason why we experience so much intolerance to wheat in our time. Our spiritual health and true life depends on recognizing Hashem as the Creator of everything. We need to return the ultimate labor of our hands to Him, in recognition that even what we have put most of ourselves into really belongs to Him, Who is the source of our life and labor. Only when we have reached this level of conscious existence, will we be able to heal our relationship with wheat completely.

Returning the Life to the Wheat

The Torah alludes to our current challenging relationship with wheat. The correct spelling of wheat in Hebrew is חִיטָה/*chitah*. However, the biblical spelling of the word for wheat, חִטָה/*chitah,* is missing the letter י/*yud* which usually follows the *chirik* (ee) vowel sound in Hebrew.[28] Without the *yud* the word חַי/*chai* – 'life' is mysteriously missing from חִטָה/*chitah* – wheat. Devoid of the *yud*, wheat is removed from the source of life, Hashem. Perhaps since wheat is identified with the Tree of Knowledge, which brought mortality to the world, it is missing the life from the Tree of Life, its antidote.[29] This could be why so many people have wheat allergies today. Furthermore, the root of the Hebrew word for wheat, implies sinning extensively and removing something from the source of life, yet it can also symbolize the elimination of sin, (חֵטְא/*chet*).[30]

At the Final Redemption, the *yud* and the *chet* will reunite in the word חִיטָה/*chitah*, wheat, to form the word חָי/*chai*, 'life'. When life will return to the wheat, it will transform its entire root and everything it represents. The wheat from the Tree of Knowledge, with all its glittering temptation, will become elevated and transformed into the fruit of the Tree of Life – the actual material manifestation of the Torah. Then the Tree of Knowledge (wheat and human technology) and the Tree of Life (Torah) will become unified. There will no longer be a gap between the spiritual and the physical, between body and soul. The *yud* represents the '*pintele yid,*' the aspect of the Jewish soul hardwired into the Divine, which can never be extinguished. Once the *yud* will infuse our bread, the source of our physical sustenance, we and the wheat will make peace, and together we will rise to a higher level of existence. Our *chayah* and *yechidah* soul levels of life will then be reawakened and activated.[31]

By pronouncing חִטָה/*chitah* as חִיטָה/*chiytah* with the inclusion of the letter *yud*, we are infusing our lower state of awareness with the *kavanah* (intention) of propelling us toward a state of Messianic

awareness. The wheat bread, the very same vehicle (Knowledge) that caused our original separation from the source of our life, will reunite us with G*d during the Messianic grandeur as it states: "For the land shall be full of the knowledge of Hashem as the water covers the sea."[32]

The Final Redemption ushered in by Mashiach will take place when we will have completed the rectification for eating from the Tree of Knowledge. It is not by chance that once our relationship with wheat is healed, the most refined and perfected human being, Mashiach, will arise specifically from Bethlehem, in Hebrew, בֵּית לֶחֶם/*Beit Lechem* – The House of Bread, to repair the world.[33] At that time the rectified wheat will reflect human refinement and the actualization of our full potential. Then "the land of Israel will [once again] bring forth bread-cakes."[34]

Reverting the Curse of Eating from the Tree of Knowledge

בְּזֵעַת אַפֶּיךָ תֹּאכַל לֶחֶם עַד שׁוּבְךָ אֶל הָאֲדָמָה... (בראשית ג, יט)

"In the sweat of your brow shall you eat bread, till you return to the ground..." (Genesis 3:19).

Bread was only introduced to our diet as a consequence of eating from the Tree of Knowledge.[35] Perhaps we are in the process of returning to the 'Edenic' lifestyle and diet consisting of fruits and vegetables alone.[36] Just as the rest of the curses resulting from eating from the Tree of Knowledge are gradually fading out, as we approach the Final Redemption, perhaps the curse of eating bread (with or without "the sweat of your brow") is also drawing to a close, as we await the day when "the Land of Israel will once again produce muffin trees."[37] Until then, sourdough whole wheat and sprouted wheat bread serve as a healthy alternative to our dilemma of whether or not to eat wheat.

Infusing our Bread with Torah

One should place both hands on the bread at the time of blessing, for the hands have ten fingers corresponding to the ten mitzvot connected with producing bread.[38] Therefore, there are ten words in the blessing of '*Hamotzi*' (Who brings forth bread...) There are also ten words in the verse "A land of wheat and barley..." (*Deuteronomy* 8:8).[39]

The ten words in the blessing:

בָּרוּךְ אַתָּה הָשֵׁם אֱלֹקֵינוּ מֶלֶךְ הָעוֹלָם הַמּוֹצִיא לֶחֶם מִן הָאָרֶץ

Blessed are you, Hashem our G*d, Sovereign of the world, Who brings forth bread from the earth, moreover, correspond to the Ten Commandments – the essence of the Torah – which we connect with our bread, infusing our eating and physical existence with the ways of the Torah.

הרואה חטים בחלום ראה שלום, שנאמר
"הַשָּׂם גְּבוּלֵךְ שָׁלוֹם חֵלֶב חִטִּים יַשְׂבִּיעֵךְ:"

*He who sees wheat in a dream has seen peace,
as it says, "He has placed peace in your borders;
He will satiate you with the fat of wheat"*[40]
(Babylonian Talmud, Berachot 57a).

⁖ *A Taste of Kabbalah – Bread with Salt*

הרבה פעמים אמרו רז"ל פת במלח, "משהעני נכנס לאכול פתו במלח",
"כך דרכה של תורה פת במלח", "פת במלח וקיתון של מים מבטלתו",
והרבה כיוצא, ונראה לי שרומז על מה שכתבתי לעיל סוד פת הוא סוד
מוחין דגדלות ודקטנות והוא סוד החסד וגבורה, ונודע שכל זמן שאין
הגבורות יורדין עד יסוד אין נמתקין, רק כשבאין ליסוד ומתעכבין יחד
אז נמתקים... והנה מלח הוא יסוד, על כן פת במלח רומז על התכללות
חסד וגבורה מוחין דגדלות וקטנות ביסוד דאקרי מלח ושם נמתקים...
וכן דרכה של תורה להמשיך המוחין ליסוד ומשם נשפעים לכל העולמות,
וזה שאמר "פת במלח תאכל", וכן מה שאמר "פת במלח וקיתון של מים
מבטלתן חלאים דמרה" שהוא מבחינת שמאל, ועל ידי המשכת החסדים
שביסוד דאקרי פת במלח... (קהלת יעקב - ערך פת)

Our Sages often speak about eating bread with salt, for example:
"When the poor comes to eat bread with salt."[41] "This is the way
of the Torah, bread with salt..."[42] "Bread with salt and a pitcher
of water..."[43] It seems to me that it alludes to the secret of bread,
which is the secret of expansive and constricted consciousness,
the secret of *Chesed* and *Gevurah*. It is known that *Gevurah* is
only sweetened when it comes into *Yesod* and remains with it.
Salt is *Yesod*, therefore bread with salt alludes to the inclusion of
Chesed and *Gevurah*, the expansive and constricted consciousness in *Yesod*, which is called salt, and there they become sweetened. This is the way of the Torah to draw down consciousness
into *Yesod* and influence all the worlds from there. This is the
meaning of "you shall eat bread with salt." Likewise, "bread
with salt and a pitcher of water counteracts the illnesses of the
gall," which are from the aspect of the left, by means of drawing down *Chesed* into *Yesod,* which is called "bread with salt..."
(Rabbi Ya'acov ben Chaim Tzemach, *Kohelet Ya'acov*).

Explanation: The above text is discussing the deeper Kabbalistic
reason for why the Talmud often recommends eating bread with
salt. In all of the citations mentioning bread together with salt, the
Hebrew word for bread is פַּת/*pat* rather than לֶחֶם/*lechem*. This is

because the word פַּת/*pat* has the *gematria* (numerical value) of 481 with the *kollel* (when counting the word itself as one). 481 equals the gematria of יָמִין/right, 110 and שְׂמֹאל/left, 371, which represent *Chesed* and *Gevurah,* respectively. *Chesed* is on the right branch of the Tree of Life, while *Gevurah* is on the left. Bread includes both *Gevurah* and *Chesed,* because it is made from wheat and water, which correspond to *Chesed,* but baked with the fire of *Gevurah.* Salt, the most fundamental of all seasonings, corresponds to *Yesod,* the channel through which the remaining sefirot merge on their way to *Malchut.* In order to access the light of the harsh judgments of *Gevurah* (from the fire of baking the bread) it needs to be sweetened by *Chesed.* This sweetening and mingling takes place in the foundation of *Yesod.* Therefore, our Sages recommended that we dip bread in salt, in order that the *Gevurah* of the bread can be properly blended with the *Chesed* of the bread by means of *Yesod,* embodied by the salt.

The Jewish way is to always dip our bread in salt, not only on Shabbat. Additional reasons for this are that our table is considered an altar,[44] and in the Holy Temple salt was offered together with every sacrifice. Salt never spoils or decays, therefore, it is symbolic of our eternal covenant with G*d and referred to as "the salt of your G*d's covenant."[45] Salt also adds taste to everything. Our bond with Hashem is supposed to add meaning and flavor to every moment of our lives, even when we are not directly involved in spiritual pursuits.

We dip the bread in salt rather than sprinkling salt on the bread because salt can also represent *Gevurah,* Divine Severity, while bread, the staff of life, primarily represents *Chesed,* Divine Kindness. We don't want to sprinkle severity on top of kindness; rather, we endeavor to overpower the severity with kindness. In addition, the gematria of the Hebrew word for bread, לֶחֶם/*lechem,* is 78. We dip the bread three times, dividing the energy of 78 into three times 26, the gematria of the name of G*d. This reminds us that "humanity does not live by bread alone, but rather by whatever comes forth from the mouth of Hashem..."[46]

Wheat Recipes

Accessing the Blessing of Whole Wheat Kernels

Wheat is most often used as flour in baking. However, the less wheat has been processed, the healthier it is. Therefore, it is important to eat the entire wheat berry, preferably whole or at least cracked. Valuable proteins, fats, minerals and vitamins are present in the germ and the outer hull.

Just as *Chesed* is expansive, wheat has the ability to extend the sunlight into the earth and the roots by means of its straight axis. We can ingest some of this sunlight when we consume whole wheat kernels. Try to eat fewer products made with flour, and more with whole grain kernels, which you can sprout or soak and cook.[47] Here are a few recipes that you can experiment with and expand.

BACK-TO-BASICS BOILED WHEAT BERRIES
A basic, filling staple to serve with goat cheese and fresh salad

2 cups organic wheat berries
4 cups water
2 tablespoons sea salt

1. Rinse the wheat berries and soak them overnight.

2. Place them in a pot with the water. Bring the pot to a boil and simmer for one and a half to two hours, then add salt.

3. Using a pressure cooker your wheat berries will be ready in 45 minutes.

This basic recipe can serve as an alternative to rice, served with any sauce and stir-fried veggies.

I like it plain with just olive oil and *za'atar*, (A common Middle Eastern spice consisting mainly of dried hyssop, sesame seeds and salt), but you can also add other herbs like basil, parsley or coriander.

(If you cook the wheat berries for closer to two hours, they will be soft and sticky and thereby avoid uncertainty regarding their blessing. See *Laws of Blessings* p. 88.)

NUTTY GREEN WHEAT BERRY SALAD

Almost a meal in itself, filled with green goodness

2 cups soaked organic wheat berries

1 cup sunflower seeds
(you may substitute different seeds or nuts)

1 bunch of chopped green onions

3 stalks chopped celery

½ cup pomegranate arils

½ cup finely chopped parsley

½ cup finely chopped cilantro

4 tablespoons olive oil

3 tablespoons lemon juice

Sea salt and freshly ground black pepper to taste

1. Prepare wheat berries according to *Back-to-Basics Boiled Wheat Berries* recipe.

2. Drain and let cool.

3. In a large bowl, combine the wheat berries with remaining ingredients.

You can experiment with the ingredients according to which greens, veggies, seeds and nuts you have on hand.

WHEAT BURGERS

A great vegetarian meal; add mashed tofu for an even better meat substitute

> 1 cup whole wheat berries
> 3 medium-sized onions
> 3 cloves of garlic
> 1 egg or 1 tablespoon freshly ground flax seeds soaked in 3 tablespoons water for 10 minutes
> 2–3 tablespoons raw oat flakes
> 1–3 tablespoons olive oil for sautéing
> 1 teaspoon dried parsley
> Sea salt and freshly ground black pepper to taste

1. Cook the wheat berries according to the *Back-to-Basics* recipe.

2. Chop the onions and sauté them until golden.

3. Add garlic and continue sautéing for approximately five more minutes.

4. Place the cooked wheat berries and the sautéed onions in the food processor.

5. Process with the S-blade until almost smooth. (You may reserve ¼ cup of the wheat berries to mix in whole for a nuttier consistency).

6. Add egg or soaked flax seeds, oats, salt and herbs.

7. Leave to steep together for about half an hour.

8. Form into burger shapes and sauté in olive oil until browned.

Variation

For a wholesome health treat, use sprouted instead of cooked wheat berries and bake instead of sautéing.

WHEAT BALLS

Children will happily eat any veggie camouflaged inside of this dish

1 cup whole wheat berries

2–3 medium-sized onions

2–3 carrots

½ cup raw oat flakes

1–3 cloves of garlic

2 eggs or soaked flax seed equivalent
(see recipe for *Wheat Burgers*)

Sea salt, freshly ground black pepper, basil and ground nutmeg to taste

Sauce

1 finely chopped onion

1 small can of tomato purée diluted with 2 cans of water
(125 gram or a little more than 7 oz.)

2 tablespoons sweetener (molasses, honey, brown sugar)

2 tablespoons lemon juice

Black pepper to taste

1. Cook the wheat berries according to the *Back-to-Basics* recipe.

2. Chop the onions and sauté them until golden.

3. Place the cooked wheat berries and the sautéed onions in the food processor with remaining ingredients.

4. Leave to steep together for about half an hour.

5. Shape into balls.

6. Prepare the sauce by sautéing the onion until golden.

7. Add the remaining ingredients and simmer for five minutes.

8. Add the balls and simmer for about 10 minutes or until ready.

WHEAT LOAF
Very tasty and hard to believe the main ingredient is wheat berries

> 1 cup whole wheat berries
>
> 2–3 onions
>
> 1½ cups wheat germ
>
> 3 eggs or soaked flax seed equivalent
> (see recipe for *Wheat Burgers*, p. 74)
>
> ½ cup corn flour or raw oat flakes
>
> 1 teaspoon each paprika and marjoram
>
> Sea salt and freshly ground black pepper to taste

1. Cook the wheat berries according to the *Back-to-Basics* recipe.

2. Place the cooked wheat berries and the chopped onions in the food processor.

3. Add the remaining ingredients, be generous with the spices, process briefly with the S-blade.

4. Press the dough into an oiled baking pan.

5. Bake at medium heat for one hour.

Variation

Separate the eggs and beat the whites until stiff before mixing into the dough for a lighter loaf.

You may add whatever you have on hand to this basic recipe, such as shredded carrots and zucchinis. Any vegetable leftovers will only add taste to the wheat-loaf. Feel free to experiment with the spices including thyme, basil, cumin, etc.

GREEN MIDDLE EASTERN TABOULI SALAD
A nice filling side dish on a warm summer day

1 cup bulgur (cracked wheat)
2 cups boiling water
1½ cups finely chopped parsley (about 1½ bunch)
½ cup finely chopped fresh mint
1 cup finely chopped green onions or chives
2 finely chopped large tomatoes
4 finely chopped cucumbers
Fresh juice of 3 lemons
3 cloves of garlic
5 tablespoons olive oil
Sea salt and freshly ground black pepper to taste

1. Pour the boiling water over the bulgur in a medium-sized bowl.

2. Place a towel over the bowl so the steam cannot escape. Set aside to steep until cool.

3. Process the garlic and herbs in the food processor and place them into a large salad bowl.

4. Chop the vegetables and herbs finely and add to the herb mixture.

5. Juice the fresh lemons and pour the juice over the salad mixture.

6. Add olive oil, black pepper and sea salt to the salad mixture.

7. Add the cooled bulgur and mix all the ingredients well.

SPROUTED WHEAT BERRIES

Adds texture and vitamins to many salads, soups and side-dishes

1. Soak one cup of organic wheat berries in a container filled with water for 24 hours.

2. Strain the water and save it in a bottle for drinking.[48]

3. Replace the container cap with screen material fastened with a thick rubber band to facilitate rinsing and drainage. Keep your container slightly slanted horizontally so that any excess water can drain out into your kitchen sink.

4. Rinse your sprouts in water and drain well daily.

    (In the summer twice a day is preferable).

It is important to use organic wheat berries. Most seeds that are not organic will rot rather than sprout. This teaches us that only organic produce is alive. If your seeds are left to stand in excess water they will rot. Avoid the disappointment of ruined sprouts by rinsing and draining thoroughly. The sprouts should be ready within three days, or when the wheat berries have sprouted ½ cm (¼ inch) tails. Make sure to rinse out, refrigerate or use before the green wheatgrass begins to grow, or it will make the sprout hard and chewy. Use wheat sprouts in salads, casseroles, stir-fries, breads and cakes and as a chewing gum substitute.

Health Benefits of Sprouted Wheat

Live grains soaked in water significantly increase valuable nutrients. Sprouting wheat increases its vitamin E 300 times.[49] Germinated wheat sprouts are an effective and economical tonic that improves general health. The seeds become living food as soon as germination takes place and valuable enzymes are activated. Once eaten, these enzymes act as catalysts that perform important functions in the body, such as: aiding digestion, neutralizing toxins, cleansing the blood and providing energy for innumerable bodily functions. Sprouted wheat is an excellent source of protein, calcium, iodine, iron, potassium, zinc, magnesium, phosphorus, B-complex and vitamin E.[50]

REJUVELAC

*The simplest way to make rejuvelac is to use the water
in which wheat berries have been soaking for 24 hours.
Here is a fancier way to make an even more potent rejuvelac.*

1. Soak 2 cups of wheat berries in purified water for 12 hours.

2. Drain and let them sprout for approximately two days, rinsing
   as needed.

3. Place the sprouted wheat berries in a 4-liter (1 gallon) jar.
   Fill it to the top with purified water, and let it sit, covered, at
   room temperature.

4. The soaking liquid becomes rejuvelac after 48 hours and has a
   slight lemony flavor.

5. Drain the rejuvelac off into another container.

6. Refill the gallon jar with more purified water and soak the
   wheat berries for 24 hours for a second batch, then feed them
   to your chickens or the birds outside.

Health Benefits of Rejuvelac

Rejuvelac is an organic fermented drink containing acidophilus
and friendly bacteria necessary for the colon. Furthermore, it
contains extra enzymes to aid in food digestion and prevents
oxidation. [51] It is highly recommended to drink rejuvelac when
taking antibiotics, in order to replace friendly bacteria killed
by the medicine.

WILD WINTER WHEATSPROUT SALAD
A delightful nutty crunchy side dish

2 cups sprouted wheat berries

½ cup sesame seeds

1 finely chopped red onion (optional)

¼ cup chopped dill

¼ cup chopped parsley

¼ cup chopped cilantro

3 tablespoons lemon juice or apple cider vinegar

3 tablespoons olive oil

¾ teaspoon sea salt

½ teaspoon freshly ground black pepper

Mix all ingredients well and serve chilled.

SPROUTED WHEAT BREAD
*So Simple, so Delicious, so Nutritious! You won't believe
it is made with only one ingredient – sprouted wheat berries!*

1. Place well drained sprouted wheat berries in the food processor.
   Don't rinse the sprouts after they have finished sprouting.

2. Add a touch of sea salt (optional).

3. Process with the S-blade for about one minute. Open the food
   processor and push down the wheat sprouts that tend to stick
   to the sides of the food processor. Continue processing until
   the berries resemble bread dough, forming a ball around the
   blade (it may take from three to five minutes).

4. Remove the ball of dough from the food processor. Shape the
   dough into several balls, one big loaf, or any shape of your
   choice.

5. Sprinkle with freshly ground corn meal or sesame seeds
   (optional).

6. Place the shaped dough on your baking pan, or in your muffin
   tray for rolls.

7. Bake on high heat for 10–15 minutes to create a nicely browned
   crust, then lower the heat and continue baking for 20–30
   additional minutes until done. (The bread should remain soft
   and moist under the crispy brown crust.)

Variation

1. Press the sprouted wheat dough into your crock pot.

2. Place the cover on your slow cooker and turn to its lowest
   setting.[52]

3. Cook the bread for approximately eight hours or until the
   bread is rich, dark brown.

The top of the bread may crack and it will have a tough, thick crust
and moist, brown bread on the inside. Because this bread is so
nutritionally dense, you only need a small piece to accompany your
salad or soup entrée. Your sprouted grain bread will stay fresh in the
refrigerator for more than a week.

The blessing for sprouted wheat bread is '*Hamotzi Lechem min ha'aretz.*'[53]

IT'S GOOD TO BE ACCUSTOMED TO EATING BREAD IN THE MORNING as it states in the Talmud:[54] "Eighty-three kinds of illnesses result from the gall, but they all are counteracted by eating bread dipped in salt in the morning, followed by a pitcher of water. It is a mitzvah to make this one's custom and thereby guard one's health in order to be healthy and strong to serve the Creator."[55]

Chacham Ben Tzion Abba Shaul ruled that one fulfills this obligation not only with bread, but also with other baked grain products. Other Rabbis hold that it is not an obligation to eat bread in the morning. According to the *Shulchan Aruch* it is '*tov*' (good) to eat bread in the morning if one is accustomed to this. The *Mishnah Berurah* explains that this is in order to perform the mitzvah to guard one's health. If one has other ways to keep healthy, it is not necessary to eat bread in the morning.[56]

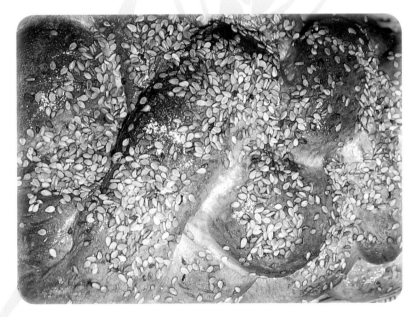

WHEATGRASS JUICE

Today wheatgrass juice has become a popular alternative to 'bread in the morning' among the health conscious. It is recommended to consume it first thing in the morning, before partaking of any other food. According to scientific research, wheatgrass can actually be an important resource for improving wheat bread.[57]

Wheatgrass is usually consumed in juice form. In order to produce wheatgrass juice you need a special juicer.[58] For optimal health benefits, drink a ¼ cup of wheatgrass juice every morning on an empty stomach five days a week, for three weeks a month. Drink your juice within six minutes of juicing. You can also receive the benefits of wheatgrass juice by chewing the stalks of wheatgrass for a long time, before discarding the remaining chewed pulp. This can serve as a chewing gum substitute which will benefit your teeth and gums greatly. Wheatgrass may have a purifying effect on water. Cut a few stalks and add to your water bottle.

You can grow your own wheatgrass on a sunny windowsill on plastic trays of 55/15 cm (8/28 inch) or any size available that fits your windowsills. Place a thin layer of good soil on the bottom of your trays and sprinkle the trays with a dense layer of wheat berries that have been soaked for 24 hours. Water your wheat berries daily, and keep them moist, as you watch them germinate, sprout and grow into fresh green grass. After seven days you can start harvesting your wheatgrass by cutting it down, while allowing it to grow back for a second batch or even a third. Keep in mind that wheatgrass is most potent from seven to ten days after sprouting.

Health Benefits of Wheatgrass

The consumption of wheatgrass in the Western world began in the 1930s by Charles Schnabel, who taught that "15 pounds of wheatgrass is equal in overall nutritional value to 315 pounds of ordinary garden vegetables, a ratio of 1:21."[59] Schnabel was able to nurse dying hens back to life by feeding them wheatgrass. The hens recovered, and produced eggs at a higher rate than healthy hens. Wheatgrass juice has increased in popularity as a general health tonic for everyone, especially people who are allergic to the gluten component of wheat. Wheatgrass is rich in vitamins and minerals. It constitutes at least 13 vitamins (several are antioxidants), including B12, a wealth of minerals and trace elements, such as selenium, all 20 amino acids and over 30 enzymes.[60] Wheatgrass contains as much magnesium as broccoli and half as much iron as spinach.[61] Its 70% chlorophyll content, which is similar in structure to hemoglobin, builds healthy red blood cells, normalizes blood pressure, provides optimal amounts of oxygen to the body, destroys carbon dioxide, promotes better metabolism and alkalizes the blood.[62] In addition, wheatgrass juice detoxifies, promotes digestion, strengthens the teeth, prevents cancer and is used as a remedy for ulcerative colitis.[63]

WONDERFUL WHEAT GERM BROWNIES
An absolutely irresistible healthy flour and sugar-free dessert

2 cups wheat germ

1 cup sweetener (honey, agave, maple syrup etc.)

2 tablespoons molasses

½ cup oil

4 eggs

1 teaspoon baking powder

1 cup shredded coconut (optional)

½–1 cup crushed walnuts or sunflower seeds (optional)

1. Mix all ingredients together in any order.

2. Press into a baking pan. If the baking pan has a larger surface the batter will resemble brownies, if the dish is smaller the batter will be more like cake.

3. Bake at medium heat for about 45 minutes.

4. Check the brownies after half an hour. They should be moist but hard enough to cut into slices that won't fall apart.

Health Benefits of Wheat germ

Wheat germ contains naturally occurring polyunsaturated fat and provides an impressive bundle of nutrients, including vitamin E, folate, phosphorus, thiamin, zinc and magnesium. Phytosterols in wheat germ may have important effects on cholesterol absorption and metabolism.[64] Because of its high oil content, improperly stored wheat germ can become rancid. Keep it refrigerated, and if possible store it in a glass jar.

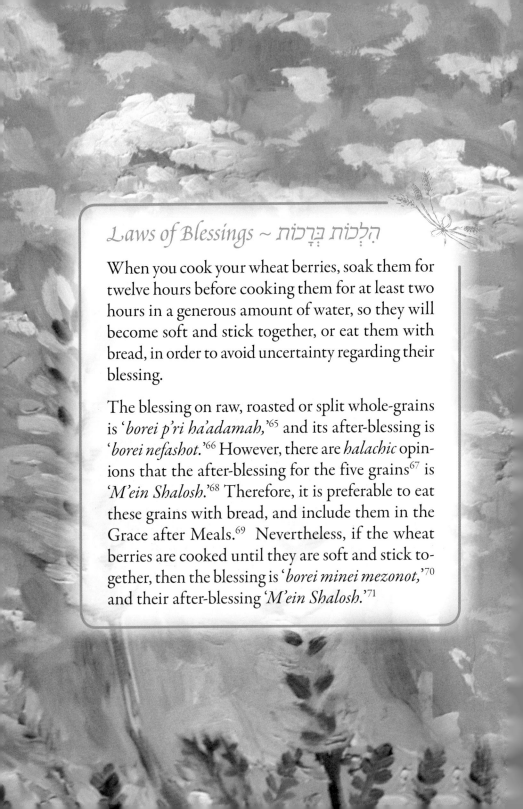

Laws of Blessings ~ הִלְכוֹת בְּרָכוֹת

When you cook your wheat berries, soak them for twelve hours before cooking them for at least two hours in a generous amount of water, so they will become soft and stick together, or eat them with bread, in order to avoid uncertainty regarding their blessing.

The blessing on raw, roasted or split whole-grains is 'borei p'ri ha'adamah,'[65] and its after-blessing is 'borei nefashot.'[66] However, there are *halachic* opinions that the after-blessing for the five grains[67] is 'M'ein Shalosh.'[68] Therefore, it is preferable to eat these grains with bread, and include them in the Grace after Meals.[69] Nevertheless, if the wheat berries are cooked until they are soft and stick together, then the blessing is 'borei minei mezonot,'[70] and their after-blessing 'M'ein Shalosh.'[71]

Hello, I'm Grandpa Grain,

I'm always happy to see you. I love having guests and I'm happy to share whatever comes my way. As the wisest of all men said: "Cast your bread upon the waters, for after many days you will find it again."[72] My wife and I have a bakery, and every Friday we send fresh-baked challah rolls and cakes to all the orphans and widows in our community. Lately, we have been turning to our grandchildren to help us with the deliveries. Whenever you come by we will enjoy a variety of baked goods together. I am especially fond of my wife's wonderful wheat germ brownies. They are supposed to be healthy, so I keep munching on them, although I really have to watch my weight. Yet, dieting is not fun, and even if the volume of my belly stretches my shirts and several buttons have popped off and gotten lost, these should be our greatest *tzuris* (trouble)! 'You only live once.' Actually, that may not be true; nevertheless I stick to the advice of the wise King Solomon: "Enjoy life with your wife, whom you love..."[73]

Endnotes

1. Genesis 15:15.

2. Wheat – חִטָּה/*chitah,* חִטִּים/*chitim* and חִטִּין/*chitin,* are mentioned 29 times in the Bible.
    Wheat – חִטָּה/*chitah* is mentioned in the Bible as a singular noun seven times, three times in the Pentateuch and four times in the rest of the Bible: Exodus 9:32; Deuteronomy 8:8, 32:14; Isaiah 28:25; Joel 1:11; Psalms 81:17; Job 31:40. **Wheat** – חִטִּים/*chitim* is mentioned in the Bible as a plural noun 21 times, 3 times in the Pentateuch and 18 times in the rest of the Bible: Genesis 30:14; Exodus 29:2, 34:22; Judges 6:11, 15:1; I Samuel 6:13, 12:17; II Samuel 4:6, 17:28; I Kings 5:25; Jeremiah 12:13, 41:8; Ezekiel 45:13; Psalms 147:14; Song of Songs 7:3; The Scroll of Ruth 2:23; I Chronicles 21:20, 21:23; II Chronicles 2:9, 2:14, 27:5. **Wheat** – חִטִּין/*chitin* (adding a *nun*) as a plural noun, is mentioned once in Ezekiel 4:9.

3. Rav Mordechai Weinberg, *Machon HaMachshava,* אלבום פרק שירה/Album *Perek Shirah* gleaned from the great commentaries on *Perek Shirah,* quoting Rabbi Chaim Kanievsky, *Perek b'Shir.*

4. The nutritional information provided for the Seven Species is based on the USDA National Nutrient Database for Standard Reference as detailed at <http://ndb.nal.usda.gov> unless specified otherwise, retrieved during the month of August, 2013. The percentage of Recommended Daily Dietary Allowance is based on *Power your Diet* <http://www.nutrition-and-you. com/. Alternative nutritional information can be found at: *The World's Healthiest Food, The George Mateljan Foundation* <http://whfoods.org/>, *Self-Nutrition Data, Know What You Eat* <http://nutritiondata.self.com/>, Dr. *J. D. Decuypere Alternative Health Care* <http://www.health-alternatives.com/>. There are infinite numbers of 'studies' on the composition of foods, some of them empirical and others scientific. The USDA was recommended to me by medical professionals because it provides accurate analysis through the use of modern lab techniques, of each particular sample tested. However, any nutritional information provided has a very great range, because there is no such thing as any two olives or dates being identical. For example, when comparing USDA's information on *Olives, pickled, canned or bottled, green* with *Olives, ripe, canned, (small to extra large),* the former has more than five times the amount of potassium. The same basic food may provide different nutritional information based on the variance of the specific sample and its growth or storage conditions. An extra rainy season, frost, poor or rich soil, and even warehouse conditions will all cause differences in the 'same' food.

Likewise, the Recommended Daily Dietary Allowance (RDA) is relative, as the nutritional requirements of various people depend on age, race, living conditions and specific needs. Nevertheless, I chose to base my summary of the mineral and vitamin content of the Seven Species on the RDA for an approximate estimation.

I generally use the following keys: 'excellent' – more than 25% RDA, 'great' – more than 15%, 'good' – more than 10%, 'contain' more than 5%, 'small amount(s)' more than 2%. For an overview on the benefits of each of the minerals and vitamins listed I recommend the University of Maryland Medical Center's excellent online database. <http://umm.edu/search-results>.

5. The vitamin and mineral content of wheat is based on USDA, *Basic Report: 20649, Wheat flour, whole-grain, soft wheat* and *Basic Report: 20072, Wheat, hard red winter.*

6. Michael Tierra, C.A., N.D., O.M.D., *Planetary Herbology* (Lotus Press, Wisconsin, 1988), p. 345.

7. Psalms 89:3.

8. Rav Yitzchak Ginsburgh, *Body, Mind, and Soul, Kabbalah on Human Physiology, Disease, and Healing,* Gal Einai Institute, Inc., Israel, 2003, p. 77.

9. Oded Borowski, *Agriculture in Iron Age Israel* (Winona Lake: Eisenbrauns, 1987), p. 57. According to the USDA's Economic Research Service, the average amount of wheat flour consumed annually per capita in the world is 164.2 pounds. This is almost 75% of total grain product consumption (199.9 lb), and more than eight times the consumption of rice (19.7 lb). <http://www.usda.gov/factbook/chapter2.pdf> retrieved June 17, 2013.

10. *Midrash Genesis Rabbah* 48:11.

11. Genesis 18:5; Bread is also offered to sustain the heart in (Judges 19:5); King David likewise reaffirms that "bread sustains the heart of man" (Psalms 104:15).

12. According to Rambam, Rabbi Moshe ben Maimon, Spain (1135–1204), referenced by Rabbi Binyamin Moshe Kohn Shauli, מרפא הבשם/*Nature's Wealth, Health and Healing Plants,* based on the *Teachings of the* Rambam (Shauli Spirituality Community Center and Synagogue publishing, Ashdod, Israel, 1989), p. 142.

13. Wolff T, Witkop C, Miller T, *et al, Folic Acid Supplementation for the Prevention of Neural Tube Defects.* US Preventive Services Task Force. Ann Int Med 2009, May 5;150(9):632–9.

14. Wheat germ extract increased death of breast cancer cells in vitro. When used in conjunction with the anti-tumor agent, Tamoxifen, wheat germ extract exhibited synergistic anti-tumor effects. Z. Marcsek, Z. Kocsis, M. Jakab, *et al, The Efficacy of Tamoxifen in Estrogen-receptor Positive Breast Cancer Cells is Enhanced by a Medical Nutriment. Cancer Biotherm Radiopharm* 2004 Dec;19(6):746–53.

Peña-Rosas JP, Rickard S, Cho S, *Wheat Bran and Breast Cancer: Revisiting the Estrogen Hypothesis*, Arch Latinoam Nutr. 1999 Dec;49(4):309–17.

15. Rambam, הנהגת הבריאות/*The Regiment of Health* 1:6.

16. Rambam, *The Regiment of Health* 1:6; Also quoted by Nisim Krispil, צמחי המרפא של הרמב"ם/*Medicinal Herbs of the Rambam*, Arad, Israel, 1989, p. 116.

17. Rambam, *The Preservation of Youth*, Essays on Health, Translated from the Original Arabic, with an Introduction by Hirsch L. Gordon, M.D., Ph.d., D.H.L,.Philosophical Library NY. p. 31

18. The eleven steps of producing bread are: זוֹרֵעַ/*zorea* – sowing, חוֹרֵשׁ/*choresh* – plowing, קוֹצֵר/*kotzer* – harvesting, מְעַמֵּר/*me'amer* – bundling, שָׁד/*dash* – trampling (separating the grains from the straw), זוֹרֶה/*zore* – winnowing (separating the grains from the chaff), בּוֹרֵר/*borer* – separating (separating the grains from pebbles), טוֹחֵן/*tochen* – grinding, מְרַקֵּד/*meraked* – sifting, לָשׁ/*lash* – kneading, אוֹפֶה/*ofe* – baking.

19. According to the view of Rabbi Yehuda, *Babylonian Talmud, Berachot* 40a. (See the *Fig* section, p. 201 for the full quote.) This concurs with the *Babylonian Talmud, Shabbat* 30b quoted in the *Introduction,* end of p. 14, where wheat is described as a tree, which in the future will produce bread-cakes.

20. Deuteronomy 4:15.

21. Based Rabbi Yitzchak Isaac Chaver, ספר יד מצרים/*Sefer Yad Mitzrayim.*

22. William Davis M D, *Wheat Belly: Lose the Wheat, Lose the Weight, and Find Your Path Back to Health* (Rodale, Inc., New York, 2011), p. 30.

23. *Babylonian Talmud, Berachot* 40a.

24. *Babylonian Talmud, Shabbat* 30b.

25. Genesis 3:19.

26. כֹּחִי וְעֹצֶם יָדִי/*kochi v'otzem yadi* (Deuteronomy 8:17).

27. Genesis 3:5.

28. Each of the seven times the word 'wheat' appears in the Bible in the singular, it is spelled חִטָּה without the *yud*.

29. See *Kli Yakar*, Rabbi Ephraim Solomon, Leczyca, Poland (1550–1619), Genesis 2:9.

30. Rabbi Matityahu Clark, *Etymological Dictionary of Biblical Hebrew* (Feldheim publishers, Jerusalem, Israel, 1999), p. 78.

31. The Hebrew letters *chet* and *yud* are acronyms for *chayah* and *yechidah* [which are the two innermost and transcendental levels of the soul]. See the Lubavitcher Rabbi, Rabbi Menachem M. Schneerson, *The Sichah of Shabbos, Parashas Pinchas,* 5700 [1940], *Sefer HaSichos* of that year, p. 159.

32. Isaiah 11:9.

33.   Mashiach is descended from King David who was born in Bethlehem (I Samuel 17:12).

34.   *Babylonian Talmud, Shabbat* 30b.

35.   Genesis 3:19.

36.   "G*d said, 'Behold I have given you every herb-bearing seed which is upon the face of the all the earth, and every tree, on which is the fruit-yielding seed; to you it shall be for food'" (Genesis 1:29).

37.   *Babylonian Talmud, Shabbat* 30b.

38.   These ten mitzvot are:
      1.   Not to plow with an ox and a donkey together
      2.   Not to sow different kinds of seeds together (*kilayim*)
      3.   Not to muzzle an ox during threshing
      4.   To leave stalks of wheat which fall to the ground for the poor (*leket*)
      5.   To leave forgotten sheaves for the poor (*shichecha*)
      6.   To leave the corners of the field (*pe'ah*)
      7.   To give tithes to the Kohen (*terumah*)
      8.   To give tithes to the Levi (*ma'aser rishon*)
      9.   To eat tithes in holiness in Jerusalem (*ma'aser sheni*)
      10. To separating a part of the bread dough for the Kohen (*challah*) (*Mishnah Berurah* 167:24).

39.   *Shulchan Aruch, Orach Chaim* 167:4.

40.   Psalms 147:14.

41.   *Babylonian Talmud, Berachot* 2b.

42.   *Ethics of our Fathers* 6:4.

43.   *Babylonian Talmud, Baba Kama* 92b.

44.   See Ezekiel 41:22 and *Ethics of our Fathers* 3:3.

45.   וְכָל קָרְבַּן מִנְחָתְךָ בַּמֶּלַח תִּמְלָח וְלֹא תַשְׁבִּית מֶלַח בְּרִית אֱלֹקֶיךָ מֵעַל מִנְחָתֶךָ עַל כָּל קָרְבָּנְךָ תַּקְרִיב: (ויקרא ב, יג) "Your every meal offering you shall season with salt, you shall not cause the salt of the covenant of your G-d to be missing from your meal offering. With all your sacrifices you shall offer salt." (Leviticus 2:13).

46.   Deuteronomy 8:3.

47.   *Helios Varer i Husholdningen*, a vegetarian cook booklet in Danish, (Dansk Helios Amba, Spring 1982), p. 10.

48.   This water is rich in acidophilus, containing beneficial bacteria which aid the digestion. Therefore, before meals, it is good to drink water in which wheat berries have been soaked. See full recipe for *Rejuvelac* on p. 80.

49.   Research undertaken at the University of Minnesota has shown that sprouting increases the nutrient density of food. During the three days of sprouting, the protein and vitamin E content can increase 300%, with vitamin C increasing 600%, while the B vitamins have been found to

increase from 20% to 1,200%, with B17, the 'anti-cancer vitamin,' 100% more than in un-sprouted seed. <http:// www.herbsarespecial.com.au/free-sprout-information/wheat.html> retrieved October 18, 2013.

50. Ann Wigmore, *The Sprouting Book*, (Avery Publishing Group Inc., New Jersey, 1986), p. 37.

51. <http://www.wigmore.org/miracles_wheatgrass.html> retrieved June 17, 2013.

52. Baking the sprouted wheat bread in a slow cooker is similar to dehydrating, retaining more of the wheat's natural nutrients and enzymes.

53. According to the *pesak* (*halachic* ruling) of Rabbi A.A. Mandelbaum author of *V'zot Habracha*, a halachic work defining blessings on various foods in our time. My husband personally brought one of my sprouted wheat breads to the Rav to examine before making his *halachic* ruling.

54. *Shulchan Aruch*, Orach Chaim 155:2. *Babylonian Talmud, Baba Kama* 92b.

55. *Mishnah Berurah* 155:11.

56. Rabbi Don Chanan, personal email correspondence.

57. Chen F, Liu S, Zhao F, Zu C, Xia G, *Molecular Characterization of the Low-molecular Weight Glutenin Subunit Genes of Tall Wheatgrass and Functional Properties of one Clone Ee34*. Amino Acids. 2010 Apr;38(4):991–9.

58. A Green Star juicer is excellent for extracting wheatgrass juice. It is less costly to use a manual wheatgrass juicer, however, it will not work for other vegetables and fruits.

59. Steve Meyerowitz, *"Nutrition in Grass." Wheatgrass Nature's Finest Medicine: The Complete Guide to Using Grass Foods & Juices to Revitalize Your Health* (Sproutman Publications, Summertown, TN 1999), p. 53.

60. Dr. Ann Wigmore, *Wheatgrass, Naturama Living Textbook*: "The most effective therapy which we have discovered for cancer consists of wheatgrass chlorophyll cocktails and live foods which are taken in an atmosphere of happiness and thankfulness." <http://www.greensmoothie.com/juice/wheatgrass.php> retrieved June 17, 2013.

61. Dr. Ann Wigmore, *The Wheatgrass Book* (Avery Publishing Group Inc., New Jersey, 1984), p. 45.

62. *The Garden of Spices, Recipes for Life*, Shoshanna Harrari (Almond Blossoming Publishing, Israel, 2009), p. 59.

63. Ben Arye E, Goldin E, Wengrower D, Stamper A., Kohn R, and Berry E. *Wheat Grass Juice in the Treatment of Active Distal Ulcerative Colitis: a Randomized Double-blind Placebo-controlled Trial*. Scand.J Gastroenterol 2002;37(4):444–449.

64. Ostlund RE, Racette SB, and Stenson VF. *Inhibition of Cholesterol Absorption by Phytosterol-replete Wheat Germ compared with Phytosterol-depleted Wheat Germ*. Am J Clin Nutr 2003;77:1385–9.

65. '...The Creator of the fruits of the earth,' recited before eating vegetables. For the full text of the blessings in Hebrew and English see *Appendix II – Blessings before Partaking of the Seven Species and their Derivatives.*

66. '...The Creator of many souls,' recited after consuming general foods without a specific after-blessing

67. Wheat, barley, spelt, rye and oats.

68. The threefold after-blessing recited after drinking wine or grape juice and after eating foods made from the seven holy fruits of Israel. For the full text of the blessing in Hebrew and English see *Appendix III – The Threefold After-Blessing ('M'ein Shalosh') for the Seven Species grown in Israel.*

69. *Shulchan Aruch, Orach Chaim* 208:4.

70. '...The Creator of different kinds of sustaining foods,' recited before eating cooked or baked dishes made with the five kinds of grains.

71. *Mishnah Berurah* 208:6.

72. Ecclesiastes 11:1.

73. Ecclesiastes 9:9.

Hordeum Vulgare ~ שְׂעֹרָה

Barley

גְּבוּרָה ~ Gevurah – Might / Restraint

Barley ~ שְׂעֹרָה   *Hordeum Vulgare*
Gevurah ~ גְּבוּרָה   *(Might / Restraint)*

הֲלוֹא אִם שִׁוָּה פָנֶיהָ וְהֵפִיץ קֶצַח וְכַמֹּן יִזְרֹק וְשָׂם חִטָּה שׂוֹרָה וּשְׂעֹרָה נִסְמָן וְכֻסֶּמֶת גְּבֻלָתוֹ: (ישעיהו כח, כה)

"When he has prepared a smooth surface, he then scatters the black seeds, and casts the cumin, and throws in wheat by rows, and barley in the marked spot, and spelt along its border" (*Isaiah* 28:25).

ושעורה מן השמאל...ולזה הסוטה מביאה מנחת שעורים, שהם כח כל הגבורות. (אריז"ל, ספר לקוטי תורה, פרשת עקב, פרק ח)

Barley from the left[1]... Therefore, the sotah (suspected adulteress) brings a barley offering, for barley embodies the power of all the gevurot (Arizal, Sefer HaLikutim, Parashat Ekev, chapter 8).

Attribute: *Gevurah* – Power/Might/Restraint
Character trait: The ability to say no (contraction)
Holiday: Pesach, when we begin to count the Omer of the Barley offering
Weekday: יוֹם שֵׁנִי/*Yom Sheni* – Second day of the week (Monday)
World: עֲשִׂיָּה/*Asiyah* – Action (hard inedible husk)
Body parts: The left shoulder, arm and hand
Shepherd: יִצְחָק/Yitzchak
Prophetess: מִרְיָם/Miriam
Numerical value: 575, equivalent to the word נִכְרְתָה/*nichreta* – 'Let us cut [a covenant]'[2]
Mentioned in the Bible: 36 times[3]
Meaning of Latin Name: A common grass of the temperate northern hemisphere and South America.

פֶּרֶק שִׁירָה
Perek Shirah
The Song of the Universe

תְּפִלָּה לְעָנִי כִי יַעֲטֹף וְלִפְנֵי הָשֵׁם יִשְׁפֹּךְ שִׂיחוֹ: (תהלים קב, א)

The Song of Barley: "A prayer of the poor, when he wraps himself and pours out his trouble before Hashem" (Psalms 102:1).

$\mathcal{B}$arley is 'poor man's food.' When a person is hungry and has nothing to eat he is happy to receive even barley. From this we may learn that when we are, G*d forbid, in trouble, we must stand with a broken heart like a pauper who stands in the doorway all wrapped up. We must, likewise, wrap ourselves and pour out our trouble in heartfelt prayer to Hashem. Then Hashem will hear our prayer and redeem us.[4]

Nutrition Facts and Information about Barley

Mineral Content of Barley[5]

Barley is an excellent source of iron, phosphorus, magnesium, manganese, selenium and copper. It is a great source of zinc and a good source of potassium, and has small amounts of calcium.

Vitamin Content of Barley

Barley is an excellent source of thiamin. It is also a great source of niacin, riboflavin and vitamin B6. Barley contains folate and small amounts of vitamin E and K.

Dietary Fiber

Barley is high in both soluble and insoluble dietary fiber (17.3g/100g, 69% of RDA).[6] Dietary fiber-rich barley-containing diets have several beneficial physiologic effects.[7]

Oriental Medicine

According to Chinese medicine, barley malt affects the spleen, stomach and lungs. It is sweet and warm.[8]

Hulled Barley Nutritional Facts/100 g

Minerals		RDA
Calcium	33 mg	3.5%
Iron	3.60 mg	45%
Magnesium	133 mg	38%
Phosphorus	264 mg	39%
Potassium	452 mg	9.5%
Sodium	12 mg	0.8%
Zinc	2.77 mg	20%
Copper	0.498 mg	55%
Manganese	1.943 mg	83%
Selenium	37.7 µg	63%
Vitamins		**RDA**
C	0.0 mg	0%
B1 (Thiamin)	0.646 mg	56%
B2 (Riboflavin)	0.285 mg	20%
B3 (Niacin)	4.604 mg	24.5%
B6	0.318 mg	15%
B9 (Folate)	19 µg	5%
A	22 IU	1%
E	0.57 mg	3%
K	2.2 µg	2%

Barley corresponds to Gevurah. The attribute of *Gevurah* is restraint – confining and removing excess. The quality of *Gevurah*, likewise, is contraction, reduction, and setting boundaries, as the prophet Isaiah emphasizes that specifically barley must be sowed within the boundary of the marked spot.[9] In the early stages of the Israelite settlement, the most important cereal was barley, because it was necessary to settle fringe areas, and barley can tolerate harsh environments.[10] While *Chesed* spreads to the lowest place, *Gevurah* has the strength to climb upward. Therefore, wheat grows mainly in the valleys, while barley can survive on the mountains. Barley's tolerance of harsh conditions is also reflected in the strong hull (boundary), which encloses each barley seed and remains intact even during threshing.

Reduces Liquids, Relieves Swellings and Infections

The Talmud warns that barley flour may cause intestinal worms.[11] However, barley has several eliminative properties that correspond to the eliminative attribute of *Gevurah*. Gargling with barley tea counteracts infections of the mouth, throat and tonsils. Applied externally, it is good for open, infected wounds.[12] Due to its contracting quality, barley is highly effective in reducing liquid when added to soup. Barley baths relieve swelling and rashes. Mixed with rose water, barley flour alleviates swollen and painful breasts. Barley sprouts also relieve swollen breasts, and moreover dry up mother's milk.[13]

Dissolves Gallstones and Kidney Stones

Barley may be an even better breakfast choice than oats for people with type 2 diabetes.[14] Due to its beta glucan soluble fiber, barley has a favorable effect on glucose/insulin metabolism.[15] Barley's insoluble fiber can prevent gallstones,[16] and may dissolve already-formed gallstones.[17] Barley tea, moreover, helps dissolve kidney stones, and it alleviates diabetes.[18]

Lowers Cholesterol

Gevurah channels the blood into the blood vessels of the circulatory system and controls blood circulation.[19] This concurs with the fact that whole-grain barley reduces the risk of coronary heart disease[20] by reducing blood LDL cholesterol.[21] This is partly because barley is a good source of niacin and partly because its high beta glucan dietary fiber binds cholesterol to bile acid,[22] eliminating it from the body.[23]

Contains Beta Glucan Soluble Fiber

Barley differs from most other grains because its beta glucan soluble fiber is found throughout the entire barley kernel. In other grains, the beta glucan is contained in the outer bran layer only.[24] Perhaps the entire barley is similar to the outer layer of other grains because barley reflects the boundary of *Gevurah*.

The Hebrew Word for Barley and Gevurah

The first letter of the Hebrew word for barley, שְׂעוֹרָה/*se'orah,* is שׂ/*sin* ('s' sound), with a *nikud* (dot) over the left arm of the שׂ/*sin* – as opposed to the שׁ/*shin* ('sh' sound), which has a dot over the right arm. This supports the fact that שְׂעוֹרָה/*se'orah* – barley is associated with *Gevurah*, the upper left branch of the Tree of Life.

Rambam teaches that barley cereal has cleansing properties. It cleans the respiratory system and dries up mucus. Barley is also cooling, especially for the eyes. Lentils have opposite qualities to barley and balance it. Therefore, a dish cooked from a mixture of barley and lentils is especially beneficial.[25]

Health Benefits of Barley Grass

Although less well known, barley grass is a powerful super-food, with comparable health benefits to wheatgrass. It is similarly high in chlorophyll content, and is an excellent source of enzymes, vitamins and minerals.[26]

Barley, the 'Multi-Tasker'

Like many grains, barley is a 'multi-tasker.' We cherish those little nutty pearls of hearty goodness often found in soups and stews or eaten as a cereal. Barley is considered one of the top five cereal grains in the world. Its grandeur is most distinguished as the centerpiece of the Shabbat table, in the famous Shabbat *cholent* (stew). Barley is also a prime ingredient in one variety of miso, the popular Japanese condiment. Only 10% of barley is used as human food, while a full third is used for brewing malt beverages. However, the majority is used for livestock feed.

Animal Food

The *sotah* (suspected adulteress) brings a barley sacrifice. "Just as her actions were animalistic, so does her sacrifice consist of animal food."[27] A sotah is a woman who secluded herself with a man whom her husband had specifically warned her not to befriend. Her inability to protect the precious boundaries of her marriage is considered an animalistic act, as we cannot expect an animal such as, for example, an ox to be faithful to any specific cow. "The superiority of the human over the animal is nothing (אָיִן/*ayin*)..."[28] The word *ayin* means 'nothing' or 'no.' In addition to the accepted interpretation, that there is no difference between man and animal, this verse can also mean that the superiority of the human being over the animal is our ability to say '*ayin*' (No!).[29] Therefore, the suspected adulteress sacrifices an offering of barley in order to rectify her animal soul, and to ingrain within her the *Gevurah* of self-restraint and setting proper boundaries.

The Boundaries of Measure

When we measure something, we determine its particular boundaries. Barley corresponds to the boundaries of measurement. The root of the Hebrew word for barley, ש-ע-ר/*sin-ayin-reish* with the ו, consists of the same letters as the Hebrew word for measurement, שִׁעוּר/*shiur*. This term is often used in Jewish law, as for example one needs to eat a certain שִׁעוּר/*shiur* – amount, in order to be required to recite an after-blessing.[30] We also use the term שִׁעוּר/*shiur* to refer to a Torah class. Many people may not be aware, however, that a שִׁעוּר/*shiur* implies that the class takes place within a certain time frame, and must begin and end on time. It is also interesting to notice that a grain of barley is used to determine the minimum measure that negative spirits may control. Therefore, the Egyptians were unable to replicate the plague of lice, "for the demon is powerless over a creature smaller than a barley seed."[31] Perhaps the reason for this is that whatever is beyond measure belongs exclusively to the Divine domain.

Establishing the Season of Spring based on the Growth of Barley

The Hebrew calendar is synchronized with the spirit of the maturing crops. Since barley is associated with a certain time measure, it makes perfect sense that one of the biblical criteria for the mitzvah of establishing the first month of the year, called "the month of spring," (אָבִיב/*aviv*),[32] is when the barley grain is אָבִיב/*aviv* – "in its spring," having sprouted forth its green ears.[33] When the barley head has not yet developed, it is a sign to add an extra month of Adar and establish a leap year. This ensures that the month of Nissan, celebrating the Exodus from Egypt, always occurs when the barley is green. Since Talmudic time, however, a fixed calendar was established. It includes seven leap years over the course of a nineteen-year cycle.

The Omer Offering

Although barley and wheat were both planted in the fall, barley matured faster and was harvested sooner. During the seven weeks between the holidays of Pesach and Shavuot, an Omer of barley, was offered at the Temple daily. The word עֹמֶר/*Omer* is a biblical measure roughly equal to two quarts or two liters.[34] It is sometimes translated as 'sheaf,' as it was a large enough amount of grain to require bundling. On Pesach, the Israelites, who had just left Egypt, were still in the process of purification from the influence of the animal-worshipping Egyptian culture. The barley offering reflects the low spiritual level of the Jewish people leaving Egypt, who were only fit to eat the less refined barley grain.[35] It would take the Jewish people forty-nine days of elevating themselves until they would reach the level of wheat during the festival of Shavuot. This was the fitting time to offer two wheat challot, reflecting the holy Torah received on this day, after being redeemed from the animal soul and *yetzer hara* (negative inclination).[36] Every year, we relive this purification process during the period of counting the Omer of barley until we reach the level of wheat.

"When Gideon came, behold, there was a man telling a dream to his friend, and he said, 'Behold, I dreamed a dream, and, lo, a slice of barley bread tumbled into the camp of Midian, and came to the tent, and smote it so that it fell, and turned it upside down, so that the tent fell down.' His fellow answered and said, 'This is nothing other than the sword of Gideon, the son of Joash, a man of Israel, G*d has delivered Midian and all the camp into his hand.'"[37]

This dream alludes to the fact that Israel's victory over Midian was in the merit of the Omer that is sacrificed on Pesach.[38] It is known that wheat represents the intellect, while barley is referred to as animal food and represents a person's animal soul. The Omer sacrifice is from barley in order to purify a person's animal soul, so that the heart by itself will be drawn after Hashem's will even without the illumination of the intellect...[39]

Overcoming Evil

The three root letters of the word barley — ש-ע-ר can be unscrambled to spell the word רָשָׁע/*rasha* which means 'wicked' or 'evil.' The origin of *Gevurah* stems from Divine restraint. G*d's nature is ultimate good, therefore, restraint and concealment of the Divine is the root of evil. When the light of *Gevurah* is blocking Divine *Chesed*, it causes *hester panim* (the hiding of G*d's face). This implies that the Divine light of *Chesed* becomes spiritually blocked from us, in the same way that the light of the sun gets blocked from our view by a cloud. Blockage of Divine *Chesed* manifests itself as *midat hadin* (the attribute of judgment). In the human psyche this aspect of *Gevurah* is reflected in our restraint from bestowing goodness upon others, when we judge them as undeserving of our kindness. However, we need to find an opening in order to unblock the light of *Gevurah* from overpowering the light of *Chesed*. We can create such an opening by turning the power of *Gevurah* into a gate – שַׁעַר/*sha'ar* by means of the three root letters of the word for barley.

Through *teshuvah*, *tefilah*, and *tzedakah* (repentance, prayer and charity) that remove evil decrees,[40] we can pierce the shell of *Gevurah*, in order to open the gate that blocks Divine *Chesed*, thus sweetening the *Gevurot* in their root.[41] The light of *Gevurah* can then be mitigated and employed to energize us to withstand temptation and perform a positive deed. When we restrain the might of *Gevurah*, we are empowered to overcome our enemies, whether from without or within (our *yetzer hara*).

כי העומר בא מן השעורים שהוא לשון שעור ומדה וקצבה והם סוד הגבורות שצריך להתגבר ולטהר עצמו בימי הספירה... (עבודת ישראל- לשבועות)

For the Omer comes from barley, and signifies measurement and ration (שִׁעוּר/shiur). This is the secret of Gevurah, as one needs to overcome oneself during the days of counting the Omer... (Rav Tzadok HaKohen of Lublin, Avodat Yisrael for Shavuot).

Accessing the Power of Storm

The root of the Hebrew word for barley, ש-ע-ר/*sin-ayin-reish,* implies a strong movement from within.[42] These letters also refer to a powerful windy storm (רוּחַ שַׂעֲרָה/*ruach sa'arah*), as contrasted to רוּחַ הַקֹּדֶשׁ/*ruach hakodesh* – (Divine inspiration). This reflects the purpose of the *kelipah* (shell) of *Gevurah* – enabling growth through strong inner movement. By giving the soul something to push and pull against, *Gevurah* manifests as an agitating wind that loosens distorted complexes in the soul for removal and/or reconstruction. Whereas ruach hakodesh reflects Hashem's bestowal upon us, the growth caused by *ruach sa'arah* results when we move toward the Divine.

וַיֹּאמֶר הָבִי הַמִּטְפַּחַת אֲשֶׁר עָלַיִךְ וְאֶחֳזִי בָהּ וַתֹּאחֶז בָּהּ וַיָּמָד שֵׁשׁ
שְׂעֹרִים וַיָּשֶׁת עָלֶיהָ וַיָּבֹא הָעִיר: (רות ג, טו)

*"He said, 'Bring the kerchief that is upon you, and hold it:' and
she held it: and he measured six measures of barley, and placed
them on it: and he went into the city" (The Scroll of Ruth 3:15).*

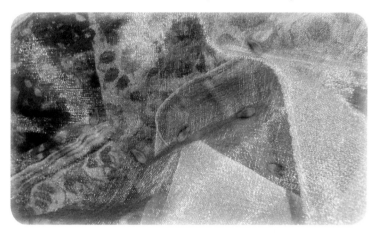

HE MEASURED SIX SHEAVES OF BARLEY – It was really (*mamash*)
six barley seeds. He hinted to her that in the future there would issue
from her a son who would be blessed with six blessings...[43]

> *But was it Boaz's practice to give gifts of six grains of barley? He
> intimated to her that six sons were destined to issue from her,
> each of whom would be blessed with six blessings, namely: David,
> Mashiach, Daniel, Chananiah, Mishael, and Azariah. David, as
> it is written "...he knows how to play [music], is a mighty man of
> valor, a warrior, wise in affairs, handsome, and Hashem is with
> him..."[44] Mashiach, as it is written, "The spirit of Hashem shall
> rest upon him: the spirit of wisdom and understanding, the spirit of
> counsel and might, the spirit of knowledge and of the fear of G*d"[45]
> (Babylonian Talmud, Sanhedrin 93b).*

⁝ *A Taste of Kabbalah – The Seeds of Blessing*

והם בסוד שעורים שהם בגבורה... ולכן אשה סוטה נבדקת ע"י מנחת שעורים
והוא מנחת קנאות וכו' על שהפרה בריתו למי שעשאה כלי וכו' וכידוע בכ"מ.
וז"ש כאן שבועז נתן לרות שש שעורים שהוא רוחא ו' דילי', אלא רמז זה לה
שעתידים שש בנים וכו' והם בסוד מ"ן דילה שהם בנין דילה כמ"ש (בראשית
ל:ג) "ואבנה גם אנכי וכו'". ולפי שבועז באמת הי' דרגא דיסוד בכלל האצי'
וכן רות נוק' כללא דכנ"י, ולכן יצאו ממנה אלו ששה בנים שהם ג"כ כלל כל
ישראל... ולכן כל א' נתברך בו' ברכות שכל א' נכלל ברזא דו', וביסוד סוד כל
הברכות כמ"ש (בראשית מט כו) "ברכות אביך גברו וכו' תהיינה לראש יוסף
וכו'". (ספר ביאורי אגדות אפיקי ים) - סנהדרין צג, ע"א)

They are in the secret of barley, which is in *Gevurah*... The sotah is
tested through the barley offering, which is the offering of jealousy,
because she broke the covenant with the one who made her a vessel
[her husband]. This is why it states that Boaz gave Ruth six barley
seeds, for he is her spirit of six. He alluded to her that in the future
six sons would descend from them. They are the principle of her
feminine waters, which is her building, as it states, "I will also be
built..."[46] Boaz was indeed on the level of *Yesod* in the world of
Atzilut (Emanation), and Ruth was the incarnation of *nukvah*
(*Malchut*) – the feminine congregation of Israel. Therefore, these
six sons who also included all of Israel descended from her... Each
of them is blessed with six blessings, for each of them is included in
the secret of six – *Yesod*/foundation, the secret of all the blessings,
as it states, "The blessings of your father are mighty... they shall
be on the head of Yosef..."[47] (Rav Yitzchak Isaac Chaver, *Beurei
Agadot, Afikei Yam*, on Babylonian Talmud, *Sanhedrin* 93a).

Explanation: The sotah is tested through barley, corresponding to
Gevurah, which implies the boundaries of a vessel. When a woman
marries, she becomes a vessel for her husband's light, for a woman only
makes a covenant with the one who made her into a vessel, as it states,
"for your maker is your husband."[48] In the physical realm, the wife becomes a vessel for her husband's seed, and enables him to fulfill the
mitzvah to be fruitful and multiply.

The woman corresponds to the lowest sefirah of *Malchut*, the feminine vessel for all of the other sefirot, as it states about *Malchut*, "It has nothing of its own."[49] By giving Ruth six barley seeds, Boaz alluded to his correspondence to the masculine *Yesod*, which includes the six middle sefirot.[50] Boaz, as the greatest of his generation, knew exactly what he was doing through Divine inspiration. As he counted six barley seeds, he alluded to their future sons, and laid the foundation for the coming of Mashiach.

The unity between Boaz's masculine *Yesod* – corresponding to the number six[51] – and Ruth's feminine *Malchut* completes and builds the *Malchut* to rise from a small point to reach full stature. This building of the feminine is the main rectification in the world, which brings redemption by building the *Shechinah* (Divine feminine in-dwelling Presence).[52] It is, therefore, the job of the man to build the woman.[53] He may accomplish this by facilitating his wife's Torah learning and helping her express her light in the world. In addition, a woman is built through begetting children. Therefore, Sarah exclaimed, "Perhaps I will be **built** through her"[54] when she gave her handmaid, Hagar, to Avraham. She had in mind that Hagar's children would be considered hers spiritually.[55]

The six barley seeds that Boaz offered Ruth correspond to the six holy descendants that she desired. Each of these six descendants also corresponds to *Yesod*, because they are all part of the foundation of Israel. Therefore, they are each blessed with six blessings. *Yesod* includes all the blessings, just as Yosef, who is the sixth shepherd corresponding to *Yesod*, included all the blessings of his father.[56]

There are four worlds: אֲצִילוּת/*Atzilut* – Emanation, בְּרִיאָה/*Beriyah* – Creation, יְצִירָה/*Yetzirah* – Formation and עֲשִׂיָּה/*Asiyah* – Action.[57] The *Yesod* of Boaz was from the highest world. When he bequeathed the six barley seeds to Ruth, he enabled his *Yesod* to receive a vessel for his holy lights to manifest within the physical world of *Malchut* corresponding to the lowest world of *Asiyah*. Thus, Boaz's gift of six barley seeds intimated ultimate unification of the highest with the lowest world, specifically through the congregation of Israel which Ruth represents.

הרואה שעורים בחלום סרו עונותיו שנאמר "וְסָר עֲוֹנֶךָ
וְחַטָּאתְךָ תְּכֻפָּר": אמר רבי זירא אנא לא סלקי מבבל
לארץ ישראל עד דחזאי שערי בחלמא:

*He who sees barley in a dream, his transgressions
have been removed, as it says, "Your transgression has
been removed, and your sin has been atoned."*[58] *Rabbi
Zeira said, "I did not go up from Babylon to the Land
of Israel until I had seen barley in a dream"
(Babylonian Talmud, Berachot 57a).*

Barley Recipes

Hulled or Pearled Barley?

Barley is one of the oldest grains ever eaten, but today this ancient grain is more likely to appear in your brew than on your dinner plate! The subtle, nutty flavor and satisfying pasta-like texture of barley is a healthier alternative to processed wheat products such as macaroni and spaghetti. Today, there are two kinds of barley on the market: hulled and pearled. The difference between them is similar to the difference between brown and white rice.

Hulled barley is the healthiest kind of barley. This whole-grain, also known as barley groats, has only the outermost hull removed, retaining its fibrous bran layers. It is, therefore, chewy and rich in fiber. However, it takes longer to cook than pearl barley, about one to two hours. I recommend soaking hulled barley overnight in water first.

Pearl barley is the form of barley you will most often find in the supermarkets. This grain has been polished – a process that removes its outer husk and bran layers, making it less nutritious than hulled barley. Pearl barley is softer and takes less time to cook, about 45 minutes. Most recipes call for pearl barley even if it's not specified. You can still substitute the healthier hulled barley as long as you adjust the recipe cooking time.

BACK-TO-BASICS BOILED BARLEY
A basic filling grain-dish in place of bread

2 cups hulled barley
4 cups water
2 tablespoons sea salt
2 tablespoons virgin olive oil
Dill, marjoram and other herbs to taste

1. Rinse the barley grains and soak them overnight.

2. Place them in a pot with the water.

3. Bring the pot to boil and simmer for one hour.

4. Add olive oil, sea salt and herbs.

BAKED BARLEY

An elegant dish, much healthier than the traditional white noodle lasagna

> 1 cup cooked barley
> 1 onion
> 2–3 carrots
> 1–2 stalks of celery
> ¼ cup ground walnuts or other nuts of your choice
> ¼ cup flax seeds or wheat germ
> 1½ cup vegetable stock
> Sea salt, freshly ground black pepper and cumin to taste
> A little olive oil for greasing and sprinkling

1. Grate the carrots, onion and celery finely.

2. Sauté the vegetables lightly.

3. Turn off the fire and add the spices.

4. Process the barley in the food processor with the S-blade until it becomes a doughy consistency.

5. Add vegetable stock and flax seeds, and let the barley steep for 10–15 minutes.

6. Grease a baking pan and layer the sautéed vegetables lengthwise with barley mixture.

7. End with the top layer of barley mixture.

8. Add the ground nuts and sprinkle with olive oil.

9. Bake at 390 F° (200 C°) with a little water on the pan for about 45 minutes or until crisp.

10. Serve with goat cheese or a bean dish and fresh salad.

BARLEY & VEGETABLE CASSEROLE A' LA RAMBAM

*A blend of mushrooms, zucchini, onion and celery with barley
for an easy garden skillet dish*

> 3 cups water
> 1 cup hulled barley
> ½ cup raw green lentils (other lentils may be substituted)
> 1 chopped onion
> 1 cup sliced mushrooms
> 2 chopped zucchini
> 2 medium stalks sliced celery
> 2 tablespoons olive oil
> 1 tablespoon miso
> 1 tablespoon lemon juice
> 2 teaspoons chopped fresh basil or ¾ teaspoon dried basil
> Sea salt and freshly ground black pepper to taste

1. Heat water to boiling point.

2. In a 3 quart saucepan, sauté onions in olive oil until translucent and slightly browned, set aside.

3. Sauté celery, mushrooms and basil in olive oil for about 10 minutes, stirring frequently until the celery is crisp and tender, set aside.

4. Return the sautéed onions to the saucepan. Add the barley and lentils, and sauté for one minute or so.

5. Pour boiling water over the barley-lentil-onion mixture.

6. Cover and simmer for about one hour, or until the barley mixture is tender and all liquid is absorbed.

7. Add the remaining sautéed vegetables. Continue sautéing over medium heat for about five minutes, stirring occasionally.

8. Add miso and lemon juice.

HEARTY BARLEY SOUP

A big pot of barley soup simmering on the stove warms the heart during stormy, rainy weather

Half a diced onion

2 diced celery stalks

2 diced carrots

Additional vegetables of your choice such as leeks, kohlrabi, parsley and celery root

2 tablespoons olive oil

8 cups water or vegetable broth

½ cup hulled uncooked barley

½ cup presoaked beans of your choice

⅓ cup crushed tomatoes or tomato sauce

2 large bay leaves

½ teaspoon of each basil, oregano and thyme

½ teaspoon sea salt and freshly ground black pepper

1 teaspoon onion powder (optional)

¼ teaspoon celery-salt (optional)

1. In a large soup pot, sauté the onions for five minutes or more until translucent.

2. Add celery, carrots and any other vegetables and continue to sauté for three to five minutes.

3. Add the remaining ingredients including the liquids and bring to a boil, then reduce heat to medium low.

4. Allow soup to simmer for at least one hour, stirring occasionally, until the barley is soft and somewhat fluffy.

5. Adjust the spices according to taste and enjoy!

MUSHROOM MEAL-IN-A-BOWL BARLEY SOUP
Serves as a cozy family meal for a cold winter night

3–6 cups sliced mushrooms

6 cups vegetable stock or water in which barley has been soaked

½ cup hulled barley soaked overnight,

(or soaked in boiling water for at least 20 minutes)

1 cup kidney beans or black eyed peas soaked overnight

2–3 cups diced onions

2–4 cloves of garlic

1 cup diced celery

2 crushed tomatoes

(you may substitute 2 tablespoons of tomato sauce)

2 tablespoons olive oil

2 bay leaves

½ teaspoon dried thyme

½ teaspoon sea salt

½ teaspoon freshly ground black pepper

1. Heat olive oil in a skillet and sauté onions for five minutes or more, until translucent.

2. Add the garlic, and then the mushrooms, celery and spices. Continue to sauté for five more minutes until slightly browned.

3. Add boiling stock or water and the beans and barley.

4. Cook, covered, on low heat from one and a half to two hours.

5. Add more water as needed, as barley may soak up the liquid.

PARVE CHOLENT

Traditional Shabbat cholent adds warmth to your bones on a freezing winter Shabbat day

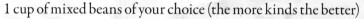

1 cup of mixed beans of your choice (the more kinds the better)

½ cup hulled barley

2 large diced onions

2 large cubed potatoes

1 large cubed sweet potato

4–6 cloves of minced garlic

2 large bay-leaves

2 tablespoons olive oil

1 tablespoon sea salt

2 teaspoons onion powder

2 teaspoons paprika

2 teaspoons freshly ground black pepper

2 teaspoons *hawaich**

2 teaspoons turmeric

A touch of ginger (optional)

4 cups or more of water as needed to cover

1. Soak the beans in water overnight. Drain them.

2. Heat olive oil in a skillet and sauté onions for five minutes or more, until translucent.

3. Add the remaining ingredients and continue to sauté for five additional minutes until slightly browned.

4. Add boiling water and cook, covered, on low heat for about one and a half hours.

5. Add water if necessary. (The cholent needs to be covered with a layer of liquid as it dries out overnight on the Shabbat hotplate).

6. Place on Shabbat hotplate (*blech*) and leave until the Shabbat day-meal.

Variation

Alternatively you can prepare your Shabbat cholent in a crock-pot.

Hawaich is a Yemenite spice mixture, used in soups, meats and vegetable dishes.

Here is a recipe to make your own hawaich:

Mix the following spices together: 5 tablespoons ground cumin,

2 tablespoons ground cardamom, 5 teaspoons ground black pepper, 3 teaspoons ground turmeric, 2 teaspoons ground coriander.

Store your hawaich spice away from direct light exposure in a tightly-covered jar.

BARLEY BEET SALAD

A complete meal in a salad bowl, including starch, veggies and protein

1 cup hulled barley soaked overnight
3½ cups stock or water in which the barley has been soaked
4 medium beets with leaves
1 small finely chopped red onion
⅔ cup crumbled goat or sheep feta cheese
3 tablespoons olive oil
3 tablespoons lemon juice
2 cloves of minced garlic
Sea salt and freshly ground black pepper to taste
A handful sliced scallions, green onions or parsley for garnish

1. Bring the water to a boil. Add the barley and sea salt.

2. Simmer covered for about one hour.

3. Roast the beets in the oven until they are tender for about 30–45 minutes. Peel and dice the beets into small cubes.

4. Soak the beet leaves and stems in natural soap water for three minutes, check them for bugs and slice them into thin strips.

5. Combine barley, beets, beet leaves, red onion and feta in your mixing bowl.

6. Whisk the lemon juice and olive oil, add the garlic and spices, and mix this dressing well with the salad.

7. Add the green garnish and serve at room temperature.

SHEPHERD'S BARLEY SALAD

A refreshing meal which can easily be packed for a nature hike or picnic

1 cup hulled barley soaked overnight

3½ cups vegetable stock or water in which the barley has been soaked

½ cup crumbled goat cheese

¼ cup sliced black olives

2 handfuls of pine nuts or sunflower seeds

¼ cup fresh basil

¼ cup chopped arugula

¼ cup olive oil

Juice of half a lemon

2 cloves of minced garlic

1. Bring water to a boil, add barley.

2. Reduce heat and simmer, covered for one hour or until barley is just tender.

3. Drain any excess liquid. Transfer to a large bowl. Cool.

4. Process olive oil, basil and garlic in food processor until smooth, mix with cooled barley.

5. Stir all remaining ingredients into cooled barley.

BARLEY BALLS

A vegetarian delight for children and adults alike

1 cup cooked hulled barley
(according to instructions 1. and 2. in *Shepherd's Barley Salad*)
2 carrots
1 parsnip or parsley root (you may substitute celery or zucchini)
1 leek
1 small bunch (about 5 stalks) parsley
1 tomato
2 tablespoons tomato purée
2 eggs
½ cup ground flax seeds or wheat germ
Sea salt, freshly ground black pepper, marjoram and nutmeg
to taste

Sauce
1 finely chopped onion
1 small can of tomato purée (125 g or 4.5 oz.)
diluted with 2 cans of water
2 tablespoons sweetener (molasses, honey, brown sugar)
2 tablespoons lemon juice

1. Cook the vegetables in a small amount of water until almost soft.

2. Process the vegetables together with the barley in food processer until minced

3. Add the remaining ingredients and steep together for about half an hour.

4. Shape into balls.

5. Prepare the sauce by sautéing the onion until golden.

6. Add the remaining ingredients and simmer for five minutes.

7. Add the balls and simmer for about 10 minutes.

Variation

Eliminate the sauce and sauté or bake according to the instructions for *Barley Burgers*.

BARLEY BURGERS

A satisfying choleserol-free alternative to fatty hamburgers

> 1 cup cooked hulled barley
> (according to instructions 1. and 2. in *Shepherd's Barley Salad*)
> 1 cup minced celery
> 2 minced onions
> ½ cup ground flax seeds
> 2 eggs or soaked flax seed equivalent
> (see recipe for *Wheat Burgers*, p. 74)
> Virgin olive oil for sautéing
> Sea salt, freshly ground black pepper, fennel seeds and nutmeg
> to taste.

1. Process celery and onions for just a few seconds in the food processor with the S-blade until minced.

2. Sauté the onions until translucent, then add the celery and continue to sauté lightly.

3. Process barley in food processer until it becomes a gooey doughy consistency.

4. Mix the sautéed vegetables with the processed barley and add the remaining ingredients.

5. Form into burger shapes and sauté in olive oil until browned.

Shortcut Variation

Skip sautéing the onions and celery separately and just process them with the barley.

Baked Variation

For a healthier choice, bake the barley burgers for about 45 minutes at medium heat or until crisp on the outside. Turn the burgers after about 25 minutes.

LEMONY BARLEY WATER

A refreshing, nourishing drink that aids the digestion

> 3 cups water in which barley was soaked for 24 hours
> 3 additional cups of water
> ¼ cup honey
> Juice and finely grated zest of two lemons
> 1 teaspoon grated ginger
> 1 teaspoon cinnamon (optional)

1. Strain barley.
2. Add remaining ingredients to barley water.
3. Mix together in pitcher and enjoy!

Laws of Blessings – הִלְכוֹת בְּרָכוֹת

When eating both barley bread and spelt bread, we make the blessing on the barley bread and have the intention to include the spelt bread, because even though the spelt bread is nicer, the barley bread is from the Seven Species.[59]

I'm pleased to introduce myself. My name is Madam Pearl. In Israel they call me *Geveret* Penina. My life is carefully scheduled. It makes me secure to follow my set routine and avoid wasted time. Every morning I do my exercise routine before eating my breakfast, which consists of one piece of fruit, two slices of barley bread with a thin layer of butter and a cup of tea. I am careful not to overeat as it pleases me to retain my upright and slim figure. I am quite strong and fit except for occasional joint pain, but I guess this is expected at my age. I must admit I'm not good at coping when things don't go according to my anticipated plan, yet I have enough self-control not to show my distress outwardly. Last week when my car broke down, I was devastated because I came late to work and missed teaching my regular child discipline class. The young generation urgently needs guidance. Our current permissive education creates confused and naughty children. In my time, children didn't need Ritalin. A little fear of old-fashioned punishment would make them shape up and sit still, as King Solomon teaches: "He that spares his rod hates his son."[60]

Endnotes

1. The sefirah of *Gevurah* is on the left branch of the Tree of Life.

2. Genesis 31:44.

3. Barley – שְׂעֹרָה/ *se'orah*, שְׂעֹרִים/*se'orim* and שְׂעוֹרִים/*se'orim* are mentioned 36 times in the Bible.
   Barley – שְׂעֹרָה/*se'orah* is mentioned in the Bible in the singular form six times, three times in the Pentateuch and three times in the rest of the Bible: Exodus 9:31 (twice); Deuteronomy 8:8; Isaiah 28:25; Joel 1:11; Job 31:40. **Barely** – שְׂעֹרִים/*se'orim* is mentioned in the Bible in the plural form 28 times, twice in the Pentateuch and 26 times in the rest of the Bible: Leviticus 27:16; Numbers 5:15; Judges 5:8, 7:13; II Samuel 14:30, 17:28, 21:9; I Kings 5:8; II Kings 4:42, 7:1, 7:16, 7:18; Jeremiah 29:17, 41:8; Ezekiel 4:9, 4:12, 13:19, 45:13; Hosea 3:2 (twice); The Scroll of Ruth 1:22, 2:17, 2:23, 3:2, 3:15, 3:17; I Chronicles 23:5; II Chronicles 2:9, 2:14. **Barley** – שְׂעוֹרִים/ *se'orim* with a וֹ/*vav* is mentioned in the Bible twice: I Chronicles 11:13; II Chronicles 2:27.

4. Album *Perek Shirah,* quoting Rav Ya'acov Emden, *HaYa'avetz* and Rav Moshe MiTrani, (*Hamabit*), *Beit Elokim.*

5. The vitamin and mineral content of barley is based on USDA, *Basic Report*: 2004, *Barley, hulled.*

6. Based on <http://nutritiondata.self.com/facts/cereal-grains-and-pasta/5678/2> retrieved June 19, 2013.

7. Dongowski G, Huth M, Gebhardt E, Flamme W., *Dietary Fiber-rich Barley Products Beneficially Affect the Intestinal Tract of Rats,* J Nutr. 2002 Dec;132(12):3704–14.

8. Michael Tierra, *Planetary Herbology,* p. 296.

9. Isaiah 28:25 as quoted at the beginning of the *Barley* section.

10. Oded Borowski, *Agriculture in Iron Age Israel*, p. 7.

11. *Babylonian Talmud, Berachot* 36a.

12. Michael Tierra, *Planetary Herbology*, p. 260.

13. Michael Tierra, *Planetary Herbology*, p. 260.

14. Behall KM, Scholfield DJ, Hallfrisch J. *Comparison of Hormone and Glucose Responses of Overweight Women to Barley and Oats.* J Am Coll

Nutr. 2005 Jun;24(3):182–8. In this study conducted by the Agricultural Research Service, barley was much more effective than oats in reducing both glucose and insulin responses.

15. Bays H, Frestedt JL, Bell M, Williams C, Kolberg L, Schmelzer W, Anderson JW. *Reduced Viscosity Barley β-Glucan versus Placebo: a Randomized Controlled Trial of the Effects on Insulin Sensitivity for Individuals at Risk for Diabetes Mellitus.* Nutr Metab (Lond), 2011 Aug 16;8;58.

16. Zhang JX, Lundin E, Hallmans G, Bergman F, Westerlund E, Petterson P. *Dietary Effects of Barley Fibre, Wheat Bran and Rye Bran on Bile Composition and Gallstone Formation in Hamsters.* APMIS. 1992 Jun;100(6):553–7.

17. Zhang JX, Bergman F, Hallmans G, Johansson G, Lundin E, Stenling R, Theander O, Westerlund E. *The Influence of Barley Fibre on Bile Composition, Gallstone Formation, Serum Cholesterol and Intestinal Morphology in Hamsters.* APMIS. 1990 Jun;98(6):568–74.

18. Rabbi Binyamin Moshe Kohn Shauli, *Nature's Wealth*, p. 250.

19. Rav Yitzchak Ginsburgh, *Body, Mind, and, Soul*, p. 78.

20. Truswell AS. *Cereal Grains and Coronary Heart Disease.* Eur J Clin Nutr. 2002 Jan;56(1):1–14.

21. Mason CM, Doneen AL. *Niacin: A Critical Component to the Management of Atherosclerosis: Contemporary Management of Dyslipidemia to Prevent, Reduce, or Reverse Atherosclerotic Cardiovascular Disease.* J Cardiovasc Nurs. 2012 Jul–Aug;27(4):303–16.

22. Behall KM, Scholfield DJ, Hallfrisch J. *Diets Containing Barley Significantly Reduce Lipids in Mildly Hypercholesterolemic Men and Women,* Am J Clin Nutr. 2004 Nov;80(5):1185–93. This study reported a 6–8% reduction in LDL cholesterol following consumption of diets containing barley with 3–6 grams of beta-glucan soluble fiber.

23. Hoang MH, Houng SJ, Jun HJ, Lee JH, Choi JW, Kim SH, Kim YR, Lee SJ. *Barley Intake Induces Bile Acid Excretion by Reduced Expression of Intestinal ASBT and NPC1L1 in C57BL/6J mice.* J Agric Food Chem. 2011 Jun 22;59(12):6798–805.

24. Aldughpassi A, Abdel-Aal el-SM, Wolever TM. *Barley Cultivar, Kernel Composition, and Processing Affect the Glycemic Index.* J Nutr. 2012 Sep;142(9):1666–71.

25. Nisim Krispil, *Medicinal Herbs of the Rambam*, p. 208.

26. <http://www.gogreen.net.nz/barleygrass-table.htm> retrieved December 18, 2012.

27. *Babylonian Talmud Sotah* 14a.

28. Ecclesiastes 3:19.

29. Rav Ruderman (1901–1987), quoted by Rabbi Frand, *Parshat Naso* <http://www.torah.org/learning/ravfrand/5762/naso.html> retrieved December 18, 2012.

30. See for example Rav Shlomo Ganzfried, Ungvar (1804–1886), קיצור שולחן ערוך/*Kitzur Shulchan Aruch*, 54:8.

31. Rashi, Exodus 8:14.

32. Exodus 23:15, 34:18; Deuteronomy 16:1.

33. The word אָבִיב/*aviv* – 'spring' is also used to describe the maturing of the barley during the month of Nissan, when the plague of hail in Egypt damaged only the barley and flax but not the wheat, which had not yet sprouted forth. "And the flax and the barley were smitten: for the barley was in the ear – אָבִיב/*aviv* and the flax was in bud" (Exodus 9:31).

34. An Omer is a dry measure of 2.2 liters (2 quarts U.S.).

35. Among the commentaries that explain this concept, see for example Rabbi Nachman of Breslov, Ukraine (1772–1810), ספר השתפכות הנפש/ *The Outpouring of the Soul, Ot* 71.

36. *Shem M'Shemuel,* Numbers, Shavuot, year 5670 (1909).

37. Judges 7:13–14.

38. Rashi, *ad. loc.*

39. *Shem M'Shemuel, Parashat Vayechi.*

40. Rosh Hashana Prayer book, *Netaneh Tokef.*

41. The Kabbalistic concept of sweetening the judgment at its root implies mitigating judgment with kindness by meditating on the root of judgment until one reaches its source in kindness.

42. Rabbi Matityahu Clark, *Etymological Dictionary of Biblical Hebrew*, p. 243.

43. Rashi, The Scroll of Ruth 3:15.

44. I Samuel 16:18. Each of the six descendants of Ruth and Boaz was blessed with six blessings; here I have only mentioned the six blessings of David and Mashiach.

45. Isaiah 11:2.

46. Genesis 30:3.

47. Genesis 49:26

48. Isaiah 54:5, *Babylonian Talmud, Sanhedrin* 22b.

49. See the *Introduction*, p. 18 endnote mark 27, Arizal, *Sefer HaLikutim, Parashat Terumah*, chapter 26.

50. *Chesed, Gevurah, Tiferet, Netzach, Hod, Yesod.*

51. Among the seven emotional sefirot, *Yesod* is the sixth sefirah.

52. The rectification through the building of the feminine is a foundation in Arizal's writings. See for example שער הכוונות/*Sha' ar HaKavanot, Drashei HaAmidah, drush* 4; *Drashei HaPesach, drush* 4, 11, 12; *Drashei Yom HaKipurim, drush* 5, שער הפסוקים/*Sha'ar HaPesukim, Parashat Naso, siman* 4.

53. Arizal, *Etz Chaim, Hechal Nukvah, Sha'ar Miyut HaYareach,* chapter 1; Sarah Schneider, *Kabbalistic Writings on The Nature of Masculine and Feminine* (A Still Small Voice, Jerusalem, Israel, 2001), pp. 52–98.

54. Genesis 16:2.

55. Genesis 16:2, with the commentaries of Rashi and Abarbanel.

56. Genesis 49:26 with Rashi's commentary.

57. Rav Shemuel Toledano, Tangiers, Morocco - Israel (1910–2003), ספר מבוא לחכמת הקבלה/*Introduction to the Wisdom of Kabbalah,* part 1, 6:1.

58. Isaiah 6:7. The word for barley – *se'orim* can be read as an abbreviation of the expression, '*sar avon*' – removal of transgression.

59. *Shulchan Aruch, Orach Chaim,* 168:4.

60. Proverbs 13:24.

Vitis Vinifera ~ עֲנָבִים

Grapes

תִּפְאֶרֶת ~ Tiferet – Harmony / Beauty

Grapes ~ גֶּפֶן *Vitis Vinifera*
Tiferet ~ תִּפְאֶרֶת *(Harmony / Beauty)*

וְיָשְׁבוּ אִישׁ תַּחַת גַּפְנוֹ וְתַחַת תְּאֵנָתוֹ וְאֵין מַחֲרִיד... (מיכה ד, ד)

"They shall sit, every man under his vine and under his fig tree: and none shall make them afraid..." (Micah 4:4).

ענבים שסחטן ולא מברך שֶׁהַכֹּל, א"ל בני שנא ושנא מפני כבוד הגפן הוא התפארת מלך בו' קצוות. (ספר הקנה - ד"ה ענין יראת המקום)

We do not bless 'shehakol' on grapes that are juiced. They made this change for the sake of honoring the grapevine,[1] for it is Tiferet, king over the six directions[2] (Sefer HaKane, Inyan Yirat Hamakom).[3]

Attribute: *Tiferet* – Harmony/Beauty

Character trait: The ability to synthesize and integrate (harmonizing)

Holiday: Purim, when we celebrate with wine feasts

Weekday: יוֹם שְׁלִישִׁי/*Yom Shelishi* – Third day of the week (Tuesday)

World: יְצִירָה/*Yetzirah* – Formation (hard inedible pit)

Body parts: The heart

Shepherd: יַעֲקֹב/Ya'acov

Prophetess: דְּבוֹרָה/Devorah

Numerical value: 133, equivalent to the word לְנַגֵּן/*lenagen* – 'to play' (an instrument)[4]

Mentioned in the Bible 216 times[5]

Meaning of Latin Name: Any of numerous woody vines of genus Vitis bearing clusters of edible berries.

פֶּרֶק שִׁירָה
Perek Shirah
The Song of the Universe

כֹּה אָמַר הַשֵׁם כַּאֲשֶׁר יִמָּצֵא הַתִּירוֹשׁ בָּאֶשְׁכּוֹל
וְאָמַר אַל תַּשְׁחִיתֵהוּ כִּי בְרָכָה בּוֹ כֵּן אֶעֱשֶׂה לְמַעַן
עֲבָדַי לְבִלְתִּי הַשְׁחִית הַכֹּל:
(ישעיה סה, ח)

*The Song of Grapes: "Thus says Hashem: As
the wine is found in the cluster, and one says,
'Do not destroy it, for a blessing is in it,' so will
I do for the sake of My servants, that I will not
destroy them all" (Isaiah 65:8).*

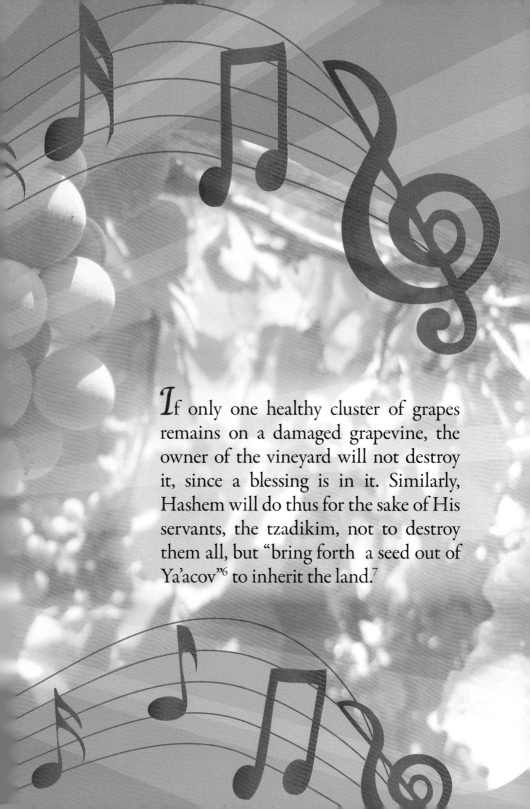

*I*f only one healthy cluster of grapes remains on a damaged grapevine, the owner of the vineyard will not destroy it, since a blessing is in it. Similarly, Hashem will do thus for the sake of His servants, the tzadikim, not to destroy them all, but "bring forth a seed out of Ya'acov"[6] to inherit the land.[7]

Nutrition Facts and Information about Grapes and Raisins

Mineral Content of Grapes[8]

Grapes are a good source of copper and contain small amounts of iron, potassium, phosphorus, magnesium, manganese, and traces of calcium. Grapes contain flavonoids, with powerful antioxidant effects.

Mineral Content of Raisins[9]

Raisins are rich in essential minerals. They are an excellent source of iron and copper, and a great source of potassium and phosphorous. They also contain a good amount of magnesium, manganese and small amounts of calcium.

Vitamin Content of Grapes[10]

Grapes are a good source of vitamins C and K. They also contain thiamin and riboflavin. Vitamins A and B6 are present in small quantities as well as traces of vitamin E and niacin.

Vitamin Content of Raisins

Raisins are a good source of riboflavin and thiamin. They also contain vitamin B6, niacin, and small amounts of vitamins C and K.

Oriental Medicine

According to Chinese medicine, grapes affect the liver and kidneys. They are sweet, sour and neutral. Their properties are blood and yin, nutritive and diuretic.[11]

Grapes and Raisins Nutritional Facts/100 g

Minerals	Grapes	Raisins	RDA	
Calcium	10 mg	28 mg	1%	2.8%
Iron	0.36 mg	2.59 mg	4.5%	31.6%
Magnesium	7 mg	30 mg	2%	8.6%
Phosphorus	20 mg	75 mg	3%	11%
Potassium	191 mg	825 mg	4%	17.6%
Sodium	2 mg	28 mg	0.2%	2.5%
Zinc	0.07 mg	0.18 mg	0.5%	1.6%
Copper	0.127 mg	0.302 mg	14%	33.2%
Manganese	0.071 mg	0.267 mg	3%	10.7%
Vitamins	**Grapes**	**Raisins**	**RDA**	
C	10.8 mg	5.4 mg	18%	9%
B1 (Thiamin)	0.069 mg	0.112 mg	6%	9.5%
B2 (Riboflavin)	0.070 mg	0.182 mg	5%	14.5%
B3 (Niacin)	0.188 mg	1.114 mg	1%	7.5%
B6	0.086 mg	0.188 mg	4%	8%
B9 (Folate)	2 μg	3 μg	0.5%	0.6%
A	66 IU	0 IU	3%	0%
E	0.19 mg	Not listed	1%	1%
K	14.6 μg	Not listed	12%	3%

Grapes correspond to Tiferet. The attribute of *Tiferet* is the perfect blend between the expansion of *Chesed* and the contraction and restraint of *Gevurah*. Therefore, grapes include both nourishing and eliminating qualities. Harmony is created when *Gevurah* contains *Chesed*, and *Chesed* tempers *Gevurah*. This harmony is called *Tiferet*, which means beautiful, because balance and harmony is the ultimate beauty within Creation. The beautiful grape clusters reflect the beauty of *Tiferet*, characterized by the balance between different and sometimes contrary components.

The Eliminating and Cleansing Properties of Grapes

Grapes contain anti-cancer properties due to the anti-inflammatory effect of their resveratrol and other antioxidants.[12] Grapes not only lower the risk of cancer; they also suppress the growth and propagation of cancer cells.[13] Due to their diuretic quality, grapes can help treat edema and urination problems.[14] They can decrease acid such as uric acid, thereby reducing the workload of the kidneys. Wine has an astringent effect and promotes the elimination of germs, mucus, and fatty deposits on the artery walls. Certain types of kidney stones can be prevented or dispelled by increasing consumption of grapes and drinking wine cooked with parsley.[15]

The Nourishing Properties of Grapes

Grapes are very nutritive and replete with iron and vitamins A, B and C.[16] Therefore, they counteract fatigue and provide instant energy. Grape seed oil nourishes the skin. It also contains a high level of antioxidants for eliminating free radicals.[17] The strong antibacterial and antiviral properties of grapes protect against infections.[18] The antioxidants present in grapes also provide a needed boost to the immune system.[19]

Grapes, Tiferet and Heart Health

Tiferet corresponds to the muscular system, with the heart – the greatest muscle in the body – as its centerpiece. Likewise, the seat of *Tiferet* is in the heart.[20] This corresponds to the fact that grapes and wine improve heart health. "Wine gladdens a person's heart..."[21] Whoever suffers from worry, fears and depression should eat grapes and drink wine daily.[22] Grapes hang in clusters that have the shape of the heart, and each grape looks like a blood cell. Grapes nourish the blood and treat blood and energy deficiency.[23] Whoever suffers from bleeding, such as nose bleeding or blood in the urine, should eat lots of grapes, especially green grapes, and drink wine in a measured way.[24] Grapes increase the nitric oxide levels in the blood, which prevents blood clots, thereby reducing the chances of a heart attack.[25] Especially the skins of purple grapes contain powerful antioxidants that prevent the accumulation of cholesterol on the artery walls.[26] Their resveratrol, a type of natural phenol, also helps prevent high blood pressure.[27] For this reason, drinking wine in moderation is considered to be healthy. Wine strengthens and speeds up the activity of the blood, straightens the stature of a person and regulates menstruation.[28]

Grapes for the Brain

Grapes promote brain health because they contain resveratrol. Therefore, grapes can stall the onset of neurodegenerative diseases and are beneficial for patients with Alzheimer's disease.[29] Raisins strengthen the activity of the brain and develop wisdom. Drinking wine strengthens the power of memory. It sharpens the person.[30]

Rambam teaches that grapes belong to the three kinds of healthy fruits that can be eaten without restriction.[31] They purify the body from toxins.[32] Grapes are excellent for the stomach. According to the Talmud, young wine is bad for the intestines, but old wine is good for the intestines.[33] Wine is very nourishing and supports digestion. In Aramaic wine is called חֲמַר/*chamar*, which has the numerical value of 248 corresponding to the 248 limbs of the body. From this we learn that wine enters each and every limb of the body.[34] The nature of grapes is warm and moist, which is excellent for old people who lack natural heat. In general, wine is good for the old and bad for the young.[35] Rambam teaches us to avoid drinking during a meal except for water mixed with wine.[36] He recommends drinking wine cooked with honey to keep the skin beautiful and youthful. He also suggests applying this mixture to the skin to alleviate hemorrhoids.[37]

Grapes – King of Fruits

כִּי תָבֹא בְּכֶרֶם רֵעֶךָ וְאָכַלְתָּ עֲנָבִים כְּנַפְשְׁךָ שָׂבְעֶךָ וְאֶל כֶּלְיְךָ לֹא תִתֵּן:
(דברים כג, כה)

"When you come into your neighbor's vineyard, then you may eat grapes until you have enough at your own pleasure: but you shall not put any in your container" (Deuteronomy 23:25).

According to Jewish law, any laborer harvesting fruit is free to eat as much as he wants from the produce while he is harvesting, as long as he doesn't take any home.[38] This law refers to any fruit picker, yet the Torah chose grapes to represent all fruits because of their importance. Grapes are among the 15 most important foods grown in the world. Approximately 71% of world grape production is used for wine, 27% as fresh fruit, and 2% as dried fruit. Grapes grow in clusters of six to 300 and can be black, blue, golden, green, purple, red, pink, brown, peach or white.[39] Jews have continually been engaged in viticulture to ensure the availability of kosher wine. The grapevine is a most versatile plant and produces grapes, raisins, grape seed oil, grape leaves, wine and grape juice. The Torah even has a special name for grape juice – תִּירוֹשׁ/*tirosh*. In the Bible, it took eight men to carry one cluster of grapes grown in the Holy Land.[40] To this day, an immense cluster of grapes carried on a pole serves as the logo for Israel's Ministry of Tourism.

Wine and Kingdom from Yehuda

Ya'acov prophesied that the Land of Judea will flow with wine like a fountain. The vines will be so productive that the grapes of only one vine will fully load one foal, while the produce of only one branch will load one ass's colt.[41] The central Judean Hills, west of Jerusalem and the southern Judean Hills including Chevron have proved to be vine-growing regions of the highest caliber.[42] This area is characterized by warm days and cool nighttime temperature – the perfect climate for growing grapes.[43]

Israel – Compared to the Grapevine

כַּעֲנָבִים בַּמִּדְבָּר מָצָאתִי יִשְׂרָאֵל... (הושע ט, י)

"I found Israel like the grapes in the wilderness..." (Hosea 9:10).

The children of Israel are compared to grapes, and G*d to the owner of the vineyard.[44] Malbim explains that when Hashem found Israel in the desert, they were as dear in His eyes as someone who finds grapes – the most important fruit – in the wilderness, where nothing grows. Just as grapes do not receive grafting, so was Israel in the wilderness pure, holy and careful to avoid immorality.[45]

The grapevine, with its beautiful clusters of grapes and foliage, symbolizes the importance of all the different segments of Israel. The children of Israel are like a grapevine. Its branches are the aristocracy, its clusters the scholars, its leaves the common people and its tendrils those in Israel that are void of learning. This is what was meant when word was sent from there: "Let the clusters pray for mercy for the leaves, for were it not for the leaves, the clusters could not exist."[46]

The harmony between the Torah scholars and the common people finds its expression in the grapevine, whose leaves cover the fruit clusters, in the same manner that the common people cover and protect the Torah scholars. Just as a grapevine has large and small clusters and the large ones hang lower, so too the Jewish people: Whoever labors in Torah and is greater in Torah seems lower than his fellow [due to his humility].[47]

The grapevine is a humble tree. It barely looks like a tree; especially in the winter without its leaves, it resembles a dreary stick. Nevertheless, the grapevine can produce the most royal wine. Israel, similarly, has been regarded as the lowest of nations, yet, from a branch of Israel's trunk will sprout forth the King Mashiach.

Just as the vine is the lowest of all trees, yet is king over them, so too Israel seems to be the least of the nations in this world. However, in the future, Israel will eventually become crowned by them and inherit the whole word, from one end to the other.[48]

מה הגפן הזו מתחלה נרפסת ברגל ואחר כך מעלין אותה על שלחנות
מלכים, כך הן ישראל בעולם הזה...,אבל לעתיד לבא (ישעיה מט, כג)
"והיו מלכים אומניך וגו'" (מדרש שמואל פרשה טז)

Just as grapes are first pressed under the feet, and then served on the royal tables: so too, is Israel downtrodden in this world, but in the next world, they will become kings (Midrash Shemuel, Parasha 16).

Wine – a Metaphor for Torah

While the grapevine is a metaphor for Israel, its wine alludes to the Torah. The numerical value of the word יין/*yayin* – 'wine' is 70. This is identical with the numerical value of the Hebrew word for 'secret' – סוד/*sod*. From this the Talmud learns נכנס יין יצא סוד/*nichnas yayin, yatza sod* – through wine it is possible to access the secrets of the Torah,[49] as long as one masters drinking without getting drunk.[50]

Rabbi Yosei bar Yehuda appreciated mature wine and compared it to the Torah scholars. "One who learns from the young is compared to one who eats unripe grapes and drinks wine from the wine-press. However, one who learns from the elderly is compared to one who eats ripened grapes and drinks mature wine."[51]

The grape wood is the least useful of all woods, as the prophet asks: "Can wood be taken from it for productive use? Could they take from it even a peg upon which to hang any vessel?"[52] Rather than trying to be like 'the other trees in the forest' known for their 'wood' – their economic political and military power, Israel exists only for her 'fruits' – the holy Torah and mitzvot, the source of life for all humanity.[53]

Symbol of Peace and Prosperity

During the peaceful period of King Solomon's reign, the children of Israel are described as dwelling securely under their grapevine and fig tree.[54] Radak explains that both Israel and all the nations will dwell under the grapevine in the future to come, when there will no longer be any wars in the world.[55]

Grapes – the Source of Blessing or Curse

Grapes teach us that we must bless both on the good and on the bad, just as we are required to recite a blessing for both wine and for vinegar. On the good we bless, "Blessed are You... Who is good and does good."[56] On the bad we bless, "Blessed are You... the true Judge."[57]

According to Rabbi Meir, the Tree of Good and Evil was a grapevine.[58] Depending on how it is used, the grapevine can either cause the greatest good or the greatest evil. Many Torah verses describe how wine brings a person to sin. After the flood, the first thing Noach planted was a grapevine.[59] Rashi explains that Noach degraded himself by planting a vineyard that supplied intoxicating drink, before growing sustainable food.[60] On the other hand, the grapes of the vine are the holiest of fruits, as the first kohen, Malkie Tzedek, brought forth bread and wine to sanctify Avraham's victory and proclaim the Divine sovereignty.[61] Wine accompanies us through the gates of holiness,[62] as it sanctifies circumcision, the Shabbat, holidays and marriages,[63] and is offered in the Temple.[64]

The practice to say *l'Chaim* – 'to life,' when drinking wine made from grapes is based on the Talmudic opinion that the fruit of the Tree of Knowledge was the grapevine, which brought death to the world. Therefore, when drinking wine we pray to attach ourselves to the Tree of Life, echoing the hope that our drinking will bring only good and not evil.

Kiddush or Havdalah?

Kiddush, the benediction recited over a cup of wine on Shabbat and holidays, means holiness or sanctification. The root of this word – ק-ד-ש is used for the first time in the Torah with respect to sanctifying and setting Shabbat aside from the remaining weekdays.[65] As part of the Jewish wedding ceremony, before the groom places the ring on his bride's finger he proclaims, "Behold you are consecrated unto me with this ring, in accordance with the Law of Moses and Israel." The Hebrew word for consecrated, מְקֻדֶּשֶׁת/*mekudeshet*, stems from the same root as the word for קִדּוּש/*Kiddush*. This word for holiness is also intimately connected with the act of separating one Jewish woman from the rest of the world to be uniquely and exclusively consecrated to her husband.

The *Havdalah* ceremony, recited over a cup of wine at the end of Shabbat, also means 'separation.' In the text of the Havdalah ritual, we praise the Creator for distinguishing between light and darkness, Israel and the nations, and separating the seventh day from the six workdays. The separation of Havdalah is through fire, as the braided Havdalah candle affirms.

> *"If the Jew doesn't make Kiddush, then the gentile will make Havdalah"* (Rav Chaim Volozhin).

If a Jew doesn't make Kiddush – sanctifying himself by maintaining a distinctly Jewish lifestyle, but rather, tries to melt into the society of the gentiles, then the non-Jew will make Havdalah for him by excluding him from certain country clubs, etc., and making the Jew realize that he is truly different.

The Jewish people are uniquely entrusted with the task of being a Holy Nation – "a kingdom of priests,"[66] whose primary mandate is to illuminate the physical realm with Hashem's light, through elevating all of Creation. In order to fulfill this purpose of holiness, the Jewish people must remain separate from all other nations. The nations of the world have an unconscious recognition that the national separation of Israel is crucial to their wellbeing, and an intrinsic part of the very fabric and purpose of Creation.

While we may sometimes be misguided by a desire to be less different than the other nations, Rav Chaim Volozhin is reminding us that we have no choice but to be separate. Yet, we do have a choice regarding our path of separation. We can remember who we are and actively pursue our separate path of holiness, or inadvertently let the nations of the world remind us by forcing us to remain separate with their flames of burning anti-Semitism.[67]

Jewish Weddings and Wine

Wine is central in wedding celebrations. Even the engagement is simply called the '*l'Chaim*' in many Jewish circles. The sanctification of the marriage under the *chuppah* (marriage canopy) cannot take place without the wine cup of blessing. Why is wine so essential in Jewish marriage ceremonies?

Whereas all other fruits decrease in value and blessing when made into juice, grapes increase their value when juiced. This is reflected in the special higher blessing we recite over wine and grape juice. Wine, therefore, delivers the powerful message that by coming together in marriage, the couple's newfound union is more valuable than their independent individualities. Therefore, it is not enough to become close and share each other's grapes. The centrality of wine in Jewish weddings teaches the new couple to transcend their individual identity and crush their grapes together until they become a new merged entity, as the Torah teaches, "Therefore, a man leaves his father and mother and cleaves to his wife and they become one flesh."[68] Although man and woman each have their own values and 'hang on their own grapevine,' the wine during Jewish wedding rituals teaches that the basic tenant of marriage is to choose wine over grapes.[69]

Separation versus Unification

Wine has a dual role in Jewish celebrations. On the one hand, it separates by elevating and consecrating the people of Israel from the mundane realm. On the other hand, it facilitates transcendence and merging of the individuals into a greater whole. This dual role reflects the energy of *Tiferet*, which is not just to synthesize between two opposites; but, moreover, to incorporate the Divine within this new union. Such fusion can only take place after separating from the mundane domain, thereby gaining freedom to merge with a higher entity within the realm of the Divine.

The Jewish Wife – A Fruitful Vine

אֶשְׁתְּךָ כְּגֶפֶן פֹּרִיָּה בְּיַרְכְּתֵי בֵיתֶךָ בָּנֶיךָ כִּשְׁתִלֵי זֵיתִים סָבִיב לְשֻׁלְחָנֶךָ:
(תהלים קכח, ג)

"Your wife is like a fruitful vine in the recesses of your home. Your children are like olive plants around your table" (*Psalms* 128:3).

The modest woman is compared to a grapevine, because it is the custom to plant the grapevine at the recesses of the house. When it grows it sends forth its branches outside of the home, toward the sun. Yet, its root remains close to home... Likewise the modest woman is worthy to sit inside... while her children go out to the field...[70]

...Although the grapevine stands at the recesses of the house, its branches and leaves reach the roof of the house and protect the entire home. Likewise, the modest wife, who dwells in the recesses of her home, guards and protects the entire home.[71]

 A Taste of Kabbalah – The Four Mystical Cups of Creation

שמצינו ד' דברים שנמשלים לגפן, כדאיתא בפ' ג"ה (דף צ"ב
ע"א), **א.** ישראל נמשלו לגפן, כמ"ש שם "ובגפן ג' שריגים", אלו
ג' שרי גיאים שיוצאין מישראל בכל דור וכו', והם ניצוצי ג' אבות
שמתגלגלים בכל דור, **ב.** העולם נדמה לגפן, **ג.** גפן זו תורה, **ד.**
ירושלים ובהמ"ק כמ"ש שם. ר"א המודעי אומר "גפן זה ירושלים
וכו'", וביציאת ישראל ממצרים נבחרו לו לעם, כמ"ש "והוצאתי
אתכם וגו', ולקחתי אתכם לי לעם", ואז היה ג"כ בריאת העולם
מחדש כמש"ל באריכות שיתנהג ע"פ סידור ניסיי למעלה מן הטבע.
ומבואר בכתוב שיצי"מ היה ע"מ לקבל התורה, כמ"ש "בהוציאך
את העם ממצרים תעבדון את האלקים על ההר הזה", ועיקר קיום
התורה והמצוות הם בא"י ובירושלים ובהמ"ק... ולכן נגד זה ד'
כוסות, כוס ראשון של קידוש נגד ישראל "אשר בחר בנו וכו'", כוס
שני סיפור יצי"מ נגד העולם שהוא יתברך שידד הטבע וחידש כל
הבריאה, שזה ענין סיפור יצי"מ זכרון הניסים והנפלאות שנעשו
במצרים, כוס שלישי בהמ"ז נגד א"י וירושלים ובהמ"ק, "על ארץ
חמדה וכו', ועל ירושלים וכו', ועל הבית הגדול וכו'", ועיקר בהמ"ז
הוא על הארץ כידוע, כוס ד' הלל הוא על התורה ומתחילין "לא לנו
וגו', כי לשמך תן כבוד", והיא התורה שכולה שמותיו של הקב"ה...
(יד מצרים - פירוש הגדה של פסח, עמ' קלז-קלח)[72]

We find four things compared to a grapevine:

1. Israel is compared to a grapevine, as it states, "...and on the grapevine there were three branches."[73] These are the three men of excellence that come forth in Israel in every generation.[74] They are the sparks of the three fathers that reincarnate in every generation.

2. The world is compared to a grapevine.

3. The Torah is compared to a grapevine.

4. Jerusalem and the Temple are compared to a grapevine.

Israel was chosen to be His people during the Exodus, as it states: "I will bring you out... and I will take you to Me for a people."[75] Then the world was as if created anew through the miracles beyond nature. The Exodus was for the sake of receiving the Torah, as it states: "When you have brought the people out of Egypt, you shall serve G*d upon this mountain."[76] True observance of the Torah and the mitzvot takes place in the Land of Israel, in Jerusalem and in the Temple.

The Four Cups on Pesach, likewise, correspond to these four things. The first cup during Kiddush corresponds to Israel when we recite "Who has chosen us, etc." The second cup that we drink during the story of the Exodus corresponds to the world, as Hashem overruled nature and renewed creation during the Exodus. This explains the importance of telling about the miracles that took place in Egypt. The third cup during Grace after Meals corresponds to the Land of Israel, Jerusalem and the Temple. The main theme of Grace after Meals is thanking Hashem for the land, as we recite: "We thank You ...for the desirable land... for Jerusalem... for the great house, etc." The fourth cup, with which we complete the *Hallel*,[77] corresponds to the Torah, as Hallel opens with "not for our sake... but give honor to Your name." This is the Torah, which in its entirety conveys the names of G*d (Rav Yitzchak Isaac Chaver, *Sefer Yad Mitzrayim, Commentary on the Haggadah of Pesach*).

Explanation: Rav Yitzchak Isaac Chaver bases his commentary on Genesis 40:10 about the grapevine in the butler's dream, that Yosef interpreted, as proof text for comparing the grapevine to the people of Israel, the world, the Torah and the Land of Israel.

וּבַגֶּפֶן שְׁלֹשָׁה שָׂרִיגִם וְהִוא כְפֹרַחַת עָלְתָה נִצָּהּ הִבְשִׁילוּ אַשְׁכְּלֹתֶיהָ עֲנָבִים:
(בראשית מ, י)

"In the vine were three branches, it was as though it budded, and its blossoms shot forth, its clusters brought forth ripe grapes" (*Genesis* 40:10).

Furthermore, Rav Yitzchak Isaac Chaver quotes the following explanation of this Torah verse from the Babylonian Talmud:

"In the vine were three branches..." Rav Chiya ben Abba said in the name of Rav, "These are the three men of excellence that come forth in **Israel** in every generation..." Rabbi Eliezer said, "'The vine' is the **world.** The 'three branches' are [the patriarchs] Avraham, Yitzchak and Ya'acov. 'It was as though it budded, and its blossoms shot forth' – these are the matriarchs. 'Its clusters brought forth ripe grapes' – these are the tribes." Rabbi Yehoshua said to him: "'The vine' is the **Torah.** The 'three branches' are Moshe, Aharon and Miriam. 'And as it was budding its blossoms shot forth' – these are [the members of] the Sanhedrin."[78] Rabbi Elazar the Modiite says: "'The vine' is **Jerusalem.** The 'three branches' are the Temple, the King and the Kohen Gadol. 'And it was as though it budded, and its blossoms shot forth' – these are the young kohanim. 'Its clusters brought forth ripe grapes' – these are the drink offerings."[79]

The allegory of the grapevine represents G*d's final goal of Creation. When the grapevine is analogous to the Jewish people, its three branches correspond to our holy fathers, Avraham, Yitzchak and Ya'acov, who fulfilled Hashem's purpose of creation. Therefore, splinters of their souls reincarnate in every generation.

All of the four interpretations of the metaphor are interconnected and lead to one another. Hashem created the world for the sake of the Torah and for the sake of the people of Israel,[80] who will fulfill the Torah in the world and specifically in the Land of Israel. Hashem renewed the Creation of **the world** by means of the miracles that took place during the Exodus, the Ten Plagues and the splitting of the Reed Sea. Since these miracles were beyond nature, it was as if Hashem created the nature of the world anew during the Exodus. Hashem enacted the Exodus in order to free **His people Israel** to serve Him by keeping **the Torah,** including its mitzvot. It is impossible to keep all of the Torah on foreign soil, as some mitzvot are dependent on the **Land of Israel.** G*d, therefore, led us to the Holy Land.

We drink four cups of wine during the Seder on the first night of Pesach. The first three cups correspond to the Jewish people, the world, and the Land of Israel respectively. The last cup, which we drink following the Hallel prayer of praise, opens with requesting that Hashem deliver us for the sake of His great name. This cup corresponds to the Torah, for its inner level, without the current spaces between the words, consists of various combinations of the letters of G*d's Holy Names. "The entire Torah is like an explication of, and a commentary on, the Ineffable Name of G*d."[81]

הרואה גפן טעונה בחלום אין אשתו מפלת נפלים שנאמר אשתך כגפן פוריה, שורקה יצפה למשיח שנאמר אֹסְרִי לַגֶּפֶן עִירֹה וְלַשֹּׂרֵקָה בְּנִי אֲתֹנוֹ:

He who sees a grapevine laden with fruit in a dream, his wife will never miscarry, as it says, "Your wife is a fruitful vine..."[82] *One who beholds a branch of a grapevine in a dream, should look forward to seeing Mashiach, as it states, "He shall tie his donkey to a small grapevine, and to a branch of a grapevine, his donkey's foal"*[83] *(Babylonian Talmud, Berachot 57a).*[84]

Grape Recipes

Seedless Grapes or Seed-bearing Fruits?

וַיֹּאמֶר אֱלֹקִים תַּדְשֵׁא הָאָרֶץ דֶּשֶׁא עֵשֶׂב מַזְרִיעַ זֶרַע עֵץ פְּרִי עֹשֶׂה פְּרִי לְמִינוֹ
אֲשֶׁר זַרְעוֹ בוֹ... וַיַּרְא אֱלֹקִים כִּי טוֹב: (בראשית א, יא-יב)

"G*d said, 'Let the earth sprout vegetation: seed-bearing plants and trees of every kind, bearing fruit with the seed in it...' And G*d saw that this was good" (Genesis 1:11–12).

Contrary to the original Divine directive, nearly all commercial grapevines today produce seedless grapes. If you go to a grocery store to buy grapes, there is a good chance that the only type of grapes you will find is seedless. These grapes have been manipulated genetically to prevent the seeds from growing. However, by eating seedless grapes you lose the important health benefits of the grape-seed oil. Moreover, on the energetic level, the seed with its ability to reproduce and maintain the species, is the life of the fruit. Spiritually, it was Hashem's will to create seed-bearing plants. Seedless grapes are, therefore, not according to the Divine intent.

The importance of Organic Grapes

It's especially important to get hold of organic grapes, wine and raisins, even if you haven't taken upon yourself to eat only organic produce. Because grapes ripen quickly, tend to mold, and attract insects, they are sprayed with more chemicals than most other crop. Organic grapes also have a sweeter, more intense flavor, and keep longer than those commercial produced. This may be because commercial produced grapes have a higher average crop yield at the expense of their nutritional quality. Grape vines managed for maximum yields produce more grapes per acre, but lower quality, less flavorful fruits.

GRANDMA'S GOODLY GRAPE JUICE

*No store-bought grape juice can compare to the fresh taste of
real homemade grape juice*

You will need 2–3 kilos (about 5 pounds) of grapes. You may
even use soft mushy ones that no one feels like eating.

1. Remove the stalks and rinse.
2. Feed through juicer.
3. Bottle and refrigerate immediately.

Variation
The old-fashioned way – a family activity

1. Place the grapes in large tub.
2. Step on them with well rinsed feet.
3. Strain juice well, bottle and refrigerate immediately.

Although the old fashioned way may be more time consuming and
messy, my family definitely prefers it, because when the seeds are
strained out, rather than crushed in the juicer, the grape juice comes
out much clearer. However, including the crushed seeds in the juice
improves the juice due to their many health benefits.

Blended Variation

1. Place the grapes in the blender and blend well, strain.
2. Pour into a bottle and refrigerate.

I find it easier and less messy to make grape juice in the blender. Keep in mind that the grape juice produced this way will come out quite foamy like a delicious grape smoothie.

Homemade grape juice will keep for up to three to four days in the refrigerator before it begins to ferment. Afterwards it can be used as an excellent wine-vinegar.

(It is important to be aware that in order to produce kosher grape juice, only a Jew may feed the grapes through the juicer, step on them and handle the juice in any way).

אמר רבי חנין בר פפא כל שאין יין נשפך בתוך ביתו כמים אינו בכלל ברכה: (תלמוד בבלי מסכת עירובין סה, ע"א)

Rabbi Chanin Bar Papa said "He who does not have wine spilled in his home like water, is not considered to be blessed" (*Babylonian Talmud, Iruvin* 65a).

GLORIOUS FROZEN GRAPE GALORE
A colorful, refreshing, healthy alternative to ice cream

When the grape harvest is abundant you can make the simplest, most delicious snack from frozen grapes.

1. Separate the grapes from their stalks.
2. Wash them well.
3. Place grapes in a freezer bag or container in the freezer.
4. Serve on a hot summer day alone or mixed with slices of other frozen fruits such as peaches, bananas, plums, etc.

Variation

1. Put a handful of seedless grapes inside the blender with a few ice cubes.
2. Blend until a slush-like mixture is formed.
3. Add some whole grapes or pieces of frozen fruit for a blend of textures. (If you like it sweeter, you may add fruit juice concentrate or honey to taste).
4. Place in freezer for a day or more.
5. Serve in colored glasses with spoons as a refreshing snack.

JEWELLED GRAPE FRUITION SALAD
A delightful treat for the eyes and taste buds alike

This fruit salad blends three of the Seven Species into a sweet refreshing treat, taking advantage of their complementary flavors and textures. The dark purple grapes resembling blueberries contrast beautifully with the ruby-colored pomegranate arils laced with coconut flakes. The cinnamon adds further zest.

1 cup small purple grapes
1 cup large green deseeded grapes cut in half
1 cup pomegranate arils (about three pomegranates)
1 apple cut into thin slices
4 sun-dried chopped figs
2 tablespoons shredded coconut
1 tablespoon pure vanilla extract
¼ teaspoon cinnamon
A few spritzes of fresh lemon juice

1. Gently blend all of the fruits together.

2. Sprinkle them with pure vanilla, cinnamon and coconut.

3. Squeeze a few drops of lemon juice on top for taste and to keep the colors from running.

4. Serve at room temperature in pretty glass bowls.

RAISIN CAROB TRUFFLES
Better than the most luxurious chocolate

10 pitted dates
¼ cup soaked raisins
2 tablespoons orange juice
¼ cup almonds
¼ cup sunflower seeds
¼ cup carob powder
1 tablespoon techina (sesame butter) or almond butter
1 teaspoon grated orange peel
1 teaspoon pure vanilla extract
¼ teaspoon cinnamon
1 pinch sea salt
For dusting: carob powder, cacao powder, or shredded coconut

1. Soak the raisins in the orange juice for 20 minutes.
2. Process the almonds and sunflower seeds in food processor.
3. Add remaining ingredients and process until it turns into a sticky dough.
4. Refrigerate for one hour.
5. Shape into balls.
6. Roll in carob powder, cacao powder, or shredded coconut.

Makes approximately 20 truffles

Variation

For a more textured truffle, do not add the whole raisins with the orange juice in the food processor, but gently fold them in whole afterwards.

RAW RAISIN ROLLIES

This yummy desert rolls into your mouth and easily disappears in no time

> 1 cup raw nuts (½ cup of almonds, ¼ cup pecans, and ¼ cup of walnuts, or use whatever combination you prefer). You may substitute any amount of the nuts with sunflower seeds and/or coconut.
>
> ¾ cup raisins
>
> ¼ cup cocoa powder
>
> 1 teaspoon pure vanilla extract
>
> Water as needed for mixture to bind without crumbling apart

1. Process the raw nuts and raisins in a food processor with the S-blade until the nuts and raisins stick together.
2. Add in the cocoa powder and vanilla extract and continue processing until all of the ingredients combine.
3. Gradually add water as needed to allow the mixture to bind together without becoming too wet.
4. Form the mixture into balls the size of your preference.
5. Dust with cocoa powder or shredded coconut.
6. Place in a sealed container in the freezer or refrigerator.

Variation

You may substitute most of the ingredients. Instead of raisins you could use dates, instead of cocoa use carob powder – experiment with different nuts and seeds. You could even try including a few handfuls of soaked chia seeds.

CHOCOLATE GRAPE LEAVES

*For patient cooks ready to make the extra effort to create
a stunning effect*

> 200 g (a little more than 7 oz.) chocolate chips
> or other chocolate
> 16 young fresh medium-sized grape leaves

1. Soak the grape leaves in natural soap water for three minutes, rinse and hold up to light to check for bugs.

2. Dry the grape leaves and arrange them vein side up on three or four baking sheets, so that the leaves do not touch one another.

3. Melt half the chocolate either in a double boiler or in the microwave for 30 seconds.

3b. Instructions for melting chocolate in double boiler: Fill a pot with water and bring it to a boil, then turn down the temperature to keep the water at a simmer.

3c. Place a small bowl filled with the chocolate on the simmering water in the pot. Stir the chocolate to prevent it from burning.

3d. When the chocolate has melted, remove bowl from the heat, wiping it dry on the bottom to prevent any moisture from affecting the chocolate.

4. Spread the melted chocolate on half of the grape leaves. Make sure their veins are facing up, because these ridges will create the design in the leaf during molding.

5. Let the chocolate cool down. Repeat this procedure with the second batch of chocolate and grape leaves.

6. When the chocolate has cooled sufficiently and solidified (after approximately two to three hours – better safe than sorry) gently peel off the grape leaves. Be careful when you peel the fragile grape leaves not to break the chocolate.

7. Serve your beautiful chocolate grape leaves at special celebrations, as decorative centerpieces on dessert platters.

GREEN FRUITY CARROT SALAD

A creative healthful green alternative to the traditional carrot raisin salad

4 cups grated carrots
¾ cup raisins
¼ cup fresh minced basil
¼ cup finely chopped chicory leaves or other greens
¼ cup sunflower seeds
Juice of 1–2 oranges
1 teaspoon cinnamon

1. Grate the carrots.

2. Add remaining ingredients.

3. Mix all ingredients together and serve.

I like how the sweetness of the raisins complement and camouflage the tarter taste of the greens.

GRAPE LEAF SMOOTHIE

Who would believe that even grape leaves provide a wild vitamin and mineral boost in a cup!

7 large grape leaves, cut into small pieces, for your blender's sake!

2 medium-sized red apples, pears, peaches or plums – or a little of each, roughly chopped

2 cups frozen strawberries

2 bananas

1 cup water

1 tablespoon spirulina (optional)

Blend everything until smooth and enjoy.

Health Benefits of Grape Leaves

Raw grape leaves are an excellent source of vitamins A and K, calcium, magnesium and manganese. They are a great source of vitamin C, riboflavin, B6 and folate, iron and copper. Grape leaves are also a good source of vitamin E and niacin and contain some phosphorous and potassium, with small amounts of thiamin and zinc.[85]

STUFFED GRAPE LEAVES

Making stuffed grape leaves is another delicious way to utilize an otherwise inedible object that originated in ancient Mesopotamia. Today, they remain popular throughout much of the Middle East.

WILD GRAPE LEAVES

Pick grape leaves in the beginning of summer when they are young and tender. Be sure to harvest the large, minty-green colored leaves; the dark, older leaves tend to be stringy and fibrous.

1 quart Mason jar
3 dozen (36) wild grape leaves
2 tablespoons sea salt
2 cups water

1. Mix the water and sea salt together in a bowl to make brine and set aside.

2. Stack the grape leaves on top of each other until you have a stack of 12.

3. Roll up this stack into a tight roll and put it in the jar.

4. Make two additional rolls of 12 to fill the jar.

5. Pour the brine over the rolls until the jar is full and cap it.

6. Leave the jar to sit out on the counter for 48 hours on a towel, as there may be a little leakage. This begins the healthy lacto-fermentation process.

7. After 48 hours place the jar in the fridge and leave it for at least a month.

8. At the end of four weeks, the grape leaves are ready to use. They will keep for a long time in the refrigerator, so you can use them anytime you are inspired to make stuffed grape leaves.

Shortcut Variation

1. Pick grape leaves, wash them well in cold water and check them for bugs.

2. Blanch the leaves in boiling, lightly salted water for about half a minute each.

3. Drain and pat dry, use right away or freeze. (Make sure the water is drained well from the grape leaves).

4. Stack about 50–60 leaves turned the same way on a piece of wax paper.

5. Roll up the wax paper, squeezing out any remaining water and place as a roll in a plastic bag in the freezer.

The grape leaves can remain indefinitely in the freezer and may be refrozen.

RICE MIXTURE

(For stuffing about three dozen medium-sized grape leaves)

2 cups water

1 cup raw brown rice

(or use part wild rice for an extra wild treat!)

2 small minced onions

¼ cup fresh minced parsley

¼ cup fresh minced mint or cilantro

(You may use ½ cup parsley if you don't have mint or cilantro).

3–4 stalks minced celery

4 tablespoons olive oil

Juice of 2 lemons

6 cloves of garlic (3–4 minced, the rest whole)

2 teaspoons sea salt

2 teaspoons turmeric

2 teaspoons hawaich (Yemenite spice mixture)

1 teaspoon freshly ground black pepper

2 red or green peppers, halved

1. Mix the ingredients from rice to mint together.

2. Add half of the second group of ingredients (not including red or green peppers) to the rice mixture.

3. Save the other half to add to the water for cooking the stuffed grape leaves.

4. If you use pickled grape leaves in brine, you may optionally soak them in hot water for one hour and drain them before use.

ASSEMBLING THE ROLLS

1. Lay out a grape leaf, vein side up, nip off the stem. On large leaves place about 1 tablespoon rice-mixture and on smaller leaves a heaping teaspoon near the stem end.

2. Carefully fold the leaf from the stem end to cover the filling. Fold the sides over, and then roll up the leaf to form a neat package. Squeeze out any extra liquid.

3. Cover the bottom of the pot with any leftover leaves.

4. Layer peppers on bottom of pot to create a base. Arrange rolled grape leaves seam side down into pot in two layers on top of the peppers.

5. Drizzle with remaining oil mixed with the spices, garlic and lemon juice. Cover with water and bring to boil.

6. Reduce heat and simmer covered for three to four hours on very low heat. Optionally spread a towel over the lid of the pot to keep all vapor inside.

7. After one and a half hours, check to see if you may need to add more water. When one of the stuffed grape leaves at the top is soft, they are all ready. Serve hot or cold.

Baked Variation

- 2¼ cups water
- 1½ cups uncooked brown rice
- 1½ cups minced onion
- 2 tablespoons olive oil
- 5 cloves of minced garlic
- 2 tablespoons lemon juice
- ½ teaspoon sea salt
- ¼ teaspoon freshly ground black pepper
- ¼ cup minced parsley
- ¼ cup fresh minced mint
- ½ cup pine nuts (optional)

1. Cook rice in water until tender.

2. Meanwhile, sauté onion in olive oil until translucent.

3. Add sea salt, freshly ground black pepper, garlic, and pine nuts to the sautéed onions, sauté for about five more minutes.

4. Allow rice to cool, then place in a bowl with the sautéed mixture. Add lemon juice, parsley and mint. Mix well. Use this mixture to fill the grape leaves.

5. Place each leaf shiny side down on a flat, clean surface.

6. Put a heaping tablespoon of filling near the stem end.

7. Fold in the sides and roll tightly.

8. Arrange the stuffed leaves onto a baking sheet brushed with olive oil.

9. Brush the tops of each roll generously with olive oil using a pastry brush.

10. Bake at 325 F° (160 C°) for about 20 minutes, until heated thoroughly.

11. Allow to cool thoroughly before brushing a second time with olive oil.

12. Make a mixture of three tablespoons lemon juice and one teaspoon sea salt. Using your pastry brush again, coat each roll generously with the lemon-salt mixture.

13. Chill thoroughly in the refrigerator and serve cold.

14. Arrange on a tray and garnish with thin slices of lemon.

Laws of Blessings ~ הִלְכוֹת בְּרָכוֹת

We bless 'borei p'ri hagafen'[86] on wine, whether it is uncooked, boiled or spiced with honey and pepper.[87] If the wine is mixed with liquor we go according to the majority of the mixture. If the majority is wine, the blessing is 'borei p'ri hagafen.' If the majority is liquor, the blessing is 'shehakol.'[88]

When there are several kinds of fruits that require the same blessing, including fruits from the Seven Species, the blessing of the Seven Species takes precedence.[89]

Among the Seven Species, the fruit mentioned first in the Torah verse takes precedence.[90] However, the verse is broken up by the repetition of the word "land."[91] According to the principle of the order of blessings, the species mentioned closer to the word 'land.' take precedence. Therefore, dates precede grapes, because dates are listed second to the second mention of "land," whereas grapes are listed third to the first "land."[92] This applies specifically to eating grapes, but if one made wine from them, which elevate them to require their own blessing of 'borei p'ri hagafen,' the blessing over the wine takes precedence. However, a dish made with any of the five kinds of grain is even more important than the blessing on the wine.[93]

Nice to meet you, I'm Mrs. Gefen. I live in the hills and treasure the cool summer nights. People think I'm pretty and I do make great efforts to preserve my beauty and always look my best. I wrap myself in purples, pinks and greens with lacy fringes. I am very open; I wear my heart on my sleeve. My skin is thin and I easily get bruised. It breaks my heart when people are insensitive. I don't like being called a social butterfly, although I do enjoy the company of friends. I really love people and share their joys with my full heart. I'll never miss a *simcha* (happy occasion to celebrate), or a wedding. I have started many volunteer groups and oversee clusters of social welfare. I'm a very spiritual woman. I can't wait to greet the Shabbat and holidays. I anticipate that my old age may transform into the prime of my life. As the Proverb goes: "Old age is a crown of glory. It is found in the way of righteousness."[94] Understanding the truth of the Torah is my passion, yet my expertise is quite versatile, balancing Torah learning with general worldly knowledge. People from far and near come to drink my words of wisdom and it is my mission to gently help guide others back on the path and give sound advice, as King Solomon teaches: "A soothing tongue is a tree of life."[95]

Endnotes

1. The general blessing "שֶׁהַכֹּל/*shehakol* – *that everything came into being by His word*' – pertains to all foods that have lost their original form, such as completely mashed fruits and vegetables. This blessing is last in the order of blessings since the more specific always takes precedence. The blessing on all other juices except grape juice is "שֶׁהַכֹּל/*shehakol*,' since the juice has lost the form of the fruit from which it was produced. However, grape juice merits the special blessing of 'בּוֹרֵא פְּרִי הַגָּפֶן/*borei p'ri hagafen* – *Creator of the fruit of the vine*' – because of its special honorable status.

2. The six directions – south, north, east, west, up and down – correspond respectively to the Six Middle Sefirot: *Chesed* (loving-kindness), *Gevurah* (restraint), *Tiferet* (harmony), *Yesod* (foundation), *Netzach* (victory), *Hod* (acknowledgement). *Tiferet* is in the center of these six *sefirot*, as illustrated by the following table:

Gevurah/גְּבוּרָה Might/Restraint	*Chesed*/חֶסֶד Loving-kindness
Tiferet/תִּפְאֶרֶת Harmony/Beauty	
Hod/הוֹד Acknowledgment/Splendor	*Netzach*/נֶצַח Victory/Endurance
Yesod/יְסוֹד Foundation/Covenant	

3. *Sefer HaKane* is a Kabbalistic commentary on the 613 mitzvot. Some ascribe this book to Rabbi Nechunia ben Hakane of the 1st century. Others hold that the book was written in Spain in the 14th century.

4. I Samuel 16:17.

5. Wine – יַיִן/*yayin*, grapevine – גֶּפֶן/*gefen*, בַּגְּפָנִים/*gefanim* and grapes – עֲנָבִים/*anavim* are mentioned 216 times in the Bible.
    Wine – יַיִן/*yayin* is mentioned in the Bible 145 times, 31 times in the Pentateuch and 114 times in the rest of the Bible: Genesis 9:21, 9:24, 14:18, 19:32, 19:33, 19:34, 19:35, 27:25, 49:11, 49:12; Exodus 29:40; Leviticus 10:9, 23:13; Numbers 6:3, 6:4, 6:20 15:5, 15:7 15:10, 28:14; Deuteronomy 14:26, 28:39, 29:5, 32:33, 32:38; Joshua 9:4, 9:13; Judges 13:4, 13:7, 13:14; I Samuel 1:14, 1:15, 1:24, 10:3, 16:20, 25:18, 25:37; II Samuel 13:28, 16:1, 16:2; Isaiah

5:12, 5:22, 16:10, 22:13, 24:9, 24:11, 28:1, 28:7, 29:9, 51:21, 55:1, 56:12; Jeremiah 13:12 (twice), 23:9, 25:15, 35:2, 35:5, 35:6, 35:8, 35:14, 40:12, 48:13, 51:7; Ezekiel 44:21; Hosea 4:11, 7:5, 9:4, 14:8; Joel 1:5, 4:3; Amos 2:8, 2:12, 5:11, 6:6, 9:14; Micah 2:11, 6:15; Habakkuk 2:5; Zephaniah 1:13; Haggai 2:12; Zechariah 9:15, 10:7; Psalms 60:5, 75:9, 78:65, 104:15; Proverbs 4:17, 9:2, 9:5, 20:1, 21:17, 23:20, 23:30, 23:31, 31:4, 31:6; Job 1:13, 1:18, 32:19; Daniel 1:5, 1:8, 1:16, 10:3; Nehemiah 2:1, 5:15, 5:18, 13:15; Song of Songs 1:2, 1:4, 2:4, 4:10, 7:10, 8:2; Lamentations 2:12; Ecclesiastes 2:3, 9:7, 10:19; The Scroll of Esther 1:7, 1:10, 5:6, 7:2, 7:7, 7:8; I Chronicles 9:29, 12:41, 27:27; II Chronicles 2:9, 2:14, 11:11.

Grapevine – גֶּפֶן/*gefen* is mentioned in the Bible in the singular form 50 times, 7 times in the Pentateuch and 43 times in the rest of the Bible: Genesis 40:9, 40:10, 49:11; Numbers 6:4, 20:5; Deuteronomy 8:8, 32:32; Judges 9:12, 9:13, 13:14; I Kings 5:5; II Kings 4:39, 18:31; Isaiah 7:23, 16:8, 16:9, 24:7, 32:12, 34:4, 36:16; Jeremiah 2:21, 5:17, 6:9, 8:13, 48:32; Ezekiel 15:2, 15:6, 17:6 (twice), 17:7, 17:8, 19:10; Hosea 10:1, 14:8; Joel 1:12, 2:22; Micah 4:4; Haggai 2:19; Zechariah 3:10, 8:12; Malachi 3:11; Psalms 78:47, 80:9, 80:15, 128:3, 105:33; Job 15:33; Song of Songs 6:11, 7:9, 7:13.

Grapevines – גְּפָנִים/*gefanim* are mentioned in the Bible in the plural form twice: Habakkuk 3:17; Song of Songs 2:13.

Grapes – עֲנָבִים/*anavim* are mentioned in the Bible 19 times, 12 times in the Pentateuch and 7 times in the rest of the Bible: Genesis 40:10, 40:11, 49:11; Leviticus 25:5; Numbers 6:3 (twice), 13:20, 13:23; Deuteronomy 23:25, 32:14 (in singular), 32:32 (twice); Isaiah 5:2, 5:4; Jeremiah 8:13; Hosea 3:1, 9:10; Amos 9:13; Nehemiah 13:15.

6. Isaiah 65:9.

7. Malbim, Isaiah 65:8.

8. The mineral and vitamin content of grapes is based on USDA, *Basic Report*: 09132, *Grapes, red or green* (*European type, such as Thompson seedless*), raw. The percentage of Recommended Daily Dietary Allowance is based on *Grapes, red or green* (*European type, Thompson seedless*), <http://www.nutrition-and-you.com/grapes.html> retrieved June 30, 2013.

9. The mineral and vitamin content of raisins is based on USDA, *Basic Report*: 09299, *Raisins, seeded.* The percentage of Recommended Daily Dietary Allowance is based on *Raisins, seedless* <http://www.nutrition-and-you. com/raisins.html> retrieved June 30, 2013.

10. There is an inconsistency between the USDA database, which lists the vitamin C as only 3.2 mg, and the *Power your Diet* website, which lists vitamin C as 10.8 mg and 18% of RDA. I'm puzzled by this inconsistency since the *Power your Diet* uses USDA as their source, and their amounts of all other vitamins and minerals match USDA's. I looked up all the kinds of grapes listed on the USDA database (besides the canned). For muscadine

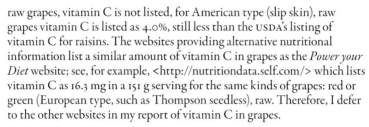

raw grapes, vitamin C is not listed, for American type (slip skin), raw grapes vitamin C is listed as 4.0%, still less than the USDA's listing of vitamin C for raisins. The websites providing alternative nutritional information list a similar amount of vitamin C in grapes as the *Power your Diet* website; see, for example, <http://nutritiondata.self.com/> which lists vitamin C as 16.3 mg in a 151 g serving for the same kinds of grapes: red or green (European type, such as Thompson seedless), raw. Therefore, I defer to the other websites in my report of vitamin C in grapes.

11. Michael Tierra, *Planetary Herbology,* p. 317.

12. Athar M, Back JH, Tang X, Kim KH, Kopelovich L, Bickers DR, Kim AL. *Resveratrol: a Review of Preclinical Studies for Human Cancer Prevention.* Toxicol Appl Pharmacol. 2007;224:274–283.

13. Waffo-Teguo P, Hawthorne ME, Cuendet M, Mérillon JM, Kinghorn AD, Pezzuto JM, Mehta RG. *Potential Cancer-Chemopreventive Activities of Wine Stilbenoids and Flavans Extracted from Grape* (Vitis Vinifera) *Cell Cultures.* Nutr Cancer. 2001;40(2):173–179.

14. Michael Tierra, *Planetary Herbology,* p. 317.

15. Rabbi Binyamin Moshe Kohn Shauli, *Nature's Wealth*, p. 101.

16. Michael Tierra, *Planetary Herbology,* p. 317.

17. Bagchi D, Bagchi M, Stohs SJ, Das DK, Ray SD, Kuszynski CA, Joshi SS, Pruess HG *Free Radicals and Grape Seed Proanthocyanidin Extract: Importance in Human Health and Disease Prevention.* Toxicology. 2000 Aug 7;148(2–3):187–97.

18. Martini S, D'Addario C, Braconi D, Bernardini G, Salvini L, Bonechi C, Figura N, Santucci A, Rossi C. *Antibacterial Activity of Grape Extracts on CagA-Positive and -Negative Helicobacter Pylori Clinical Isolates.* J Chemother. 2009 Nov; 21(5):507–13.

19. Rowe CA, Nantz MP, Nieves C Jr, West RL, Percival SS. *Regular Consumption of Concord Grape Juice Benefits Human Immunity.* J Med Food. 2011 Jan–Feb;14(1–2):69–78.

20. Each of the Ten Sefirot corresponds to a different body part. See for example Ra'avad on *Sefer Yetzirah* 1:3.

21. ‫...וְיַיִן יְשַׂמַּח לְבַב אֱנוֹשׁ‬ (Psalms 104:15).

22. Rabbi Binyamin Moshe Kohn Shauli, *Nature's Wealth*, p. 100.

23. Michael Tierra, *Planetary Herbology,* p. 317.

24. Rabbi Binyamin Moshe Kohn Shauli, *Nature's Wealth*, p. 100. The high content of Vitamin C and bioflavonoids in grapes can help prevent nosebleeds by strengthening the blood vessel walls. Shi J, Yu J, Pohorly JE, Kakuda Y *Polyphenolics in Grape Seeds-Biochemistry*

and Functionality. J Med Food. 2003 Winter;6(4):291–9. Grape seed extract has extensive benefits by improving blood circulation through the strengthening of blood vessels.

25. Zern TL, Wood RJ, Greene C, West KL, Liu Y, Aggarwal D, Shachter NS, Fernandez ML. *Grape Polyphenols Exert a Cardioprotective Effect in Pre- and Postmenopausal Women by Lowering Plasma Lipids and Reducing Oxidative Stress.* J Nutr. 2005 Aug;135(8):1911–7. This study showed that polyphenols found in grapes beneficially affect key risk factors for coronary heart disease in women.

26. Stein JH, Keevil JG, Wiebe DA, Aeschlimann S, Folts JD. *Purple Grape Juice Improves Endothelial Function and Reduces the Susceptibility of LDL Cholesterol to Oxidation in Patients with Coronary Artery Disease.* Circulation. 1999 Sep 7;100(10):1050–5.
Lipid Research Laboratory headed by Dr. Michael Aviram at the Rambam Medical Center in Israel found that grapes contain an abundance of powerful antioxidants counteracting atherosclerosis.

27. Rodrigo R, Gil D, Miranda-Merchak A, Kalantzidis G. *Antihypertensive role of polyphenols.* Adv Clin Chem. 2012;58:225–54.

28. Rabbi Binyamin Moshe Kohn Shauli, *Nature's Wealth*, p. 101.

29. Wang YJ, Thomas P, Zhong JH, Bi FF, Kosaraju S, Pollard A, Fenech M, Zhou XF. *Consumption of Grape Seed Extract Prevents Amyloid-Beta Deposition and Attenuates Inflammation in the Brain of an Alzheimer's Disease Mouse.* Neurotox Res. 2009;15(1):3–14.
Ho L, Yemul S, Wang J, et al. *Grape Seed Polyphenolic Extract as a Potential Novel Therapeutic Agent in Tauopathies. Journal of Alzheimer's Disease.* 2009; 16(2):433–439.
Ono K, Condron MM, Ho L, et al. *Effects of Grape Seed-Derived Polyphenols on Amyloid ß-Protein Self-Assembly and Cytotoxicity. Journal of Biological Chemistry.* 2008; 238(47): 32176–32187.
Wang J, Ho L, Zhao W, et al.. *Grape-Derived Polyphenolics Prevent Aß Oligomerization and Attenuate Cognitive Deterioration in a Mouse Model of Alzheimer's Disease. Journal of Neuroscience.* 2008; 28(25);6388–6392.

30. Rabbi Binyamin Moshe Kohn Shauli, *Nature's Wealth*, p.100.

31. Rambam, *Mishneh Torah, Hilchot Deot* 4:11.

32. Rambam, *Regiment of Health* 1:10.

33. *Babylonian Talmud, Nedarim* 66a.

34. *Midrash Tanchuma, Parashat Shemini,* 5, quoted by Rambam, *Regiment of Health* 1:10.

35. Rabbi Binyamin Moshe Kohn Shauli, *Nature's Wealth*, p. 101.

36. Rambam, *Mishneh Torah, Hilchot Deot* 4:2.

37. Nisim Krispil, *Medicinal Herbs of the Rambam,* p. 95.

38. Based on Rashi's commentary on Deuteronomy 23:25.

39. According to the 2002 report of the Food and Agriculture Organization, 75,866 square kilometers (29,291 square miles) of the world is dedicated to grapes <https://www.newworldencyclopedia.org; http://faostat.fao.org/site/339/default.aspx>retrieved November 21, 2013.

40. Rashi, Numbers 13:23.

41. Rashi, Genesis 49:11.

42. Rabbi Binyamin Moshe Kohn Shauli, *Nature's Wealth,* p. 99.

43. See for example Isaiah 5; Ezekiel 17:1–10; Jeremiah 2:21.

44. Jeff Cox. *Vines to Wines: The Complete Guide to Growing Grapes and Making Your Own Wine.* (Storey Publishing; 3ʳᵈ ed., 1999).

45. Malbim, Hosea 9:10.

46. *Babylonian Talmud, Chulin* 92a.

47. *Midrash Leviticus Rabbah* 36: 2. See this Midrash for a wealth of additional grapevine metaphors.

48. Based on *Yalkut Shimoni Genesis* 39:146, *Midrash Leviticus Rabbah* 36:2.

49. *Babylonian Talmud, Iruvin* 65a.

50. Rashi, *ad. loc.*

51. *Ethics of our Fathers* 4:20.

52. Ezekiel 15:3.

53. Rabbi Samson Raphael Hirsch, Germany (1808–1888), Psalms 80:9–12.

54. I Kings 5:5; see also Micah 4:4 quoted in the beginning of the *Grape* section, p. 147.

55. The Radak, Rabbi David Kimchi, Narbonne France (1160–1235), Micah 4:4.

56. בָּרוּךְ אַתָּה הַשֵׁם אֱלֹקֵינוּ מֶלֶךְ הָעוֹלָם הַטוֹב וְהַמֵּטִיב./*baruch...hatov v'hametiv.* (*Shulchan Aruch, Orach Chaim* 122:1).

57. בָּרוּךְ אַתָּה הַשֵׁם אֱלֹקֵינוּ מֶלֶךְ הָעוֹלָם, דַּיַן הָאֱמֶת./*baruch... dayan emet* (*Midrash Leviticus Rabbah* 36:2); (*Shulchan Aruch, Orach Chaim* 122:2).

58. *Babylonian Talmud, Berachot* 40a. See full quote in the *Fig* section, p. 201

59. Genesis 9:20.

60. Rashi, *ad. loc.* based on the word וַיָּחֶל/*Vayachel* used in the Torah verse, which can mean both 'began' and 'profaned.'

61. Genesis 14:18–19.

62. For example in Genesis 14:18.

63. Rabbi Binyamin Moshe Kohn Shauli, *Nature's Wealth*, p. 97.

64. Wine is often offered with the animal sacrifice; examples of which can be found in Numbers 15:5 and 15:10.

65. Genesis 2:3.

66. Exodus 19:6.

67. Taught by my neighbor, Daniel Winston.

68. Genesis 2:24.

69. Charlie Harary, *Jewish Weddings and Wine*:
The Secret to a Jewish Marriage is Hidden in the Wine
<http://www.aish.com/f/m/Jewish_Weddings_and_Wine.html>
retrieved July 25, 2013.

70. Rabbeinu Bachaya, Bachaya ben Asher ibn Halawa, Spain (1263–1340), Genesis 34:1.

71. Malbim, Psalms 128:3.

72. I have adapted the Hebrew writing of Rav Yitzckak Isaac Chaver slightly. For the sake of clarity I have enumerated the four things the grapevine is compared to. Based on careful reading, and comparing the text with the Talmudic passage quoted by Rav Yitzchak, as well as his writing at the end of p. 136, I believe there is a printing error in his book. The original reading of the part I have changed reads as follows: שהעולם נדמה לגפן, כמ"ש גפן זו תורה וכו'
I have changed this to: ב. העולם נדמה לגפן, ג. גפן זו תורה

73. Genesis 40:10.

74. *Babylonian Talmud, Chulin* 92a.

75. Exodus 6:6–7.

76. Exodus 3:12.

77. The Hallel prayer consisting of selected Psalms concludes the Pesach Seder. Hallel is also recited on festivals and *Rosh Chodesh* (New Moon).

78. The Jewish Supreme Court.

79. *Babylonian Talmud, Chulin* 92a.

80. Rashi, Genesis 1:1.

81. Rabbi Yosef Gikatilla, 13th century Spanish kabbalist, student of Rabbi Avraham Abulafia.

82. Psalms 128:3.

83. Genesis 49:11.

84. גֶּפֶן/*gefen* – the grapevine symbolizes the people of Israel. עִירֹה/*iro* – translated as "donkey" can also mean His city; i.e., Jerusalem. שׂרֵקָה/

soreka – translated as "branch of a grapevine" refers to Israel, בְּנֵי אֲתֹנוֹ/*benei atono* – translated as "his donkey's foal" can also mean they shall build His Temple (Rashi, Genesis 49:11).

85. *Self-Nutrition Data, Know What You Eat*
    <http://nutritiondata.self.com/facts/vegetables-and-vegetable-products/3038/2> retrieved July 25, 2013.

86. 'Creator of the fruit of the vine,' recited before drinking wine and grape juice.

87. *Shulchan Aruch, Orach Chaim* 202:1.

88. The *Rama*, Rabbi Moshe Isserles, Kraków, Poland (1520–1572),
    Shulchan Aruch, Orach Chaim, 202:1.
    Regarding a mixture of wine with water, the wine retains its '*borei p'ri hagafen*' even if the wine is less than half of the mixture (See the *Rama, Shulchan Aruch, Orach Chaim* 204:5).

89. *Shulchan Aruch, Orach Chaim* 211:1.

90. "...A land of wheat, and barley, and vines, and fig trees, and pomegranates; a land of olive oil and honey" (Deuteronomy 8:8).

91. "A **land** of wheat, and barley...a **land** of olive oil and honey."

92. *Shulchan Aruch, Orach Chaim* 211:4.

93. The *Rama, Shulchan Aruch, Orach Chaim* 211:4.

94. Proverbs 16:31.

95. Proverbs 15:4.

Ficus Carica ~ תְּאֵנִים

Figs

נֶצַח ~ Netzach –
Victory / Endurance / Tenacity

Figs ~ תְּאֵנָה *Ficus Carica*
Netzach ~ נֵצַח (Victory / Endurance)

הַתְּאֵנָה חָנְטָה פַגֶּיהָ וְהַגְּפָנִים סְמָדַר נָתְנוּ רֵיחַ קוּמִי לָךְ רַעְיָתִי יָפָתִי
וּלְכִי לָךְ: (שיר השירים ב, יג)

"The fig tree has put forth her green figs, and the vines in blossom gave their scent. Arise, go, my beloved, my beauty, go for yourself" (*Song of Songs* 2:13).

תאנה לוקחת מנצח... (אריז"ל, ספר הליקוטים - פרשת עקב - פרק ח)

The fig takes [its consciousness] from Netzach (Arizal, Sefer HaLikutim, Parashat Ekev, chapter 8).

Attribute: *Netzach* – Victory/Endurance

Character trait: The ability to go against obstacles (Tenacity)

Holiday: Tu b'Shevat, when we eat dried figs from Israel

Weekday: יוֹם רְבִיעִי/*Yom Revi'i* – Fourth day of the week (Wednesday)

World: בְּרִיאָה/*Beriyah* – Creation (completely edible)

Body parts: The right hip, and leg

Shepherd: מֹשֶׁה/Moshe

Prophetess: חַנָּה/Chana

Numerical value: 456, equivalent to the word מֵאֲחֻזַּת/*ma'achuzat* – 'of the possession'[1]

Mentioned in the Bible 44 times[2]

Meaning of Latin Name: Ficus derives from the Hebrew word פַּג/*pag* meaning 'unripe fig.'[3] *Carica* refers to a Roman province in southwest modern-day Turkey near the Dalaman River, known for its cultivation of figs.

פֶּרֶק שִׁירָה

Perek Shirah

The Song of the Universe

נֹצֵר תְּאֵנָה יֹאכַל פִּרְיָהּ...
(משלי כז, יח)

The Song of Figs: "He who guards the fig
tree shall eat its fruit..." (Proverbs 27:18).

As soon as each fig ripens, we must pick it to prevent it from becoming buggy. Therefore, we must guard the fig tree daily to see if any new fig has ripened, and pick it right away. Similarly, in our relationship with Torah, he who guards the Torah constantly will merit "to eat its fruit" – enjoy its spiritual reward.[4]

Nutrition Facts and Information about Figs

Mineral Content of Figs[5]

Dried figs are rich in essential minerals. They are an excellent source of iron, copper and manganese, and a great source of calcium, magnesium and potassium. Dried figs are also a good source of phosphorous. Fresh figs contain iron, potassium, magnesium, manganese, copper and small amounts of calcium, phosphorous and traces of zinc and selenium.

Vitamin Content of Figs

Dried figs are a good source of vitamin K. All figs contain thiamin, riboflavin, vitamins A, B6 and K. Vitamin C, niacin, folate and vitamin E are present in small amounts.

Oriental Medicine

In Ayurvedic medicine the fig is used as a blood tonic and mild laxative.[6] Figs promote health, vitality, strength and tranquility nourishing the mind and body.[7] In Chinese medicine, figs are either neutral or yang, depending upon usage. They are known to alleviate hormonal imbalances, moisten lungs, lubricate the colon, and be valuable for pain in the joints.[8]

Figs Nutritional Facts/100 g

Minerals	Dried Figs	Fresh Figs	RDA	
Calcium	162 mg	35 mg	16%	3.5%
Iron	2.03 mg	0.37 mg	28%	5%
Magnesium	68 mg	17 mg	16%	4%
Phosphorus	67 mg	14 mg	10%	2%
Potassium	680 mg	232 mg	15%	5%
Sodium	10 mg	1 mg	0.6%	0%
Zinc	0.55 mg	0.15 mg	3.5%	1%
Copper	0.287 mg	0.070 mg	33%	8%
Manganese	0.510 mg	0.128 mg	>100%	5.5%
Selenium	0.6 µg	0.2 µg	3%	<1%
Vitamins	**Dried Figs**	**Fresh Figs**	**RDA**	
C	1.2 mg	2 mg	2%	3%
B1 (Thiamin)	0.085 mg	0.060 mg	7%	5%
B2 (Riboflavin)	0.082 mg	0.050 mg	6.5%	4%
B3 (Niacin)	0.619 mg	0.400 mg	4%	2.5%
B6	0.106 mg	0.113 mg	5%	5.5%
B9 (Folate)	9 µg	6 µg	2.5%	1.5%
A	10 IU	142 IU	<1%	5%
E	0.35 mg	0.11 mg	3%	1%
K	15.6 µg	4.7 µg	13.5%	4%

Figs correspond to Netzach. The attribute of *Netzach* is endurance, longevity and conquest. Actually the word *Netzach* means victory. Pliny the Elder noted that ancient sports warriors, called gladiators, were fed a diet of figs to bring out their strength and stamina.[9] Fresh or dried, figs are wonderful remedies for physical debility, exhaustion and anemia. The fig tree reflects everlasting fruitfulness, since it has one of the longest ripening periods, spanning more than three months from midsummer to fall.

Netzach and the Endocrine System

Netzach corresponds to the endocrine system, which generates new cells and structures within the body, perpetuates vitality, and aids the body to overcome the obstacles that stand in the way of its growth and development.[10]

Promote Longevity

Fig trees, which originated in the Mediterranean region, can be a hundred years old and a hundred feet tall (about thirty meter). When King Chezkiyahu was mortally ill, he repented and was granted an additional fifteen years to live. Isaiah told him, "'Take a cake of figs.' They took and laid it on the boil, and he recovered."[11] Most commentaries explain that Chezkiyahu's recovery was an incredible miracle, since placing figs on a boil would naturally cause it to worsen and putrefy.[12] Perhaps the fig was chosen to restore the life of the king, not as a physical remedy but rather as a spiritual sign, because of its quality of *Netzach* and longevity.

Preserve Life, Reproduction and Vitality

Figs are highly alkaline. Therefore, they regulate the pH of the body, which is vital for self-preservation.[13] Figs are full of seeds and grow in pairs. Hashem in His great wisdom created figs to resemble the male reproductive organs. They increase the mobility and quantity of male sperm to overcome male sterility and impotence.[14] For women too, figs are beneficial. Among the fruits richest in fiber, they protect against post-menopausal breast cancer.[15] Moreover, ground fig leaves mixed with wine are helpful for women in difficult labor.[16]

Stimulate Blood Circulation

Figs are naturally restorative since they increase the blood flow and rejuvenate. Rabbi Avraham Ibn Ezra writes that "fresh or dried figs stimulate blood circulation and thus preserve life."[17] For this reason figs are excellent for heart patients and for the elderly. They stimulate and refresh the body, cleanse the blood, improve circulation, add color to the skin, and stimulate the appetite.[18]

Highly Restorative

Figs are highly nutritive due to their high glucose content, the most assimilative of all sugars. It is told that Rabbi Yochanan was once gripped with a powerful hunger. He sat at the east of a fig tree and was healed.[19] He learned about the revitalizing power of the fig from King David, who revived a person who hadn't eaten for three days by feeding him a cake of figs.[20]

Strengthen the Bones

The high calcium content of figs strengthens the bones, the most enduring part of the human body. Additionally, the potassium in figs may also counteract the increased urinary calcium loss caused by the high-salt Western diet.

Rambam teaches that figs, grapes and almonds are always the healthiest fruits whether fresh or dried.[21] He recommends ripe fresh figs for old people in the summer, and dry figs in the fall, while cautioning about other fruits. Figs are excellent for the liver and soften it. The healing properties of figs cannot be underestimated since they help alleviate constipation and keep the bowels moving,[22] which is one of the main tenets of longevity and health.[23] Whoever suffers from constipation will benefit from eating figs and drinking water in which figs have been soaked.[24] Culpepper recommends figs as a soothing nutritious mild laxative that can be given to children.[25] Five grams of fiber contained in three figs aids healthy bowel function and prevents constipation. Figs and other laxative foods, such as grapes, berries, pears, melons, squashes, and cucumbers should be eaten before all food and not together with the main part of the meal.[26] Figs are also helpful for other digestive problems. They are used to treat infections of the stomach, intestines and urinary tract.[27] Figs have high vitamin B content and other elements essential for intestinal function and regulation.[28] According to Rambam, a mixture of dried figs, walnuts and rue is a powerful antidote for poisons.[29]

Remove Warts

The milky juice of unripe figs is a known remedy for removing warts.[30] It also treats sores and softens both calluses and warts.[31]

Alleviate Coughs

Figs are accepted in Mediterranean folk medicine as a remedy for various respiratory disorders including colds and coughs.[32] Drinking tea made from water in which figs have been boiled alleviates a dry cough.[33]

The Eternity of the Torah Compared to Figs

נֹצֵר תְּאֵנָה יֹאכַל פִּרְיָהּ וְשֹׁמֵר אֲדֹנָיו יְכֻבָּד: (משלי כז, יח)

"He who guards the fig tree shall eat its fruit and he who watches his master will be honored" (*Proverbs* 27:18).

The Torah is compared to figs, because unlike most fruits, such as the olives, grapes and dates, which are picked at one time, the figs are picked gradually. This is the way of the Torah: Learn a little today, but tomorrow a lot, since the Torah cannot be learned in one year or two. About this it states, "He who guards the fig tree shall eat its fruit" – the fruit of Torah.[34]

Malbim explains that we need to watch the fig tree very carefully by picking its fruits daily, since the figs ripen one by one. Likewise, we need to heed our teachers daily in order to glean the fruits of their wisdom.[35] An example of this is Yehoshua – Moshe's disciple, "who did not depart out of his master's tent" of Torah.[36] By means of this, he became honored with divine prophecy.[37]

Scripture likens the Torah to a fig tree whose fruits are not finished at one time. Likewise, the root of the eternal Torah itself is in the upper realm, beyond any boundary and measure. Only when it comes into this physical world does it receive a boundary. As it states, "Longer than the earth is its measure..."[38] Therefore, whenever a person delves deeply into Torah, he will find new matters that he didn't grasp beforehand, even if he had learned and repeated it often. No matter how fluent he is in the words of Torah, he benefits from reviewing them constantly. Every moment he discovers new concepts, according to the root of his *neshamah* (higher soul). Since each person's soul is constantly renewed, everyone who puts effort into his Torah learning will continually discover new and deeper meanings.[39]

למה נמשלו דברי תורה כתאנה מה תאנה זו כל זמן שאדם ממשמש בה
מוצא בה תאנים אף דברי תורה כל זמן שאדם הוגה בהן מוצא בהן טעם:
(תלמוד מסכת עירובין נד, ע"א-ב)

*Why are the words of the Torah compared to a fig tree? Just as
a fig tree whenever a person shakes it, he will find figs, so does
the Torah always yield new teachings, whenever a person studies
them (Babylonian Talmud, Iruvin 54a).*

Figs – The Cause of Downfall and Rectification

...כְּבִכּוּרָהּ בְּטֶרֶם קַיִץ אֲשֶׁר יִרְאֶה הָרֹאֶה אוֹתָהּ בְּעוֹדָהּ בְּכַפּוֹ יִבְלָעֶנָּה:
(ישעיה כח, ד)

*"As the first-ripe fig before the summer, which when one looks
upon it, while it is still in his hand, he eats it up" (Isaiah 28:4).*

In the words of the
Prophets the fig is
a symbol of peace
and prosperity.[40]
The fig tree whose
leaves provided the
clothing for Adam
and Eve, is the first
fruit tree described
in the Torah, as it states, "Both of their eyes were opened, and they
knew that they were naked; and they sewed fig leaves together, and
made themselves loincloths."[41] For this reason Rabbi Nechemiah
holds that the Tree of Knowledge was a fig tree, since the same matter that caused the downfall of humanity was used as rectification.[42]
The first human beings chose to cover themselves explicitly with
fig leaves, because they understood the principle that rectification
is engendered through the exact means that caused the original destruction.[43] In addition to serving as clothing – לְבוּשׁ/*levush* to cover

up the embarrassment of Adam and Eve, the fig tree alludes to the rectification of the spiritual garments of the soul: thought, speech and action. You'll never see a flower on a fig tree, because the flower is contained inside the fruit itself. In this way, the fig tree embodies the quality of *tzniut* (modesty), by covering its own beauty and keeping its light within.

דתניא אילן שאכל ממנו אדם הראשון רבי מאיר אומר גפן היה שאין לך דבר שמביא יללה על האדם אלא יין שנאמר וישת מן היין וישכר רבי נחמיה אומר תאנה היתה שבדבר שנתקלקלו בו נתקנו שנאמר ויתפרו עלה תאנה רבי יהודה אומר חטה היתה שאין התינוק יודע לקרות אבא ואמא עד שיטעום טעם דגן: (תלמוד בבלי מסכת ברכות מ, ע"א)

It is taught in the Mishnah, about the Tree that the first man ate from, Rabbi Meir says it was a grapevine, as there is nothing which brings wailing upon a person as much as wine, as it states: "He drank from the wine and he became drunk."[44] *Rabbi Nechemiah says it was a fig tree, for through the thing that caused the destruction, they became rectified, as it states*: "They sewed fig leaves together."[45] *Rabbi Yehuda says it was wheat, for the baby does not know to call Daddy and Mommy until he has tasted the taste of grain* (Babylonian Talmud, Berachot 40a).

The Maharal explains that the differences of opinion between the Rabbis of the Talmud regarding the identity of the Tree of Knowledge is based on which part of the soul is more susceptible to temptation. When Chava was first tempted to eat from the Tree of Knowledge she "saw that the tree was good for food, and that it was a delight to the eyes, and that the tree was desirable to make one wise."[46] Each of the three ways that the Tree of Knowledge tempted the first woman corresponds to the three aspects of the soul.

The desire for the tree because it is "good for food" corresponds to the lowest part of the soul, the *nefesh* which is connected with eating and physical survival. Figs revive the nefesh and rouse the appetite. They are the kind of fruits that a person just can't stop eating, being both sweet and sticky. The organ connected to the nefesh is the liver. It purifies the food from toxins and aids digestion. Corresponding to the *ruach* (spirit), grapes are "a delight to the eyes." They affect emotions, just as the ruach is the seat of emotions ruled by the heart. The desire "to become wise" emanates from the intellectual soul – the neshamah corresponding to wheat, which affects the brain as Rabbi Yehuda stated.

A person's existence in the world depends on all the three aspects of his soul being in balance, without being drawn excessively after physical, emotional or intellectual gratification. This explains why "jealousy, physical desire, and honor seeking take a person out of this world."[47] Jealousy is when the emotions exceed their boundary. Desire is when a person is drawn excessively after his physicality. Honor seeking is an excessive desire for intellectual gratification.[48]

Table of Correspondence between Fruits, Soul Part and Character

חלקי נפש **Soul part**	מידה **Character**	חלקי פסוק (בראשית ג, ו) **Part of Torah Verse**	עצי פרי **Fruit tree**	רב **Rabbi**
נֶפֶשׁ *Nefesh*	הַתַּאֲוָה Desire	"כִּי טוֹב הָעֵץ לְמַאֲכָל" *"the tree was good for food"*	תְּאֵנָה Fig	נֶחֶמְיָה Nechemiah
רוּחַ *Ruach*	הַקִּנְאָה Jealousy	"וְכִי תַאֲוָה הוּא לָעֵינַיִם" *"it was a delight to the eyes"*	גֶּפֶן Grape	מֵאִיר Meir
נְשָׁמָה *Neshamah*	הַכָּבוֹד Honor-seeking	"וְנֶחְמָד הָעֵץ לְהַשְׂכִּיל" *"the tree was desirable to make one wise"*	חִטָּה Wheat	יְהוּדָה Yehuda

 Health benefits of Fig leaves

Fig leaves have repeatedly been shown to have anti-diabetic properties and may reduce the amount of insulin needed by people suffering from diabetes.[49] Figs, especially black figs, are also rich in potassium which helps to control blood sugar. Fig extract has been scientifically proven to treat diabetes and reduce hyperglycemia.[50] Studies indicate that figs stimulate insulin secretion significantly. Therefore, figs may in the future be developed as an oral anti-diabetic agent.[51]

Purifying from Death

The fig tree is mentioned several times in the Mishnah and Talmud. Specifically fig wood was used in the ritual of burning the Red Heifer, which purifies from the impurity of death, originally caused by eating from the Tree of Knowledge.[52] The fact that fig wood is used in purifying from death reflects its spiritual quality of *Netzach* that is associated with the preservation of life. In addition, fig wood burns beautifully without smoking and it is no wonder it is singled out as the preferred wood for the sacrifices of the Temple.[53]

Figs before Grapes

Grapes and figs are often mentioned together in the Bible.[54] In most of the verses, grapes precede figs.[55] However, when the Jews complained in the wilderness, they mentioned figs before grapes: "Why have you made us come up out of Egypt to bring us to this evil place? It is no place of seed, or of figs, or of vines or of pomegranates, nor is there any water to drink."[56] It is possible that the Jewish people who complained in the wilderness mentioned figs before other fruits, because figs are associated with the lowest part of the soul, connected to cravings for food. Since the Israelites were weary of their spiritual existence in the wilderness where they ate only the spiritual manna, they were brought to the lowest level of physical desire. *Ba'al Haturim* explains that the fig is mentioned first in this verse, because it follows directly after the section about the Red Heifer,[57] where fig wood was used.[58]

The fig is associated with *Netzach*, which also means eternity – the ability to overcome death and mortality. Therefore, it makes sense that fig wood was chosen for the ritual of the Red Heifer, used in Temple times to purify from the impurity of contact with the dead.

The prophet Habakkuk mentions figs before grapes in his prayer, where he places his entire trust in Hashem:

כִּי תְאֵנָה לֹא תִפְרָח, וְאֵין יְבוּל בַּגְּפָנִים, כִּחֵשׁ מַעֲשֵׂה זַיִת...וַאֲנִי בַּהֹשֵׁם אֶעְלוֹזָה
אָגִילָה בֵּאלֹקֵי יִשְׁעִי: (חבקוק ג, יז-יח)

*"For though the fig tree shall not blossom, neither shall fruit be
in the vines: the labor of the olive shall fail... yet I will rejoice in
Hashem... of my salvation" (Habakkuk 3:17–18).*

Metzudat David explains that the fig that did not blossom yet refers to the people of Israel, for they still had not acquired sufficient
strength and courage to face the enemy in war. This fits in with the
essential quality of figs, *Netzach*, which can refer to victory.

רמי בר יחזקאל איקלע לבני ברק חזנהו להנהו עיזי דקאכלן תותי תאיני
וקנטיף דובשא מתאיני וחלבא טייף מנייהו ומיערב בהדי הדדי אמר היינו
זבת חלב ודבש: (תלמוד בבלי מסכת כתובות קיא, ע"ב)

*Rami bar Yechezkel once paid a visit to Bene-Berak where he
saw goats grazing under fig trees while honey was flowing from
the figs, and milk ran from them, and these mingled with each
other. "This is indeed," he remarked, "[a land] flowing with
milk and honey" (Babylonian Talmud, Ketubot 11b).*

🌱A Taste of Kabbalah – Light, Shells, Souls and Fruit

וכן יש בקליפה עצמה, יש בחינה שהיא קליפה מלגאו ומלבר, והיא
אותה הבחינה שכבר נתבררו הניצוצות של הקדושה שהיה בתוכה,
ואותם שכבר נתבררו הם הכל טוב, מוח מלבר ומלגאו. וכנגד שני
בחינות אלו אמר הכתוב (תהלים א, ג) "והיה כעץ שתול על פלגי
מים, אשר פריו יתן בעתו", זו היא הנשמה שבתוכו שהיא פריו ממש,
ועליהו לא יבול, זה הוא כנגד נשמת הצדיק החופפת עליו. וז"ש ועלהו
שהוא מקיף עליו, לא יבול. ועל השנית שהוא הכל רע, אמר לא כן הרשעים
כי אם כמוץ, והמוץ הוא קליפה ואין בו שום מוח:
וכנגד אלו יש באילנות, כי התאנה היא כנגד מה שנתברר שהכל טוב,
ואילני סרק הכל רע, שהכל קליפה. ויש אילנות שהפרי שהוא המוח
הוא מלגאו, והקליפה חופפת עליו מבחוץ, כגון אגוזים ורימונים,
וכנגדם בקליפה, שלקחה ניצוץ הקדושה בתוכה לחיות אליה, והיא
חופפת עליה כקליפה על המוח, וזהו כנגד אותו שנשמתו טהורה
והקליפה חופפת עליו, ולכן יש לו מידות רעות כדאמרן. ויש אילנות
שהמוח מלבר והקליפה שהוא הגרעין מבפנים, כגון זתים ותמרים
וענבים וכיוצא, והוא כנגד זה בקליפה, כשניצוץ הקדושה שנפלה שם
היתה גדולה, ולא יכלה לסבול כל אותו האור בקרבו, ונכנסה הקליפה
בתוך הקדושה, ועושה הקדושה מקיף עליו לבר, והוא כנגד הרשע
שבא עליו נשמת צדיק לתקן אותו:
(ספר הליקוטים - פרשת ויצא - פרק לו)

There are two kinds of kelipah, the kind that is inside of the
fruit (the pit) and that which surrounds it. The kind of person whose holy sparks both inside and surrounding him are
clarified is completely good, inside and out. Corresponding
to these two aspects Scripture states, "and he shall be like a
tree planted by streams of water, that brings forth fruits in its
season."[59] This refers to the neshamah within, which is really
its fruit. "Its leaf also shall not wither,"[60] refers to the soul of
the tzadik which covers him. Therefore, it states: "its leaf,"
which covers it, "shall not wither." About the second kind of
person, who is completely evil, it is said: "not so the wicked, they

are like the chaff"[61] – a shell that has no fruit inside it. There are trees corresponding to each of these kinds of people. The fig tree corresponds to the kind of person who is completely good, whereas the fruitless tree corresponds to the kind of person who is completely evil – completely kelipah. There are trees with fruit covered by a shell on the outside, like nuts and pomegranates. They correspond to a kelipah that took a holy spark inside of it to keep alive through it. The kelipah covers the spark like the shell covers the fruit. This corresponds to the kind of person whose soul is pure but is surrounded by a shell; therefore he has negative character traits. There are also trees whose fruit surrounds the interior kelipah – the pit – like olives, dates and grapes. They correspond to a shell whose holy spark fell there, because it was so great that it was unable to contain all of its light within. Therefore, the kelipah entered inside of the holy, and caused the holiness to surround it from the outside. This corresponds to the wicked, whom the soul of a tzadik came to rectify (Arizal, *Sefer HaLikutim, Parashat Vayetze*, chapter 36).

Explanation: According to Arizal, the main purpose of our lives is to reveal Hashem's light and uncover it from the shells, where it may be trapped, both in the world and within our soul. This work may take several reincarnations. A good person has mastered revealing Hashem's light both within his soul, by means of his inner goodness, and outwardly, by means of good character traits and deeds. This work has two aspects:

1. Removing the interior kelipah and revealing the light within our soul (Inner Light/purity of soul).

2. Removing the exterior shell and revealing the light that surrounds our soul (Surrounding Light/good character traits).

There are various levels of people: Those who have rectified the inner light of their soul, and those who have rectified their sur-

rounding light, those who have rectified none of these aspects, and those who have rectified both. These people respectively correspond to different kinds of trees. Those who have rectified their inner light correspond to fruits with a hard outer shell, such as nuts and pomegranates. Those who have rectified their surrounding light correspond to fruits that have only a kelipah inside of them, in the form of a hard pit, such as olives, dates and grapes. They have such high souls that their lights are too great to be contained within the shell. Those who have rectified both their inner and surrounding lights correspond to the fig, which is wholly edible. It has neither a hard shell nor pit.

Fruitless trees	For example the willow tree	No lights	An evil person inside and out
Fruits with peels	For example nuts and pomegranates	Inner lights	A good and pure person with negative character traits
Fruits with a hard pit	For example olives and dates	Surrounding lights	A wicked person whom a righteous person came to rectify

הרואה תאנה בחלום תורתו משתמרת
בקרבו שנאמר נֹצֵר תְּאֵנָה יֹאכַל פִּרְיָהּ:

*He who sees a fig tree in a dream, his Torah
will be preserved within him, as it says, "He
who guards the fig tree shall eat its fruit…"*[62]
(Babylonian Talmud, Berachot 57a).

Fig Recipes

Enjoying the Goodness of Figs

למה נמשלה תורה לתאנה אלא כל הפירות יש בהם פסולת, תמרים יש
בהם גרעינים, ענבים יש בהם חרצנים, רמונים יש הם קליפין, אבל תאנה
כלה יפה לאכול: (ילקוט שמעוני יהושע - פרק א - רמז ב)

Why is the Torah compared to a fig? The other fruits have inedible parts (the dates and grapes have pits, the pomegranate has a hard peel), but the fig is completely good for eating (Yalkut Shimoni Yehoshua 1:2).

Checking Figs for Bugs

Figs are notorious for bugs and are very hard to check. Cut off the bottom of the fig, as often little white worms attach themselves there. Rub on the outside vigorously, straighten out all folds, and cut open. Cut off the opening and inspect the entire fruit, both inside and on its outside skin. Look for little white worms that look very much like the pistils. If you find any discard the entire fig. Remove any areas that are black or darker than the rest of the fig.

FRESH FIGS
A burst of sweetness melting in your mouth

Figs are cherished for their sweetness and soft texture. They consist of a pliable skin enclosing a sweet, even softer, fleshly interior filled with edible seeds. A fig is a very delicate fruit. It has the shortest life span of any fruit in the market. Therefore, about 90% of the world's fig harvest is dried. Here are some tips for selecting and storing fresh figs:

1. Choose slightly soft, wrinkled fruits that have a plump feel with no signs of mold.

2. When picking figs from the tree, look for ripe fruits with a drop of nectar dripping from them. If the fig doesn't come off easily without breaking its hard point attached to the tree, wait another day to pick it.

3. Arrange the figs in a shallow basket so they are not touching each other. The basket rather than a plastic bag, or a plate helps air circulation and prevents water condensation, which will make the figs rot. Your figs may keep in the fridge up to five days in the basket, so make sure you eat them quickly!

4. You can eat the entire fig, except perhaps for the hard point where it hung from the tree. Just be sure to wash before enjoying!

Once they are harvested, they only last about a week.

FRESH FIG FRUIT SALAD

The smoothness of figs perfectly complemented by crisp apples

½ cup fresh chopped figs
½ cup chopped crunchy apples
½ cup deseeded halved grapes
¼ cup shredded coconut
A few spritzes of lemon juice for garnish

1. Mix all fruits together gently.

2. Add the coconut

3. Squeeze the lemon juice on top of the fruits.

You can play with the amounts and varieties of fruits according to what you have available. The contrast between the soft figs and the crunchy apples balance each other nicely.

SUN-DRIED FIGS

A perfect energizing treat for an exhausted Mom

Figs will dry well outside on hot, sunny days. They should dry in about three to five days if whole, and in about half the time when cut open. They will also dry well in a car parked in the sun.

1. Wash the ripe figs, leaving stems on.
2. Cut the figs completely in half until the stem and turn the cut side upwards on the drying rack.
3. Cover the figs with a piece of cheesecloth or nylon net to keep insects away.
4. Put the drying rack on a table, or a car or a roof in full sun.

   (In moist climates, it is recommended to bring the figs inside every day at sundown, to avoid mold).
5. Dry the figs until the outside is leathery, but pliable. The inside should be soft, with no sign of juice.

For longest storage life: Place the dried figs in the refrigerator or freezer in moisture-proof bags or containers. Figs can be stored at room temperature if they are completely dried. To store for extended periods (more than six months) first reheat the figs at 70–80°C (160–180° F) for 10–15 minutes, then place them in moisture proof containers.

Dried figs are rich in fibre, potassium, calcium, magnesium and iron, and are useful in baking as a nourishing alternative for sugar.

FIG & ALMOND NOSH

A healthy nosh that will satisfy your hunger and sugar cravings at any time

15 almonds
5 sun dried figs

1. Open up the figs and check carefully for little white worms or other bugs.
2. Cut each fig into three to four bite size pieces.
3. Mix in the almonds and place in a bowl or bag to go.

If you don't have time to eat breakfast before leaving your home, the fig & almond nosh will provide energy, protein, vitamins and minerals on your way.

RAW FIG BARS
A nutritious mineral packed dessert and snack

Crust
1 ½ cups mixed nuts and seeds (sunflower and almonds)
4 small apples
4 dates
3 tablespoons techina
1 teaspoon vanilla extract
1 cup shredded coconut

Filling
1 cup roughly chopped dried figs
1 tablespoon honey
Water to cover

1. Process the nuts in the food processor with the S-blade.

2. Core and cut apples into coarse wedges and add to the food processor.

3. Add the remaining crust ingredients and process until smooth.

4. Press half of the nut dough into a 20 x 16 cm (8 x 6 inch) baking pan.

5. Place the figs in a small bowl, cover with hot water, and soak for 10 minutes.

6. Check carefully both the figs and the soaking water for bugs.

7. Remove the figs from the water and place in the food processor.

8. Add the honey and 1 tablespoon of the soaking liquid, purée until smooth and spreadable.

9. Spread the fig mixture on the nut dough and cover with the remaining nut dough.

10. Cover the baking pan with saran wrap, and place in the freezer for one hour.

11. Remove the baking pan from the freezer and cut into bar sized pieces.

12. Store your fig bars in the freezer, and remove them about 15 minutes before serving.

FRUITY FIG & RAISIN BALLS
A warming nutrition-packed irresistible dessert or snack

1 cup ground almonds
5 dried figs
½ cup pitted dates
¼ cup raisins
1 teaspoon pure vanilla extract
½ teaspoon cinnamon
¼ teaspoon ground cloves
Grated peel of half an orange
A pinch of nutmeg
A pinch of sea salt

1. Place all the ingredients (except the raisins) in a food processor, and process with the S-blade until well combined.

2. Add the raisins by hand.

3. Form into balls, refrigerate or freeze.

RAMBAM'S CHAROSET RECIPE
An authentic recipe by the Rambam[63]

Charoset is a mixture that resembles straw.[64] This is to commemorate the mortar of the bricks that the Israelite slaves had to produce in Egypt. Here is a simple way to make charoset:

1. Soak figs or dates.

2. Cook or mash them until they are moist.

3. Knead everything in vinegar.

4. Add whole *shibolet nerd* (spikenard) or *eizov* (hyssop) and the like.

FABULOUS FRESH FIG SPREAD
A great way to get the most out of soft and mushy figs

2 cups fresh picked figs
2 tablespoons lemon juice
1 tablespoon honey

1. Simmer figs with the lemon and honey for about 20 minutes.

2. Mash them as they cook.

3. Purée the fig mixture in a food processor or blender.

The purée freezes well and makes an excellent cookie filling, sauce for ice cream or poached pears, or a spread for sandwich or toast.

Laws of Blessings ~ הִלְכוֹת בְּרָכוֹת

We bless *'shehakol'* on water in which raisins or figs were soaked or have been cooked. However, there is an uncertainty regarding the after-blessing as whether to bless *'borei nefashot'* or *'M'ein Shalosh.'*[65] Therefore, a G*d-fearing person will only drink this water as part of a meal with bread. Alternatively, he may drink this water together with one of the Seven Species, in order to be required to recite both *'M'ein Shalosh'* [for the Seven Species] and *'borei nefashot'* [for the water].[66]

I'm Victor Frank and I am a survivor. My secret is: Never give up! "Nothing can stand in the way of one's will." I have been through a lot, but I hang in there. I have suffered many hardships but I keep moving forward in life no matter what. I have been around for a very long time. I have planted seeds and seen them flourish. I survived colon cancer and a massive heart attack. I went through a near death experience but came back, because of my super strong will to live! I have a purpose and a mission to teach the world how to overcome obstacles and live fulfilled lives. When I was young I couldn't get a job, it was disempowering when the rejections piled up and every door seemed to close. Yet, I kept trying, taking new courses and adding new skills. In the end I opened up my own company and became self-employed. For years we were in deficit. Everyone told me to close down the business, but I kept it going. After ten years of hard work from dawn to sundown, the company finally began to flourish. Still, I will not become complacent. "A wise man is strong; and a man of knowledge increases strength."[67]

Endnotes

1.   Numbers 35:8.

2.   Fig – תְּאֵנָה/te'ena, figs – תְּאֵנִים/te'enim, fig-cake – דְּבֵלָה/develah and fig-cakes – דְּבֵלִים/develim are mentioned 44 times in the Bible.
      Fig – תְּאֵנָה/te'ena is mentioned in the Bible in the singular form 22 times, 3 times in the Pentateuch and 19 times in the rest of the Bible: Genesis 3:7; Numbers 20:5; Deuteronomy 8:8; Judges 9:10, 9:11; I Kings 5:5; II Kings 18:31; Isaiah 34:4, 36:16; Jeremiah 5:17, 8:13; Hosea 2:14, 9:10; Joel 1:7, 1:12, 2:22; Michah 4:4; Habakkuk 3:17; Haggai 2:19; Zachariah 3:10; Proverbs 27:18; Song of Songs 2:1.
      Figs – תְּאֵנִים/te'enim is mentioned in the Bible in the plural form 17 times, once in the Pentateuch and 16 times in the rest of the Bible: Numbers 13:23; II Kings 20:7; Isaiah 38:21, 36,16; Jeremiah 8:13, 24:1, 24:2 (three times), 24:3 (twice), 24:5, 24:8, 29:17; Ezekiel 24:12; Amos 4:9; Nachum 3:12; Nehemiah 13:15.
      Fig-cake – דְּבֵלָה/develah is mentioned in the Bible in the singular form three times: I Samuel 30:12; II Kings 2:20; Isaiah 38:21.
      Fig-cakes – דְּבֵלִים/develim are mentioned in the Bible in the plural form twice: I Samuel 25:18, I Chronicles 12:41.

3.   Song of Songs 2:13.

4.   Rav Mordechai Weinberg, Album *Perek Shirah,* quoting Rabbi Chaim Kanievsky, *Perek b'Shir.*

5.   The vitamin and mineral content of figs is based on USDA, *Basic Report:* 09094 *Figs, dried, uncooked* and *Basic report*: 09089, *Figs, raw.* The percentage of Recommended Daily Dietary Allowance is based on *Fig fruit* <http://www.nutrition-and-you.com/fig-fruit.html> retrieved June 30, 2013.

6.   Candis Cantin Kiriajes, AHG, *Tonic Herb Theory for the Western Herbalist* <http://www.planetherbs.com/case-studies/tonic-herb-theory-for-the-western-herbalist.html> retrieved August 21, 2013.

7.   Christine Schrum, *Sweet & Sattvic: Tone Your Body & Mind with Figs* <http://www.experienceayurveda.com/2012/05/sweet-sattvic-tone-your-body-mind-with-figs/> retrieved August 21, 2013.

8.   Jacqueline M. Newman, *Food as Herbs, Health, and Medicine, Fruits as Food and Medicine*: part 1, *Summer Volume*: 2000 Issue: p. 19.

9.   Gaius Plinius Secundus, Roman author, naturalist, and philosopher (23–79 CE), p. 258.

10.   Rav Yitzchak Ginsburgh, *Body, Mind, and, Soul*, p. 86.

11.   II Kings 20:7.

12.   See Rashi and Radak, *ad. loc.*

13.   Robert O. Young, *The pH Miracle*, Warner books, May 1, 2003. Will Johnson, *Top 5 Alkaline Fruits & Their Benefits*, Feb 16, 2007.

14.   Rabbi Binyamin Moshe Kohn Shauli, *Nature's Wealth*, p. 258. Figs also strengthen male sexual performance and increase sexual desire.

15.   Suzuki R, Rylander-Rudqvist T, Ye W, Saji S, Adlercreutz H, Wolk A. *Dietary Fiber Intake and Risk of Postmenopausal Breast Cancer Defined by Estrogen and Progesterone Receptor Status – a Prospective Cohort Study among Swedish Women*. Int J Cancer. 2008 Jan 15;122(2):403–12. Study involving 51,823 postmenopausal women for an average of 8.3 years showed a 34% reduction in breast cancer risk for those consuming the most fruit fiber compared to those consuming the least.

16.   Rabbi Binyamin Moshe Kohn Shauli, *Nature's Wealth*, p. 258.

17.   Ibn Ezra, Habakkuk 3:17.

18.   Rabbi Binyamin Moshe Kohn Shauli, *Nature's Wealth*, p. 258.

19.   *Babylonian Talmud, Yoma* 83b, *Midrash Ecclesiastes Rabbah* 7:18.

20.   I Samuel 30:12.

21.   Rambam, *Mishneh Torah, Hilchot Deot* 4:11.

22.   Nisim Krispil, *Medicinal Herbs of the Rambam*, p. 211.

23.   Rambam, *Mishneh Torah, Hilchot Deot* 4:13.

24.   Rabbi Binyamin Moshe Kohn Shauli, *Nature's Wealth*, p. 258.

25.   *Culpepper's Color Herbal*, David Potterton (Sterling Publishing Co., Inc. New York, 1992), p. 75.

26.   Rambam, *Mishneh Torah, Hilchot Deot* 4:6.

27.   Rabbi Binyamin Moshe Kohn Shauli, *Nature's Wealth*, p. 258.

28.   Gilani AH, Mehmood MH, Janbaz KH, Khan AU, Saeed SA.J *Ethnopharmacological Studies on Antispasmodic and Antiplatelet Activities of Ficus Carica*. Ethnopharmacol. 2008 Sep 2;119(1):1–5.

29.   Nisim Krispil, *Medicinal Herbs of the Rambam*, p. 211.

30.   *Culpepper's Color Herbal*, p. 75.

31.   Rabbi Binyamin Moshe Kohn Shauli, *Nature's Wealth*, p. 258.

32.   Nisim Krispil, *Medicinal Herbs of the Rambam*, p. 211.

33. Rabbi Binyamin Moshe Kohn Shauli, *Nature's Wealth,* p. 258.

34. *Midrash Numbers Rabbah* 12:9.

35. Malbim, Proverbs 27:18.

36. Exodus 33:11.

37. *Midrash Numbers Rabbah* 12:9.

38. Job 11:9.

39. Rav Yitzchak Isaac Chaver, ספר אור תורה, ליקוטים/*Sefer Ohr Torah, Likutim.*

40. For example, in Micah 4:4; Joel 2:24; Zechariah 3:10.

41. Genesis 3:7.

42. *Babylonian Talmud, Berachot* 40a.

43. The Maharal, *Gur Aryeh,* Genesis 3:7.

44. Genesis 9:21.

45. Genesis 3:7.

46. Genesis 3:6.

47. *Ethics of our Fathers* 4:22.

48. The Maharal, *Derech HaChaim*, Commentary on *Ethics of our Fathers* 4:22.

49. Serraclara A, Hawkins F, Pérez C, Domínguez E, Campillo JE, Torres MD. *Hypoglycemic Action of an Oral Fig-Leaf Decoction in Type-I Diabetic Patients.* Diabetes Res Clin Pract. 1998 Jan; 39(1):19–22.

50. Pèrez C, Canal JR, Torres MD. *Experimental Diabetes Treated with Ficus Carica Extract: Effect on Oxidative Stress Parameters.* Acta Diabetol. 2003 Mar;40(1):3–8.

51. Adam Z, Khamis S, Ismail A, Hamid M. *Ficus deltoidea: A Potential Alternative Medicine for Diabetes Mellitus.* Evid Based Complement Alternat Med. 2012;2012:632763.

52. *Mishnah, Tractate Parah* 3:8.

53. *Mishnah, Tractate Tamid* 2:2.

54. 19 times altogether.

55. Figs only appear before grapes three times in the Bible: Joel 2:22; Habakkuk 3:17; Song of Songs 2:13.

56. Numbers 20:5.

57. Numbers, chapter 19.

58. Rabbi Ya'acov ben Asher, Cologne, Germany (1269–1343), Numbers 20:5.

59. Psalms 1:3.

60. Psalms 1:3.

61. Psalms 1:4.

62. Proverbs 27:18.

63. *Charoset* is a traditional dish eaten during the Pesach Seder symbolizing the mortar of the bricks that the Israelite slaves produced.

64. Rambam, *Commentary on the Mishnah, Tractate Pesachim*, chapter 10:3.

65. The *Rosh*, Rabbi Asher ben Yechiel-Ashkenazi, Germany-Toledo, Spain (1250 or 1259–1327), holds that one makes the '*M'ein Shalosh*' after-blessing for water in which raisins or figs were soaked.

66. *Shulchan Aruch, Orach Chaim*, 202:11.

67. Proverbs 24:5.

Punica Granatum ~ רִמּוֹן

Pomegranates

הוֹד ~ Hod ~ Splendor / Majesty

Pomegranates ~ רִמּוֹן *Punica Granatum*
Hod ~ הוֹד *(Splendor / Majesty)*

אֶל גִּנַּת אֱגוֹז יָרַדְתִּי לִרְאוֹת בְּאִבֵּי הַנָּחַל לִרְאוֹת הֲפָרְחָה הַגֶּפֶן הֵנֵצוּ
הָרִמֹּנִים: (שיר השירים ו, יא)

"I went down into the garden of nuts to see the fruits of the valley, and to see whether the vine had blossomed, whether the pomegranates were in flower" (Song of Songs 6:11).

רמון בהוד גי' נוריאל... (אריז"ל, ספר לקוטי תורה - פרשת עקב)

The pomegranate originates in Hod, and the numerical value of רִמּוֹן*/rimon, plus the kollel equals that of the angel* נוּרִיאֵל*/Nuriel*[1] *(Arizal, Sefer Likutei Torah, Parashat Ekev).*

Attribute: *Hod* – Acknowledgement/Thanksgiving/Splendor/Majesty

Character trait: The ability to show empathy (humility)

Holiday: Rosh Hashana, when we pray that our merits increase like the seeds of the pomegranate

Weekday: יוֹם חֲמִישִׁי/*Yom Chamishi* – Fifth day of the week (Thursday)

World: עֲשִׂיָּה/*Asiyah* – Action (hard inedible peel)

Body parts: The left hip, and leg

Shepherd: אַהֲרֹן/Aharon

Prophetess: אֲבִיגַיִל/Avigail

Numerical value: 296, equivalent to the word הָאָרֶץ/*ha'aretz* – 'the land'[2]

Mentioned in the Bible 31 times[3]

Meaning of Latin Name: A small genus of fruit-bearing shrubs or small trees

פֶּרֶק שִׁירָה

Perek Shirah

The Song of the Universe

...כְּפֶלַח הָרִמּוֹן רַקָּתֵךְ מִבַּעַד לְצַמָּתֵךְ:
(שיר השירים ד, ג)

The Song of Pomegranates: "Your cheek is like
a segment of pomegranate behind your veil"
(Song of Songs 4:3).

The Song compares the essence of the soul itself to a "segment of pomegranate," full of 613 seeds. The soul's essence, filled with spiritual Divine Light, is called "your cheek," because it seems as if it is empty without anything in it. Yet, it is still full like the rind of the pomegranate...[4]

Nutrition Facts and Information about Pomegranate

Mineral Content of Pomegranates[5]

Pomegranates contain phosphorus, iron, copper, manganese, small amounts of magnesium and zinc, as well as traces of calcium and selenium.

Vitamin Content of Pomegranates

Pomegranates are a great source of vitamins C and K and a good source of folate. They contain thiamin, riboflavin and vitamin E as well as small amounts of vitamin B6 and niacin.

Oriental Medicine

According to Chinese medicine, pomegranates affect the stomach and colon. They are bitter, sweet, astringent, neutral and demulcent. The fruit is considered a blood tonic in Ayurvedic medicine.[6]

Pomegranates Nutritional Facts/100 g

Minerals		RDA
Calcium	10 mg	1%
Iron	0.30 mg	4%
Magnesium	12 mg	3%
Phosphorus	36 mg	5%
Potassium	236 mg	5%
Sodium	3 mg	0.2%
Zinc	0.35 mg	3%
Copper	0.148 mg	18%
Manganese	0.119 mg	5%
Selenium	0.5 µg	1%
Vitamins		**RDA**
C	10.2 mg	17%
B1 (Thiamin)	0.067 mg	5.5%
B2 (Riboflavin)	0.053 mg	4%
B3 (Niacin)	0.293 mg	2%
B6	0.075 mg	3.5%
B9 (Folate)	38 µg	9.5%
A	0 IU	0%
E	0.65 mg	4%
K	16.4 µg	14%

Pomegranates correspond to Hod. The attribute of *Hod* is a soft majestic glow. Likewise, the pomegranate is a very majestic fruit, and even has a crown. The pomegranate is mentioned often in the beautiful nature descriptions of Song of Songs. It is one of the most celebrated, fascinating, and mysterious fruits in history.

Easily Adaptive to Various Conditions

The pomegranate has been cultivated over the entire Mediterranean region since ancient times. Being adaptable to new conditions is a quality of the reflective, supple energy of *Hod*. Therefore, the pomegranate easily adapts itself to different conditions. Just as *Hod* is connected with humility, the pomegranate is best suited for growing in the valleys.

Hod and the Immune System

Hod is related to the Hebrew word תּוֹדָה/*todah,* meaning recognition and thanksgiving. *Hod* corresponds to our immune system, since a healthy immune system is able to recognize friends from foes.[7] Today, unfortunately, certain people fight against themselves and their friends while befriending their adversaries. The rapid growth rate of autoimmune illnesses may be a reflection of this inability to distinguish between friend and foe – sweet and bitter.[8]

Separating Sweet from Bitter

Every cluster of pomegranate is encased by an intricate membranous compartment of bitter, white, fleshy pith. When preparing a whole pomegranate for eating, we get to practice separating the exceptionally sweet seeds from their extremely bitter peel. This process may help us get in touch with our true desire for the sweet (friend) rather than the bitter (foe).

The Pomegranate and the Star of David

Pomegranates develop from a flower in the shape of a six-pointed Star of David, which takes on the form of a crown as the fruit grows. The crown – כֶּתֶר/*Keter* – is the highest of the Ten Sefirot. *Keter* is the manifestation of our true willpower, which is a reflection of the Upper Will.[9] When we get in touch with our true divine will, our immune system is strengthened to fight against its opponents. It is likely that the famous six-pointed Star of David was inspired by the 'crown' of the pomegranate.

Pomegranates Boost the Immune System

In Hebrew the Star of David is called מָגֵן דָּוִד/*Magen David* – literally, 'the shield of David.' Therefore, it is not surprising that the pomegranate corresponds to the immune system, which protects the body against outside invaders that cause illness. Antioxidant vitamins and trace elements are essential for efficient functioning of the immune system.[10] Because of their high antioxidant content, pomegranates boost the immune system. They specifically protect against arthritis, a common autoimmune illness. Pomegranate extract, obtained from the juice, seed and peel, helps alleviate rheumatoid arthritis and osteoarthritis by reducing the damage to cartilage and joints.[11] The antioxidant level in pomegranate juice is higher than that of other natural juice, including blueberry, cranberry and orange juice. It has three times the antioxidant power of red wine or green tea.[12] In particular, the phenolic components have potent antioxidant activity.[13]

A Natural Skin Treatment

It is possible that the name רִמּוֹן/*rimon* is derived from the language of רָם/*ram* – 'high and uplifted,' since the pomegranate swells up like the apple, which is called תַּפּוּחַ/*tapuach* – 'inflated' in Hebrew. Pomegranate peel keeps the skin smooth and tight. It has astringent qualities that help reduce wrinkles and promote youthful and glowing skin.[14] Powder from pomegranate peel has, therefore, been used since ancient times in various cosmetics.[15] Several skin-care products today contain pomegranate extract. Topical application of the peel extract was shown to restore a variety of enzymes that enhance the skin.[16] The fruit extract has been shown to heal damage caused by sunburn.[17] It is also used too treat mouth sores.[18]

Balancing the Hormones

The sefirah of *Hod*, which corresponds to the immune system, works together with the sefirah of *Netzach*, which corresponds to the endocrine system that is in charge of hormone production. Pomegranates contain estrone, a natural estrogen, which is also produced by the human body. Therefore, pomegranates may improve menopausal symptoms of depression and bone loss.[19] Dr. Michael Aviram suggests that pomegranate juice might also be useful for erectile dysfunction.[20]

Rambam teaches that pomegranates are among the fruits that can be eaten as dessert after a meal since they harden the bowels. For this reason we should not eat too many of them.[21] Eaten moderately, pomegranates strengthen the stomach when eaten with bread.[22] According to Chinese medicine, pomegranate peel, bark and root, which are slightly toxic, are used to calm the stomach and cure digestive problems, including diarrhea due to cold and deficiency.[23] The sour kind of pomegranate, especially, is excellent against diarrhea.[24] Moreover, Rambam recommends drinking pomegranate juice to alleviate headaches caused by hangover. He would also use pomegranate peel to heal open wounds.[25] In folk medicine, a tea made from pomegranate husks was used as a gargle to treat mouth sores and throat irritation.[26]

Ancient Symbol of Healing

The pomegranate is a powerhouse of health. It is one of the best remedies for expelling intestinal worms.[27] Both pomegranate juice and water in which pomegranate peel has been boiled will do the job.[28] From time immemorial, the pomegranate has been valued as a symbol of healing and considered the centerpiece of many traditional folk medicine practices. Ancient Persians believed that pomegranate seeds made their warriors invincible. In China the fruit symbolized longevity. Today it is one of the main fruits whose medicinal benefits are increasingly being evidenced by medical studies.[29] Pomegranate juice has been nominated 'America's new elixir.'[30] Apart from being healthy, it is also delicious.

Preventing and Treating Heart Ailments

Pomegranate juice may lower the risk for cardiovascular disease and combat it by decreasing LDL (bad cholesterol) and increasing HDL (good cholesterol).[31] Research conducted by Professor Michael Aviram, head of lipid research at the Technion Institute in Israel, found that pomegranate extracts prevent LDL oxidation, the first stage in the formation of plaque in the arteries.[32] PubMed currently lists 32 papers published on pomegranates by Dr. Aviram. Among them are studies on the anti-hypertensive effects of pomegranate juice,[33] and on reduction of carotid stenosis (narrowing of the two major arteries that carry oxygen-rich blood from the heart to the brain).[34] Since pomegranates can stop platelets from clumping together to form clots, they thin the blood and reduce the formation of fatty deposits on artery walls.[35] Pomegranates contain the antioxidants ascorbic acid and polyphenolic flavonoids, which have a beneficial effect on the lipid profile and blood pressure of patients on dialysis.

Therefore, it may not be surprising that in Ayurvedic medicine the pomegranate is used as a blood tonic.[36] Furthermore, the pomegranate promotes general heart health. A study conducted by another Israeli physician, Dr. Batya Kristal, indicated that the consumption of pomegranate juice may lower the risk of cardiovascular disease in patients on dialysis. She recommends that pomegranate juice be added to diets designed to improve heart health. Moreover, Dr. Kristal and her team of researchers from Western Galilee Hospital in Nahariya found that kidney patients on dialysis who drank a few cups of pomegranate juice every week lowered their chances of infection, the second-leading killer of the more than 350,000 Americans on dialysis.[37]

Preventing and Curing Cancer

Israeli researchers have found that pomegranate extracts contain ultra-powerful antioxidants that are toxic to most breast cancer cells, but leave healthy cells unharmed.[38] It is interesting to note that the pomegranate resembles a woman's breast with all of its glands. Research headed by Dr. Ephraim Lansky from The Israel Institute of Technology in Haifa has discovered that pomegranate seed oil replaces the estrogen often prescribed to protect postmenopausal women against heart disease and osteoporosis, while selectively destroying estrogen-dependent cancer cells.[39] The results of his research, cited in *The Journal of the National Cancer Institute, The Journal of Ethnopharmacology, The European Journal of Cancer Prevention, The Journal of Breast Cancer Research and Treatment* and many other publications, showed that extracts of pomegranate juice, pomegranate peel, and pomegranate seed-oil all have cancer-inhibiting properties. Pomegranates contain a high level of antioxidants called flavonoids, effective in counteracting various cancer radicals. Those facing high risk of breast and prostate cancer may benefit from drinking pomegranate juice to reduce the risk of developing cancer.[40] Regular consumption of pomegranates may also fight existing cancer cells in the body. Pomegranate oil and juice have been shown to have potential in developing novel anti-cancer drugs from a natural compound and in preventing many types of cancer.[41]

The Pomegranate in Judaica

The glory of the pomegranates adorned the entrance of the Holy Temple in Jerusalem. The capitals of the two pillars that stood in front of King Solomon's Temple were engraved with pomegranates. "On the capitals of both pillars... were the two hundred pomegranates in rows all around."[42] The hem of the robe of the High Priest was adorned with pomegranates woven from sky-blue, purple and scarlet yarn interspersed with golden bells.[43] In the Talmud the pomegranate is mentioned as a decoration in the sukkah.[44] The pomegranate also appeared on the ancient coins of Judea. Until this day, we come across the pomegranate in the form of silver crowns on Torah scrolls, on *ketubah* (marriage contract) illustrations, challah covers and many other Judaic ceremonial objects, all included in what can be called 'pomegranate Judaica.'

The Pomegranate's Mitzvah Seeds

The abundant seeds of the pomegranate symbolize fruitfulness, mitzvot and good deeds. For this reason, pomegranates occupy a prime place in the Rosh Hashana Seder, when we recite a prayer that our merits will increase like pomegranates.

כְּחוּט הַשָּׁנִי שִׂפְתוֹתַיִךְ וּמִדְבָּרֵיךְ נָאוֶה כְּפֶלַח הָרִמּוֹן רַקָּתֵךְ מִבַּעַד לְצַמָּתֵךְ:
(שיר השירים ד, ג)

*"Your lips are like a thread of scarlet, your speech is beautiful.
Your cheek is like a segment of pomegranate behind your veil"*
(Song of Songs 4:3).

ואמר רבי שמעון בן לקיש אל תיקרי רקתך אלא ריקתיך שאפילו ריקנין
שבך מליאין מצות כרמון על אחת כמה וכמה אלא...
(תלמוד בבלי מסכת עירובין יט, ע"א)

*Rabbi Shimon ben Lakish said: "Don't read it "your cheek"
(רַקָּתֵךְ/rakatech), but "your empty ones" (רֵיקָתַיִךְ/rakatayich),
for even the empty ones among you are full of mitzvot like the
pomegranate..." (Babylonian Talmud, Iruvin 19a).*

An average-sized pomegranate contains approximately 600 edible seeds under its thick red covering.[45] Our Sages teach that the amount of seeds in the pomegranate corresponds to the 613 mitzvot.[46]

The pomegranate looks like one fruit, but when you open it, it is filled with a multitude of mini-fruits. Likewise, some people might seem simple and void of mitzvot, but when you get to know them better, they turn out to be filled with mitzvot.

The Prayers of the Sinners

The pomegranate alludes to the sinners of Israel who are full of mitzvot like a pomegranate.[47] Without "the empty ones of Israel" represented by the humble pomegranate, there can be no communal prayer, since "any prayer that does not include the sinners of Israel is not called prayer."[48] We learn this from the hem of the High Priest's robe. Only when the golden bells are alternating with pomegranates, shall "its sound be heard when he comes into the Holy Place before Hashem."[49] This can be understood to mean that only when the sinners of Israel are included, will our prayer be heard.[50]

The Good Deeds of the Wicked Compared to Pomegranates

There is a difference between the good deeds of the righteous and those of the wicked. The good deeds of the righteous are clean and pure, like the clear light in heaven. Unlike those of the wicked. Even their good deeds are mixed with self-interest. This is similar to the pomegranate, whose fruit is surrounded by lots of bitter white membranes and peel.[51] However, the pomegranate arils seem all the sweeter in contrast to their bitter encasing. Likewise, when people who are not mitzvah observant perform a mitzvah such as a kosher wedding ceremony or circumcision, the holiness of their mitzvot seems to reverberate on an even a higher level than the mitzvot performed by habitual mitzvah observers. According to Rabbi Nachman "even the sinners of Israel are full of mitzvot like a pomegranate" implies that even the few mitzvot kept by the Jews who do not follow the Torah, save them from sinking into impurity. Eventually these mitzvot will arouse them to complete repentance. Their mitzvot give them the power to rise from the mundane to the holy, from impurity to purity, and ultimately transform everything to good.[52]

The Pomegranate's Silent Torah

וְעָשִׂיתָ עַל שׁוּלָיו רִמֹּנֵי תְּכֵלֶת וְאַרְגָּמָן וְתוֹלַעַת שָׁנִי עַל שׁוּלָיו סָבִיב וּפַעֲמֹנֵי
זָהָב בְּתוֹכָם סָבִיב: פַּעֲמֹן זָהָב וְרִמּוֹן פַּעֲמֹן זָהָב וְרִמּוֹן עַל שׁוּלֵי הַמְּעִיל סָבִיב:
וְהָיָה עַל אַהֲרֹן לְשָׁרֵת וְנִשְׁמַע קוֹלוֹ בְּבֹאוֹ אֶל הַקֹּדֶשׁ לִפְנֵי הָשֵׁם וּבְצֵאתוֹ וְלֹא
יָמוּת: (שמות כח, לג-לה)

*"You shall make pomegranates of sky-blue, and of purple, and
of scarlet, round about its hem: and bells of gold between them
round about: A golden bell and a pomegranate, a golden bell
and a pomegranate, upon the hem of the robe round about. It
shall be upon Aharon when he comes to minister: and its sound
shall be heard when he goes in to the Holy Place before Hashem,
and when he comes out, that he does not die"* (Exodus 28:33–35).

Whenever a person has free time, he should busy himself with words
of Torah, rather than sitting idly. When he is unable to study Torah,
he should make himself as a mute who is unable to open his mouth.
This is alluded to by the bells and the pomegranates that bedecked
the hem of the Kohen Gadol's robe. The sound produced by the
golden bells symbolizes the voice of Torah, whereas the silent pomegranates allude to the required silence when not learning Torah, and
the need to desist from tittle-tattle.[53]

It is no coincidence that Aharon the High Priest wears pomegranates on his robe. He is the Shepherd that corresponds to the
sefirah of הוֹד/*Hod*, associated with the pomegranate, which is related to the Hebrew word הֵד/*hed* – meaning 'echo and reflection.'
He reflects the greatness of Moshe our teacher, who is represented
by the sefirah of נֵצַח/*Netzach*. In the same way, the pomegranate
reflects the sound of Torah by its silence, not counteracting the
Torah through idle speech. When acting in tune with the humble,
reflective pomegranate, one can rest assured that "his voice will be
heard when he comes to the Holy."[54] His voice of Torah, untainted
by evil speech, will reach its destination and be accepted by G*d.

The silence of the pomegranate also symbolizes the learning of the mystical teachings of Kabbalah, which means 'to receive.' It requires the initiate to listen silently and receive from his teacher. Experiencing the mystical tradition of Kabbalah is compared to entering 'the Garden of Pomegranates' or *Pardes Rimonim*, the title of a book by the 16th century mystic, Rabbi Moshe Cordovero, the *Ramak*.[55]

נַשְׁכִּימָה לַכְּרָמִים נִרְאֶה אִם פָּרְחָה הַגֶּפֶן פִּתַּח הַסְּמָדַר הֵנֵצוּ הָרִמּוֹנִים שָׁם
אֶתֵּן אֶת דֹּדַי לָךְ: (שיר השירים ז, יג)

"Let us get up early to the vineyards: let us see if the vine has flowered, if the vine blossoms have opened, if the pomegranates are in flower: there I will give you my love" (*Song of Songs* 7:13).

הנצו הרמונים אלו התינוקות שיושבין ועוסקין בתורה ויושבין שורות
שורות כגרעיני רמונים: (מדרש רבה שיר השירים ו, כו)

"If the pomegranates are in flower" – These are the little children who sit in rows and study Torah like the seeds of a pomegranate (*Midrash Song of Songs Rabbah* 6:26).

Rashi explains that when the pomegranates are in flower, they are compared to the masters of Talmud who are ripe with wisdom and worthy to teach.[56] Malbim adds that when we perform Torah and mitzvot out of love of G*d, it engenders a pleasant scent desirable to Hashem, which brings us eternal life. In return, He, rewards the 'soul of our deeds' and the heart of our worship with His ever-lasting love.[57]

שְׁלָחַיִךְ פַּרְדֵּס רִמּוֹנִים עִם פְּרִי מְגָדִים כְּפָרִים עִם נְרָדִים:
(שיר השירים ד, יג)

"Your shoots are like an orchard of pomegranates, with pleasant fruits, henna and nard[58] *(Song of Songs 4:13).*

❁ A Taste of Kabbalah – The Pomegranate: Outer Garment for Eternal Life

אילה שלוחה הנותן הנותן אמרי שפר... ונפתלי מזאת הבחי' של הנוק'. רמון בהוד
גי' נוריאל והוא מט"ט כשתסיר ממטטרון ט"ט גי' ח"י נשאר רמון כי ט"ט
באמצע מטטרון הוא חיות ותוכיות הרמון כי מ' מימין ורון משמאל והם
סוד הקליפה הנק' רמון ובתוכם ח"י ט"ט ואכל וחי לעולם וכן ר"מ תוכו
אכל וקליפתו זרק ובחיות אין אחיזה לחיצוני' אבל בלבוש והוא הרמון יש
להם אחיזה, ובזה ג"כ תבין סוד הפסוק והחיות רצוא ושוב רצוא כמנין רמון
אותיות צואר וזהו רצוא צואר דאמא עילאה שהוא גרון ועד הוד איתפשטת
והח"י הוא ושוב כמנין שדי אדאיהי למטה מהחיות ואיהי כללות כולם...
(ספר לקוטי תורה - פרשת עקב)

"Naftali is a hind let loose: he gives goodly words..."[59] Naftali is
from the aspect of the feminine (nukvah)... The pomegranate
is in *Hod*, the gematria of Nuriel (296). When you remove the
ט"ט – the two letters of *tet,* which together have the numerical
value of eighteen חַי/*chai* – life, from the name מֶטָטְרוֹן/Met-
tatron [the prince of the ministering angels], you are left with
the letters of רִמּוֹן/*rimon*/pomegranate. The double *tet* in the
middle of מֶטָטְרוֹן/Mettatron is the vitality and internal part of

the pomegranate. The letter מ/*mem* remains on its right, and רוֹן
/*ron* on its left. They are the secret of the shell called rimon –
pomegranate. Within it is the *chai* – life of the double *tet.* "By
eating [it] he will live forever."[60] Likewise, about Rabbi Meir it
states: "He ate its inside and cast away its husk."[61] The extrane-
ous forces have no grip on the inside vital part; however, they
do have a grip on the garment, which is the pomegranate. From
this we can also understand the secret of the verse "...the Chayot
run and return."[62] The Hebrew word for running, רָצוֹא/*ratzo,*
has the same letters as the Hebrew word for neck, צַוָּאר/*tzavar.*
This word has the same gematria as רִמּוֹן/*rimon.* The running,
the neck of the upper mother that is the throat, extends into
Hod. The חַי/*chai* – life, which is וְשׁוֹב/*vashov* – and returning,

has the gematria of the name of G*d, יְדַּ-שַׁ/Shad*dai (314) which includes all... (Arizal, *Sefer Likutei Torah, Parashat Ekev*).

Explanation: The tribe of Naftali and the pomegranate are connected as they are both associated with the sefirah of *Hod*.[63] About Naftali it states: "Naftali is a hind let loose: he gives goodly words."[64] *Hod* from the left side of the Tree of Life has the ability to differentiate between good and evil, to recognize friend from foe and extract the kernels of truth from within its external impurity. In this way *Hod*, which resides directly under *Gevurah*, applies the action of *Gevurah* in a deeper way, where the opposite forces are more closely intertwined, and the further refined filter of *Hod* is required.

The angel נוּרִיאֵל/Nuriel, which has the same numerical value as the word רִמּוֹן/*rimon*, is the guardian of the fire within, or the in-dwelling light. Nuriel is the mystical fifth angel, who helps humans calibrate the vibrations of Uriel, Raphael, Gavriel and Michael.

The letters of מֶטַּטְרוֹן/Mettatron (the angel who led the children of Israel during the Exodus)[65] are identical with רִמּוֹן/*rimon* with two additional letters of ט/*tet*. Since *tet* is the ninth letter of the Hebrew alphabet, the two *tets* together have the numerical value of eighteen, חַי/*chai*, which means 'life.' The רִמּוֹן/*rimon* is therefore the outer garment for this eternal life force represented by the double internal *tet*.

The Talmud teaches that Rabba bar Shila met Eliyahu the Prophet and said to him: "What is the Holy One, blessed be He, doing?" He answered him: "He had uttered a doctrine in the name of all other rabbis, except that of Rabbi Meir." He asked him, "Why?" Eliyahu answered, "Because Rabbi Meir learned a doctrine from the mouth of Acher." Rabba bar Shila asked him again: "Why? Rabbi Meir found a pomegranate. He ate its inside and cast away its husk."[66] Acher refers to Elisha ben Abuya, a great Torah scholar, who became a heretic when entering the 'orchard.'[67] Nevertheless, his devoted student, Rabbi Meir, continued to learn from him. Rabbi Meir had mastered the delicate skill of *Hod*. Therefore, he had the ability to acknowledge and learn from Elisha Ben Abuya, by extracting his

inner eternal vital truth, while discarding his words of heresy. This inner filtering work of *Hod* is rightfully described as 'eating the inside of a pomegranate while casting away its husk.' The pomegranate is the garment for eternal life. Its seeds of pure sweetness closely entrapped within its bitter encasing call for the filtering energy of *Hod*, necessary for its consumption.

In the Book of Ezekiel, the highest angels called Chayot are described as running and returning. The word רָצוֹא/*ratzo* – 'running' has the same numerical value (296) as רִמּוֹן/*rimon*, because running extends outwardly, like the tribe of Naftali (the quick runner),[68] associated with *Hod*. The purpose of running is וָשׁוֹב/*vashov* – to return with "goodly words" as Naftali does. The word וָשׁוֹב/*vashov* – 'and return' has the same numerical value as the Name of G*d, שַׁדַּי/*Shad*dai* and the highest angel, מֶטָטְרוֹן/Mettatron (314), which includes the additional numerical value of חַי/*chai* – eighteen added to the numerical value of רִמּוֹן/*rimon* and רָצוֹא/*ratzo* – running. Running without returning is missing the חַי/*chai* – life, and may breach the proper boundaries of life, as when Aharon's sons met their death while running toward closeness with the Divine.[69] Also today, there are people who in their excited desire to approach the Divine miss the proper boundaries of Jewish law. It is only through 'returning' that the 'running' is attached to life and reaches its true goal.

The name of G*d, שַׁ-דַּי/*Shad*dai* can mean abundantly blessed with all manner of blessings like the mother's breast, which shares the same name. In addition שַׁ-דַּי/*Shad*dai* is also the acronym of שׁוֹמֵר דְּלָתוֹת יִשְׂרָאֵל/*Shomer D'latot Yisrael* – Guardian of the Doors of Israel. In its capacity to act as a filter, allowing only what is appropriate to enter. The name שַׁ-דַּי/*Shad*dai* stands for מִי שאמר לעולמו די /*Mi she'amar l'olamo **dai*** – "He Who said to His world: 'Enough!'" This is the true application of *Hod*, teaching us that 'less is more.' Life is created through the power of שַׁ-דַּי/*Shad*dai* – enough – sifting the excess away. This name of G*d appears first in the Bible when G*d commands Avraham to circumcise himself, cutting away the foreskin from his organ of procreation.[70]

Another way to rectify רָצוֹא/*ratzo* – 'running' is alluded to in the letters of the word which can be unscrambled to spell out צַוָּאר/*tzavar* – 'neck.' The neck is a narrow channel that *Hod* flows through, connecting the head with the rest of the body. The narrow neck acts as a filter allowing only the passage of what is appropriate. On the front side of the neck, the throat sifts the thoughts to express only the deepest kinds of speech.

הרואה רמונים בחלום זוטרי פרי עסקיה כרמונא רברבי רבי
עסקיה כרמונא פלגי אם תלמיד חכם הוא יצפה לתורה שנאמר
אַשְׁקְךָ מִיַּיִן הָרֶקַח מֵעֲסִיס רִמֹּנִי ואם עם הארץ הוא יצפה
למצוות שנאמר כְּפֶלַח הָרִמּוֹן רַקָּתֵךְ מאי רקתך אפילו ריקנין
שבך מלאים מצות כרמון:

He who sees pomegranates in a dream, if they are small,
his business will flourish like a pomegranate. [He will have
many customers] If they are big, his business will increase
like a pomegranate. [His customers will make large orders].
If they are split open, a talmid chacham (Torah scholar),
may anticipate to learn more Torah, as it says, "I shall give
you to drink from the spiced wine, from the juice of my
pomegranate."[71] An unlearned person may anticipate mitzvot,
as it states, "Your cheek" (רַקָּתֵךְ/rekatech) is like a section
of pomegranate."[72] What is the meaning of רַקָּתֵךְ/rekatech?
...Even the simplest (literally, 'empty ones') among you are full
of mitzvot like a pomegranate [is full of seeds]
(Babylonian Talmud, Berachot 57a).

Pomegranate
Recipes

Pure Pleasure of Pomegranate Seeds

You can extract the health benefits of pomegranates in several ways. Juice the pomegranates or use as syrup, nectar, or concentrate. I prefer just eating a full bowl of plain pomegranate seeds with a spoon or sprinkling them over salads and fruit desserts, as a garnish. I even decorate cakes with these beautiful ruby-looking seeds.

Most of the fiber you get from eating pomegranates comes from their seeds, so do not spit them out after enjoying the juice, but crunch on them. Also very young children will love popping these tantalizing seeds into their mouths. They may even prefer them over synthetic candies. Young children just can't get enough of them! Even toddlers will delight in picking them out of the peel, and can be busied with this activity for long time periods. Make sure to dress your youngsters in clothes you don't care about, as the juice of pomegranates will stain.

A handy tip to remember when purchasing pomegranates is that the heavier the pomegranate, the more seeds it will have.

GUIDE FOR ASPIRING POMEGRANATE OPEN-UPPERS
The art of separating the tasty jewels from their bitter pith

Opening a pomegranate is like a treasure hunt, because a pomegranate is a fruit that has 'chambers.' In order to open this beautiful, divine gift and reveal all the tasty jewels inside, we need to enter the pomegranate's hidden chambers. By carefully opening its wrapping and separating the pomegranate's chambers, its goodness will pop open for us to marvel and enjoy its vibrant red, ruby-looking seeds.

1. Place your pomegranate(s) on a kitchen counter that can easily be wiped clean, or lay paper towels on the surface where you'll be cutting, as it's difficult to avoid juice splattering.

2. To properly open the pomegranate without cutting into the seeds, we need to sculpt it carefully. With a small paring knife, just barely piercing the skin, gently cut a circle the size of a small skullcap around the top edge of the pomegranate (its crown).

3. Pull away the pomegranate skin along your circular cutting lines.

4. Discover the approximately six different 'fruit chambers,' each section separated by a white line of pith. Using those pithy dividers as a guide, gently pierce the skin of the fruit without cutting all the way through. Cut down the sides of the pomegranate following where the individual sections seem to be. You'll make about six different cuts working around the pomegranate, cutting each line downward all the way to the bottom.

5. Gently press the pomegranate from its center to pry it open. Pull out each chamber independently with your hands, while penetrating the skin.

6. Serve sections of pomegranates in a bowl for yourself, your family and guests to simply bite into. Your hands and teeth will easily separate the heavenly fruits from their peel and pith. The arils (seed sacs) will burst into the mouth with their sweet, tart flavor, ending with a crunch.

7. If you want to remove the pomegranate seeds completely from their husks, simply flip each of the pomegranate sections over in your hand. Extract the pomegranates arils manually and remove the pith. The pith is easy to remove in a bowl of water, as it will float to the top.

8. The pomegranate arils are to be enjoyed whole, seed and all. Serve them in cups or small bowls with a spoon, or use them in various recipes.

The arils will keep in the refrigerator for several days and may be frozen. However, if you freeze them they will lose their crunchiness.

Variation

If you are not going to serve pomegranate sections, but you are looking to extract all the pomegranate arils easily from the pith to eat with a spoon or mix into salads, here is a slightly different way of opening a pomegranate. Before you cut into the pomegranate, hit every part of the whole unopened pomegranate well with the back of a wooden spoon or special 'kitchen hammer.' This will loosen the arils and make them easily detach from the pith. Afterwards, follow steps 2–4 to get ready to open the pomegranate. Pull the pomegranate open over a large bowl of water. Use your fingers to gently massage the arils, which will now easily fall into the water. Remove the big pieces of pith with your hands. The small pieces of pith will float to the top of the water and as you pour off the water, most of them will also wash away. Remove the last bits of pith. If a little remains, it will only add to the cleansing effect of the pomegranate! You may want to use disposable rubber gloves while opening pomegranates to avoid staining your hands.

HOMEMADE POMEGRANATE JUICE

A way to reduce the time-consuming job of extracting the pomegranate seeds from the peels

1. Cut the pomegranate in half and squeeze the juice with your lemon juicer.

   (It's even better to make pomegranate juice with a special citrus fruit juicer, if you have one).

2. Place half the pomegranate in between the two parts of the metal device and push down the upper fruit-shaped metal cup which presses the fruit from above.

3. The juice will trickle down through the holes into the cup placed at the bottom of the device.

BLENDED POMEGRANATE COCKTAIL
A way to use mushy or frozen pomegranate arils

1. Fill your blender about one third full with pomegranate arils.

2. Process them in the blender for about five minutes.

3. You may experiment with adding a touch of spice such as cinnamon, nutmeg or cloves.

The pomegranate arils will turn into a milky pinkish drink. The the seeds will give your cocktail a grainy texture.

NUTTY POMEGRANATES
A scrumptious, rejuvenating snack

2 cups pomegranate arils
¼–½ cup chopped walnuts

For a sweet breakfast treat or a filling afternoon snack, try mixing pomegranate seeds with walnuts. You can either add more or less nuts depending on your preference. You may also mix the pomegranate arils with honeydew melon. Eat with a spoon, yum!

POMEGRANATE YOGURT DIP

A delightful relish, adding flavor to any brunch

1 large pomegranate

2 cups chilled plain yogurt

3 tablespoons chives

½ cup pomegranate juice

(If you don't have a way to make your own pomegranate juice, pomegranate juice is easily found in most health food stores, where you can find a variety of organic products).

⅓ cup finely chopped fresh cilantro

1 teaspoon sea salt

1 teaspoon freshly ground black pepper

1. Separate the seeds from the pomegranate. (Letting them soak in water will allow the seeds to sink and the pulpy flesh will rise to the top).

2. Combine the yogurt, pomegranate juice, scallions, cilantro, and sea salt in a mixing bowl.

3. Gently fold in the pomegranate seeds.

4. Chill for at least half an hour to let the flavors blend before serving.

Can be made in advance and refrigerated overnight.

POMEGRATED CARROT SALAD
A Mediterranean variation of the traditional Ashkenazi carrot salad

4 cups grated carrots
¾ cup fresh pomegranate arils
A small bunch of freshly chopped basil leaves
1 handful of nuts or seeds
(I use a mixture of almonds and sunflower seeds)
Fresh juice of 1–2 lemons
¼–½ cup of coconut milk (optional)
1 teaspoon cinnamon
1 teaspoon ginger (optional)
Coconut flakes to taste

1. Mix everything together.
2. Marinate for one hour before serving.

TENDER POMEGRANATE TABOULI

A colorful, refreshing side-dish

1 cup cracked wheat (bulgur)
1 bundle finely chopped parsley (approximately ⅔ cup)
1 bunch finely chopped fresh mint or ½ cup dry (optional)
½ cup finely chopped green onions or scallions
½ cup pomegranate arils
1 finely chopped cucumber (optional)
2 lemons
2 tablespoons olive oil
Sea salt, freshly ground black pepper & allspice to taste

1. Pour boiling water over cracked wheat.

2. Soak cracked wheat in water for at least one hour. Pour out extra water (may be used in soup or to steam veggies etc.)

3. Soak the parsley, green onions and mint in natural soap water for three minutes, rinse.

4. Process parsley, green onions and mint in the food processor until very fine.

5. Mix finely chopped herbs and onions with the soaked bulgur.

6. Add the pomegranate arils and chopped cucumber.

7. Pour juice of two lemons on the tabouli and add olive oil and seasoning.

QUINOA POMEGRANATE ALMOND DELIGHT
Simple, elegant and nutritious

1 cup pomegranate seeds
1 tablespoon olive oil
2 cloves of chopped garlic
½ chopped onion
1 teaspoon sea salt
1 cup white quinoa
2 cups water
½ cup slivered almonds
½ cup chopped fresh mint

1. Sauté garlic and onion in olive oil until lightly browned in a medium saucepan over medium heat.

2. Add quinoa and sea salt to the saucepan and cover with water.

3. Bring the mixture to a boil. Cover, reduce heat and simmer for about 20 minutes.

4. Remove quinoa from saucepan to cool.

5. Mix in the mint, slivered almonds and pomegranate seeds. Add olive oil to taste.

ANTI WRINKLE POMEGRANATE PEEL FACIAL CREAM

Will moisturize your face and keep your skin youthful

½ cup almond oil
½ cup grape seed oil
¼ cup coconut oil
1 cup shea butter
1 pomegranate peel
2 aloe vera leaves

4–8 drops essential lavender oil (or other essential oil)
4–8 drops of vitamin E oil (optional)

1. Dry the pomegranate peel and grind it into a powder.
2. Take two leaves of aloe vera (from your or your neighbor's garden) and cut into pieces.
3. Blend the aloe vera in a blender and strain.
4. Add remaining ingredients.
5. Whip everything in the blender until it becomes creamy.
6. Place the cream in glass jars or wide-mouthed containers.

Since this thick moisturizing cream is water-free, it will not need refrigeration.

Laws of Blessings ~ הִלְכוֹת בְּרָכוֹת

One who eats less than a כְּזַיִת/*kezayit* – an olive size amount of food (approximately 28 cc or 1 fl. oz.) or drinks less than a רְבִיעִית/*revi'it* (86 cc or 2.9 fl. oz.) of liquid recites its suitable blessing before consuming it, but recites no after-blessing. There is a halachic opinion that one needs to recite an after-blessing for every food that is a whole creation. This refers to a food that still remains in its whole original form, the way Hashem created it, such as one grape or one aril of pomegranate, even if it is smaller than an olive size.[73] Therefore, it is recommended to eat enough to equal a kezayit, when eating a whole fruit. However, it is only called 'a whole creation' if one ate it whole. If he removed even one seed from the fruit, then it no longer is a whole creation.[74]

We bless on fruit seeds, if they are sweet '*borei p'ri ha'etz*,' but if they are bitter, we do not bless on them at all. If they are improved through cooking, we bless on them '*shehakol*.'[75]

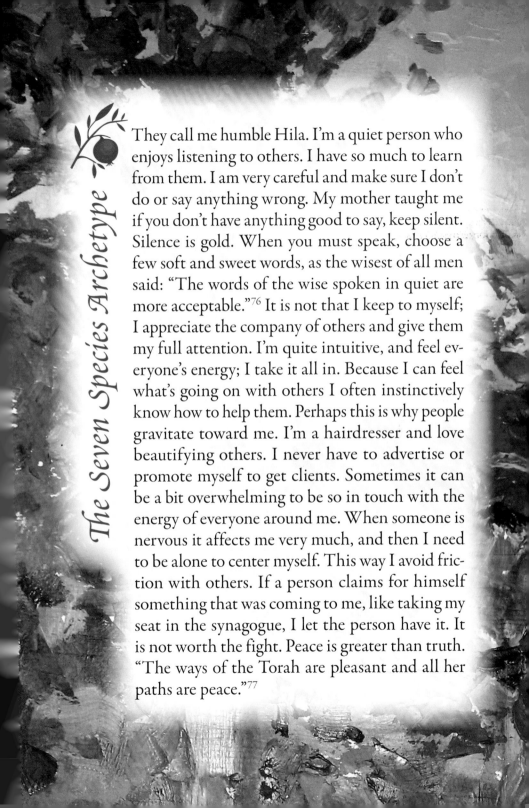

They call me humble Hila. I'm a quiet person who enjoys listening to others. I have so much to learn from them. I am very careful and make sure I don't do or say anything wrong. My mother taught me if you don't have anything good to say, keep silent. Silence is gold. When you must speak, choose a few soft and sweet words, as the wisest of all men said: "The words of the wise spoken in quiet are more acceptable."[76] It is not that I keep to myself; I appreciate the company of others and give them my full attention. I'm quite intuitive, and feel everyone's energy; I take it all in. Because I can feel what's going on with others I often instinctively know how to help them. Perhaps this is why people gravitate toward me. I'm a hairdresser and love beautifying others. I never have to advertise or promote myself to get clients. Sometimes it can be a bit overwhelming to be so in touch with the energy of everyone around me. When someone is nervous it affects me very much, and then I need to be alone to center myself. This way I avoid friction with others. If a person claims for himself something that was coming to me, like taking my seat in the synagogue, I let the person have it. It is not worth the fight. Peace is greater than truth. "The ways of the Torah are pleasant and all her paths are peace."[77]

Endnotes

1. Nuriel (light of G*d) is one of the Hashem's archangels.

2. Genesis 1:1.

3. Pomegranate – רִמּוֹן/*rimon*, רִמֹּן/*rimon*, pomegranates – רִמּוֹנִים/*rimonim* and רִמֹּנִים/*rimonim* is mentioned 31 times in the Bible.
   Pomegranate – רִמּוֹן/*rimon* is mentioned in the singular form nine times, four times in the Pentateuch and five times in the rest of the Bible: Exodus 28:44 (twice); Numbers 20:5; Deuteronomy 8:8; I Samuel 14:2; Joel 1:12; Haggai 2:19; Song of Songs 4:3, 6:7. רִמֹּן/*rimon* (without the ו/*vav*) is mentioned twice in Exodus 39:26. **Pomegranates** – רִמּוֹנִים/*rimonim* is mentioned in the plural form ten times, once in the Pentateuch and nine times in the rest of the Bible: I Kings 7:20; Jeremiah 52:22 (twice), 52:23; Song of Songs 4:13; II Chronicles 3:16, 4:13 (twice). רִמֹּנִים/*rimonim* (without the ו/*vav*) is mentioned ten times, three times in the Pentateuch and seven times in the rest of the Bible: Exodus 28:33, 39:25; Numbers:13:23; I Kings 7:18, 7:42; II Kings 25:17; Jeremiah 52:23; Song of Songs 6:11, 8:2.

4. Malbim, Song of Songs 4:3.

5. The vitamin and mineral content of pomegranates is based on USDA, *Basic Report*: 09286, *Pomegranates, raw*. The percentage of Recommended Daily Dietary Allowance is based on *Pomegranate, fresh* <http://www.nutrition-and-you.com/pomegranate.html> retrieved June 30, 2013.

6. Michael Tierra, *Planetary Herbology*, p. 344.

7. Rav Yitzchak Ginsburgh, *Body, Mind, and Soul*, p. 96.

8. Rambam describes this 'mental illness' in *Mishneh Torah, Hilchot Deot* 2:1, where he quotes this phrase from Isaiah 5:20.

9. Rabbi Shneur Zalman of Liadi, *Tanya, Igeret Hakodesh,* chapter 29.

10. Wintergerst ES, Maggini S, Hornig DH. *Contribution of Selected Vitamins and Trace Elements to Immune Function. Ann Nutr Metab* 2007, 51(4):301–23.

11. Shukla M, Gupta K, Rasheed Z, Khan KA, Haqqi TM. *Consumption of Hydrolyzable Tannins-Rich Pomegranate Extract Suppresses Inflammation and Joint Damage in Rheumatoid Arthritis. Nutrition* 2008, 24:733–743.

12. Using the Trolox Equivalent Antioxidant Capacity test. See Noda Y, Kaneyuki T, Mori A, et al. *Antiont Activities of Pomegranate Fruit Extract and its Anthocyanidins*: Delphinidin, Cyanidin, and

Pelargonidin. J Agric Food Chem. 2002;50(1): 166–71.
Aviram M, Rosenblat M. *Pomegranate Protection against Cardiovascular Diseases*. Evid Based Complement Alternat Med. 2012;2012:382763.

13. Gil MI, Tomás-Barberán FA, Hess-Pierce B, Holcroft DM, Kader AA. *Antioxidant Activity of Pomegranate Juice and its Relationship with Phenolic Composition and Processing*. J Agric Food Chem 2000. 48(10):4581–9.

14. Aslam MN, Lansky EP, Varani J. *Pomegranate as a Cosmeceutical Source: Pomegranate Fractions Promote Proliferation and Procollagen Synthesis and Inhibit Matrix Metalloproteinase-1 Production in Human Skin Cells*. J Ethnopharmacol. 2006 Feb 20;103(3):311–8.

15. Rabbi Binyamin Moshe Kohn Shauli, *Nature's Wealth,* p. 234.

16. Chidambara Murthy KN, Jayaprakasha GK, Singh RP. *Studies on Antioxidant Activity of Pomegranate (Punica Granatum) Peel Extract Using in Vivo Models*. J Agric Food Chem. 2002 Aug 14;50(17):4791–5.

17. Sarfaraz S, Afaq F, Mukhtar H. *Photochemopreventive Effect of Pomegranate Fruit Extract on UVA-Mediated Activation of Cellular Pathways in Normal Human Epidermal Keratinocytes*. Photochem Photobiol. 2006 Mar–Apr;82(2):398–405.

18. Rabbi Binyamin Moshe Kohn Shauli, *Nature's Wealth,* p. 234.

19. Mori-Okamoto J, Otawara-Hamamoto Y, Yamato H, Yoshimura H. *Pomegranate Extract Improves a Depressive State and Bone Properties in Menopausal Syndrome Model Ovariectomized Mice*. J Ethnopharmacol. 2004 May;92(1):93–101.

20. Azadzoi KM, Schulman RN, Aviram M, Siroky MB. *Oxidative Stress in Arteriogenic Erectile Dysfunction: Prophylactic Role of Antioxidants*. J Urol. 2005 Jul;174(1):386–93.

21. Rambam, *Mishneh Torah, Hilchot Deot* 4:6.

22. Nisim Krispil, *Medicinal Herbs of the Rambam,* p. 194.

23. Michael Tierra, *Planetary Herbology,* p. 402.

24. Rabbi Binyamin Moshe Kohn Shauli, *Nature's Wealth,* p. 234.

25. Nisim Krispil, *Medicinal Herbs of the Rambam,* p. 194.

26. Michael Tierra, *Planetary Herbology,* p. 344.

27. Michael Tierra, *Planetary Herbology,* p. 402.

28. Rabbi Binyamin Moshe Kohn Shauli, *Nature's Wealth,* p. 234.

29. A PubMed search for *Punica Granatum* (pomegranate) performed August 20, 2013, yielded 659 studies.

30. Jacob Schor, ND, *Pomegranate People: The Alchemist and the Capitalist,* Naturopathy Digest, April, 2006.

31. Aviram M, Dornfeld L, Rosenblat M, Volkova N, Kaplan M, Coleman R, Hayek T, Presser D, Fuhrman B. *Pomegranate Juice Consumption Reduces Oxidative Stress, Atherogenic Modifications to LDL, and Platelet Aggregation: Studies in Humans and in Atherosclerotic Apolipoprotein E-Deficient Mice.* Am J Clin Nutr May 2000;71(5):1062–76.

32. Kaplan M, Hayek T, Raz A, Coleman R, Dornfeld L, Vaya J, Aviram M. *Pomegranate Juice Supplementation to Atherosclerotic Mice Reduces Macrophage Lipid Peroxidation, Cellular Cholesterol Accumulation and Development of Atherosclerosis.* J Nutr August 2001;131(8):2082–9.

33. Aviram M, Dornfeld L. *Pomegranate Juice Consumption Inhibits Serum Angiotensin Converting Enzyme Activity and Reduces Systolic Blood Pressure. Atherosclerosis.* 2001 Sep;158(1):195–8.

34. Aviram M, Rosenblat M, Gaitini D, Nitecki S, Hoffman A, Dornfeld L, Volkova N, Presser D, Attias J, Liker H, Hayek T. *Pomegranate Juice Consumption for 3 Years by Patients With Carotid Artery Stenosis Reduces Common Carotid Intima-Media Thickness, Blood Pressure and LDL Oxidation.* Clin Nutr. 2004 Jun;23(3):423–33.

35. *Pomegranate Juice Consumption Reduces Oxidative Stress...* Mattiello T, Trifirò E, Jotti GS, Pulcinelli FM. *Effects of Pomegranate Juice and Extract Polyphenols on Platelet Function.* J Med Food. 2009 Apr;12(2):334–9. Mohan M, Patankar P, Ghadi P, Kasture S. *Cardioprotective Potential of Punica Granatum Extract in Isoproterenol-Induced Myocardial Infarction in Wistar Rats.* J Pharmacol Pharmacother. 2010 Jan;1(1):32–7.

36. Michael Tierra, *Planetary Herbology,* p. 402.

37. Shema-Didi L, Sela S, Ore L, Shapiro G, Geron R, Moshe G, Kristal B. *One Year of Pomegranate Juice Intake Decreases Oxidative Stress, Inflammation, and Incidence of Infections in Hemodialysis Patients: a Randomized Placebo-Controlled Trial.* Free Radic Biol Med. 2012 Jul 15;53(2):297–304.

38. Mehta R, Lansky EP. *Breast Cancer Chemopreventive Properties of Pomegranate (Punica Granatum) Fruit Extracts in a Mouse Mammary Organ Culture.* Eur J Cancer Prev. 2004 Aug;13(4):345–8. In his article, *Pomegranate Seed Oil Causes Breast Cancer Cells To Self-Destruct,* cited on ObGyn.Net, Lansky revealed his findings that the seed oil and the rind may have anti-carcinogenic properties effective in suppressing a variety of cancers including breast and prostate.

39. Newman RA, Ph.D. and Lansky EP, M.D. (with Block ML).

Pomegranate: The Most Medicinal Fruit. Basic Health Publications, 2007. 1st. Khan GN, Gorin MA, Rosenthal D, Pan Q, Bao LW, Wu ZF, Newman RA, Pawlus AD, Yang P, Lansky EP, Merajver SD. *Pomegranate Fruit Extract Impairs Invasion and Motility in Human Breast Cancer.* Integr Cancer Ther. 2009 Sep;8(3):242–53. Tran HN, Bae SY, Song BH, Lee BH, Bae YS, Kim YH, Lansky EP, Newman RA. *Pomegranate (Punica Granatum) Seed Linolenic Acid Isomers: Concentration-Dependent Modulation of Estrogen Receptor Activity.* Endocr Res. 2010 Jan;35(1):1–16.

40. A two-year study conducted by Dr. Pantuck and colleagues from University of California, Los Angeles, showed that men with rising prostate-specific antigen (PSA) levels after definitive prostate cancer therapy who drank 8 oz. daily of pomegranate juice had significantly longer PSA doubling times. See Rettig MB, Heber D, An J, Seeram NP, Rao JY, Liu H, Klatte T, Belldegrun A, Moro A, Henning SM, Mo D, Aronson WJ, Pantuck A. *Pomegranate Extract Inhibits Androgen-Independent Prostate Cancer Growth through a Nuclear Factor-KappaB-Dependent Mechanism.* Mol Cancer Ther. 2008 Sep;7(9):2662–71.

41. Lansky EP. *Anticancer Pharmacognosy of Punica granatum*, Ph.D. thesis, Leiden University, 2008. With Introduction, Conclusion, Summary and ten peer-reviewed publications. Adhami VM, Khan N, Mukhtar H. *Cancer Chemoprevention by Pomegranate: Laboratory and Clinical Evidence.* Nutr Cancer. 2009;61(6):811–5.

42. I Kings 7:18, 20.

43. Exodus 28:33–34.

44. *Babylonian Talmud, Beitza* 30b.

45. <http://wiki.answers.com/Q/How_many_seeds_are_there_in_a_pomegranate> retrieved August 20, 2013.

46. Malbim, Song of Songs 4:3.

47. *Babylonian Talmud, Iruvin* 19a.

48. *Babylonian Talmud, Keritot* 6b.

49. Exodus 28:35.

50. Rabbi Moshe Chaim Ephraim Sudilkov, Poland (1748–1800), *Degel Machane Efraim,* on *Parashat Tetzaveh.*

51. Rabbi Moshe Teitelbaum, Hungary (1759–1841), *Yismach Moshe, Genesis* 6b.

52. Rabbi Nachman of Breslau, Ukraine (1772–1810), *The Book of Straight Advice, Awe and Service.*

53. Rabbi Yisrael Meir Kagan, *Chafetz Chaim on the Torah, Parashat Tetzaveh.*

54. Exodus 28:35.

55. Rabbi Moshe ben Ya'acov Cordovero, quoted in the *Introduction* endnote 85 and 88.

56. Rashi, Song of Songs 7:13.

57. Malbim, Song of Songs 7:13.

58. Spikenard, a flowering plant of the Valerian family.

59. Genesis 49:21.

60. Genesis 3:22

61. *Babylonian Talmud, Chagigah* 15b.

62. Ezekiel 1:14.

63. The *Leshem*, Rabbi Shlomo Elyashiv, Lithuania-Israel (1841–1925), ספר לשם שבו ואחלמה /*Sefer Leshem, Sh'vo V'achlama, introduction and gates* 7:5.

64. Genesis 49:21.

65. Rashi, Exodus 23:21.

66. *Babylonian Talmud, Chagigah* 15b.

67. *Babylonian Talmud, Chagigah* 14b: "Four entered the Orchard (*Pardes*). They were Ben Azzai, Ben Zoma, *Acher* [literally, 'the other,' referring to Elisha ben Abuya], and Rabbi Akiva...Acher gazed and cut the plantings [i.e. he became a heretic]. Rabbi Akiva entered in peace and departed in peace..."

68. *Midrash Genesis Rabbah* 98:17.

69. Leviticus 10:2.

70. Genesis 17:1.

71. Song of Songs 8:2.

72. Song of Songs 4:3.

73. *Shulchan Aruch, Orach Chaim* 202:1.

74. The *Rama, Shulchan Aruch, Orach Chaim* 202:1.

75. *Shulchan Aruch, Orach Chaim* 202:3.

76. Ecclesiastes 9:17.

77. Proverbs 3:17.

Olea Europaea ~ זַיִת

Olives

זְיוֹד ~ Yesod – Foundation

Olive Oil ~ שֶׁמֶן זַיִת   Olea Europaea
Yesod ~ יְסוֹד   (Foundation)

וַאֲנִי כְּזַיִת רַעֲנָן בְּבֵית אֱלֹקִים בָּטַחְתִּי בְחֶסֶד אֱלֹקִים עוֹלָם וָעֶד:
(תהלים נב, י)

"But I am like a fresh green olive in the house of G*d. I trust in the love of G*d forever and ever" (Psalms 52:10).

ארץ זית שמן ודבש, זית שמן, יסוד הוא נקרא זית שמן:
(אריז"ל, ספר הליקוטים - פרשת עקב - פרק ח)

"The land of olive oil and honey. Yesod is called olive oil" (Arizal, Sefer HaLikutim, Parashat Ekev, chapter 8).

Attribute: *Yesod* – Foundation/Covenant

Character trait: The ability to overcome temptation (holiness)

Holiday: Chanukah, when we kindle the menorah (candelabra) with olive oil

Weekday: יוֹם שִׁשִׁי/*Yom Shishi* – Sixth day of the week (Friday)

World: יְצִירָה/*Yetzirah* – Formation (hard inedible pit)

Body parts: The male sexual organ, the skin

Shepherd: יוֹסֵף/Yosef

Prophetess: חֻלְדָּה/Chuldah

Numerical value: 417 + 390 = 807, equivalent to the word תַּאֲוַת/*ta'avat* – 'to the utmost bounds'[1]

Mentioned in the Bible 109 times[2]

Meaning of Greek/Latin Name: Oil from Europe

Perek Shirah
The Song of the Universe

...אָז יְרַנְּנוּ עֲצֵי הַיָּעַר מִלִּפְנֵי הַשֵׁם כִּי בָא
לִשְׁפּוֹט אֶת הָאָרֶץ: (דברי הימים א, טז, לג)

The Song of the Trees: "Then the trees of the forest will sing before G*d, Who has come to judge the earth" (I Chronicles 16:33).

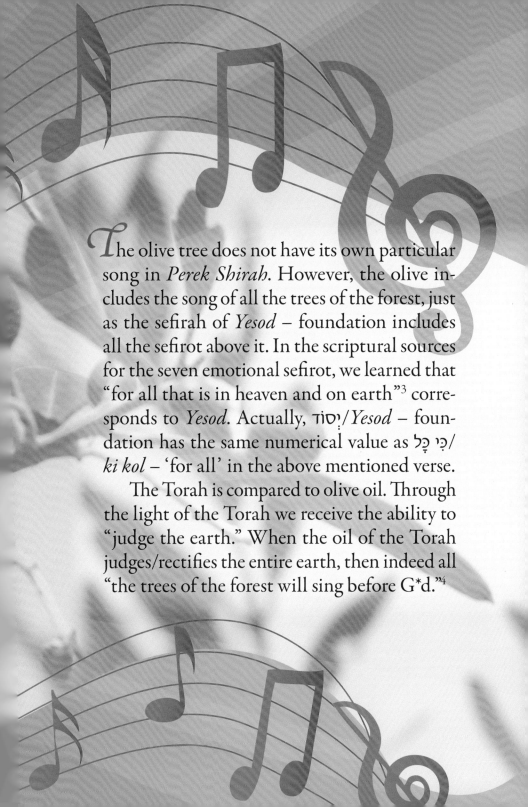

The olive tree does not have its own particular song in *Perek Shirah*. However, the olive includes the song of all the trees of the forest, just as the sefirah of *Yesod* – foundation includes all the sefirot above it. In the scriptural sources for the seven emotional sefirot, we learned that "for all that is in heaven and on earth"[3] corresponds to *Yesod*. Actually, יְסוֹד/*Yesod* – foundation has the same numerical value as כִּי כָל/ *ki kol* – 'for all' in the above mentioned verse.

The Torah is compared to olive oil. Through the light of the Torah we receive the ability to "judge the earth." When the oil of the Torah judges/rectifies the entire earth, then indeed all "the trees of the forest will sing before G*d."[4]

Nutrition Facts and Information about Olives

Mineral Content of Olive Oil[5]

Olive oil contains iron and traces of calcium and potassium.

Vitamin Content of Olive Oil

Olive oil is an excellent source of vitamins E and K.

Mineral Content of Olives[6]

Olives are an excellent source of iron and a good source of potassium and copper. They also contain calcium, and traces of magnesium, phosphorous, selenium and zinc.

Vitamin Content of Olives

Olives are a good source of vitamins A and E. They contain traces of niacin and vitamins C, B6 and K.

Oriental Medicine

According to Chinese medicine, olives affect the spleen and liver. They are sweet, neutral, demulcent, emollient, nutritive and laxative.[7]

Olive Oil and Olives Nutritional Facts/100 g

Minerals	Olive Oil	Olives	RDA	
Calcium	1.00 mg	88.0 mg	0%	9%
Iron	0.56 mg	3.30 mg	7%	41%
Magnesium	0.00 mg	4.00 mg	0%	1%
Phosphorus	0.00 mg	3.00 mg	0%	<1%
Potassium	1.00 mg	8.00 mg	0%	17%
Sodium	2.00 mg	735 mg	0.1%	49%
Zinc	0.00 mg	0.22 mg	0%	2%
Copper	0.00 mg	0.251 mg	0%	28%
Selenium	0.00 mg	0.9 µg	0%	1.5%
Vitamins	**Olive Oil**	**Olives**	**RDA**	
C	0.00 mg	0.9 mg	0%	1%
B1 (Thiamin)	0.00 mg	0.003 mg	0%	0%
B2 (Riboflavin)	0.00 mg	0.00 mg	0%	0%
B3 (Niacin)	0.00 mg	0.037 mg	0%	<1%
B6	0.00 mg	0.009 mg	0%	<1%
B9 (Folate)	0.00 µg	0.00 µg	0%	0%
A	0.00 IU	403 IU	0%	13.5%
E	14.35 mg	1.65 mg	95%	11%
K	60.2 µg	1.4 µg	50%	1%

Olive Oil corresponds to Yesod. The attribute of *Yesod* is to guard the holy, exclusive covenant between the Israelites and Hashem and between husband and wife. Likewise, the olive tree will not accept a graft from another tree; all its shoots are its own.[8] This reflects the purity and perfection of the attribute of *Yesod,* represented by the reproductive system, which brings forth the foundation of new life. Olive oil supports the health of the ovaries.[9] A mixture of olive oil, crushed garlic and cumin eaten before breakfast strengthens sexual performance.[10] Drinking a teaspoon of olive oil every morning before breakfast is helpful against stones in the urinary tract.[11]

Olive Oil – The Foundation of Life

Olive oil is the foundation of most Mediterranean foods and is used in various salad dressings and stir-fried vegetables. It is rich in antioxidants that reduce blood LDL (bad cholesterol), while it simultaneously raises HDL (good cholesterol), thereby protecting against heart disease.[12] Moreover, it protects the heart by lowering blood pressure.[13] Studies have indicated that increasing olive oil consumption may protect against strokes.[14] Several molecular components of olive oil, called phenols, have the potential to protect against cancer,[15] especially of the bowels.[16] Studies further indicate that olive oil is effective in colon cancer prevention.[17] The Mediterranean diet rich in olive oil has been connected in several studies with beneficial anti-aging effects (anti-chronic diseases and increased longevity),[18] reducing the risk of morbidity and mortality.[19] The antioxidants and other micronutrients in olive oil slow down the natural aging process and prevent bone loss and osteoporosis.[20] Thus olives can truly be called 'the foundation of life.'

The Connection between Yesod and the Skin

The sefirah of *Yesod* corresponds not only to the male reproductive organ but also to the skin, as a way of extension. When the foreskin of the male procreative organ is removed during circumcision, it also refines the rest of the skin, making it capable of reflecting spiritual light.[21]

The daughters of the tribe of Asher were known for their beauty because they anointed themselves in olive oil. Some of them even married High Priests who were anointed in olive oil.[22] It is told that Rabbi Chananya remained youthful because his mother rubbed him in olive oil.[23] Also today, our skin receives a natural shine and glow from the enriching olive oil used in cosmetic products and natural herbal therapy.

The Effectiveness of Olive Oil to Heal the Skin

There are vital antioxidants and nutrients in olive oil that make it beneficial for the skin. Olive oil is listed as a functional agent that can prevent and help treat wrinkles.[24] Up to 80% of the content of olive oil is oleic acid, the component in the olive oil contributing to its health benefits. Oleic acid is used as an enhancer for topical products to better permeate the skin's layer.[25] It delivers essential vitamins and nutrients to the skin cells. Topical use of virgin olive oil and coconut oil has moisturizing and antiseptic properties, helpful in treating contact dermatitis.[26]

A Natural Eye-Makeup Remover

Extra-virgin olive oil is safe to use on the face, and it does not clog the skin's pores. It is an excellent alternative for synthetic eye-makeup removers. Use a high-quality olive oil to help reduce the wrinkles around your eyes. Gently massage the olive oil into the skin around your eyes every morning and evening. Do not tug or pull on your skin when applying the olive oil, in order to avoid damaging and stretching the skin in this delicate area.

Rambam teaches us that keeping the bowels soft is one of the most important principles in healing.[27] Therefore, olive oil is a valuable medicinal oil since it loosens the stool and cleans the liver and digestive tract.[28] One or two tablespoons taken in the evening act as an efficient demulcent laxative.[29] A young person may soften his bowels by eating well-cooked salty foods marinated in olive oil early in the morning. Alternatively, he may drink the liquid of boiled spinach or cabbage with olive oil, fish brine and salt.[30] Olive oil supports gastrointestinal health. It aids the digestive process and boosts the metabolism.[31] It soothes the stomach by activating the secretion of bile and pancreatic hormones which help digestion. Olive oil, moreover, heals intestinal pain, strengthens the stomach, and protects against ulcers by coating the stomach.[32] The mono-saturated fats present in olive oil, help break down fat in fat cells, thereby preventing excess weight-gain.[33]

Furthermore, according to Rambam, olive oil alleviates even difficult coughs.[34] Rubbing olive oil on the chest is helpful against coughs, especially for infants. Children's coughs may be successfully treated with olive oil and honey. Olive oil mixed with egg yolk is good against cough and hoarseness.[35]

Olive oil's versatility includes other healing properties as well. Massaging the scalp with olive oil alleviates dandruff.[36] In addition, massages with olive oil have been used to treat muscle pain, joint pain and arthritis.[37] The olives also possess numerous healing properties. Rambam teaches that olives strengthen the stomach and stimulate the appetite.[38] Green olives pickled in lemon and garlic counteract diarrhea.[39]

Assaf the Healer[40] wrote that "olive oil soothes intestinal pains, aids the digestive process, alleviates disorders of the mouth and teeth, and is beneficial for head injuries. Applied to the scalp, it prevents hair loss by strengthening the hair roots. It, moreover, increases hair growth."[41]

Israel – Compared to Olives

"Just as olive oil brings light into the world, so do the people of Israel bring light into the world."[42]

The olive tree laden with fruits is praised for its beauty. However, olives are bitter fruits that become tasty and pleasant only when cured. Since the children of Israel are compared to olives, this implies that Israel's spiritual work is transforming the useless, or even negative, to become good, useful and positive.

"Hashem called your name a leafy olive tree, fair with goodly fruit."[43] Israel is compared to the olive tree because it is perpetually fresh and its leaves are moist the entire year. In the beginning when you performed His will, Hashem called your name a fresh olive. Its leaves never wither, symbolizing that you would always succeed. You would do good and beautiful deeds, compared to the fruits of the olive, as its oil is for the honor of G*d and people...[44]

Just as olive oil does not mix with other liquids, Israel does not mix with idol-worshippers. How do we know this? It states, "I will separate you from the nations to be for Me..."[45] Moreover, even if you put this oil into several liquids it remains on top of them all. Likewise, Israel is on top of all the idol-worshippers as it states, "Hashem your G*d placed you uplifted on all the nations of the earth."[46]

The righteous who take refuge in the protection of G*d are compared to the evergreen olive tree.[47] Rabbi Yehoshua son of Levi asked: "Why is Israel compared to the olive? Just as the olive leaves do not fall from the tree neither in the summer nor winter, likewise Israel can never be completely nullified in this world or in the coming world." Rabbi Yochanan asked: "Why is Israel compared to the olive? Just as the olive only brings forth its oil when beaten, so Israel only returns to be good through difficulties and hardships."[48]

אֶשְׁתְּךָ כְּגֶפֶן פֹּרִיָּה בְּיַרְכְּתֵי בֵיתֶךָ בָּנֶיךָ כִּשְׁתִלֵי זֵיתִים סָבִיב לְשֻׁלְחָנֶךָ:

(תהלים קכח, ג)

"Your wife shall be like a fruitful vine in the recesses of your home, your children [shall be] like olive plants round about your table" (*Psalms* 128:3).

Just as olives cannot be grafted so will none of your children be defective.[49]

The olive tree carries its fruits for nine months, like a woman. As a reward for her modesty, she will not miscarry, but give birth to healthy children after nine months of gestation.[50]

The "olive saplings" are compared to "your children" because they are the shoots that sprout from the roots of the olive tree and protect the trunk. If the tree is cut down, they ensure its continued existence.

The Menorah – The Emblem of Israel

It is evidently by Divine Providence that the secular State of Israel chose as its emblem the image of the Menorah (Candelabra), framed by two olive branches. This image mirrors the prophecy of Zechariah, who had a vision of "a golden menorah... and two olive trees by it, one upon its right side, and the other upon its left side."[51] The Menorah, lit every evening by the Kohanim, would cause the Shechinah to enter the *Mishkan* (Tabernacle) and Temple. Although Hashem has no need for our light, the Menorah was lit in the House of Hashem, for the sake of the honor of the Temple, where the Shechinah dwelled.[52] The Menorah would elevate Israel before the nations, who exclaimed: "How can Israel light before Hashem, Who gives light to all?"[53] Therefore, the emblem of Israel symbolizes how the nation of Israel is meant to be a vessel for the in-dwelling presence of the Shechinah, in our mission to be "a light unto the nations."[54] The Jewish nation is to accomplish this mission by example rather than force, as the prophet teaches: "Not by might, nor by power, but by My spirit, says Hashem of Hosts."[55]

The Power of Oil to Connect the Holy with its Spiritual Essence

Oil has the power of binding several substances together, including the power to connect the physical with the spiritual realm. Therefore, the holiest elements, such as the vessels in the Temple and the Kohanim, were anointed with olive oil.[56] The oil would connect and manifest the physical existence of these holy entities with their otherworldly spiritual essence. The initiation of a new king in Israel, moreover, took place through anointing.[57] This is why every king in Israel is called מָשִׁיחַ/Mashiach which means anointed. It is not surprising that in Yotam's parable, when the trees "went to anoint a king over themselves," the olive was the first to be chosen.[58]

The Torah Compared to Olive Oil

The Torah is compared to olive oil that tastes bitter in the beginning, but becomes sweet in the end. In the same way, living a Torah life can be difficult in the beginning but very rewarding in the end as it states, "Though your beginning was small, yet your end will be very great."[59] Just as the oil keeps continually without spoiling, also the words of Torah are eternal. Just as the light of the olive oil burns perpetually in the Menorah, so does the light of Torah shine forever.[60] Olive trees live longer than most other fruit trees. They may continue to produce fruits for a thousand years. In Israel there are olive trees that are more than two thousand years old!

Crushing the Olives Produces Light

In order to become a Torah scholar, one must at times disregard the needs of the body for the sake of the light of the soul. This corresponds to the process of crushing the olives (the body) in order to produce the olive oil (the Torah).[61]

Why is the Olive Chosen as the Standard Size of Eating?

The standard measure of eating in the Torah that requires an after-blessing is a כְּזַיִת/kezayit – 'like the volume of an olive.' Less than this amount is not called eating according to Jewish law.[62] The olive is chosen as the standard Torah measure of eating, because the olive with its oil clothed within it corresponds to the body with its soul (nefesh). The body, which is connected to forgetfulness, corresponds to the olive, whereas the soul, associated with memory, corresponds to its oil. Since the purpose of eating is to elevate and illuminate the soul from within the body, the definition of eating is according to the size of an olive, representing both body and soul. When we eat in a spiritual way "to satisfy our soul,"[63] we elevate the soul and memory from within the forgetfulness of the body. Therefore, the standard Torah measurement is a kezayit (olive size), since all Torah mitzvot are performed through the soul clothed within the body.[64]

The Olive Leaf, the Dove, Freedom and Healing

וַתָּבֹא אֵלָיו הַיּוֹנָה לְעֵת עֶרֶב וְהִנֵּה עֲלֵה זַיִת טָרָף בְּפִיהָ וַיֵּדַע נֹחַ כִּי קַלּוּ הַמַּיִם
מֵעַל הָאָרֶץ: (בראשית ח, יא)

The dove came in to him toward evening: with a freshly plucked olive leaf in her mouth. So Noach knew that the waters were abated from off the earth (Genesis 8:11).

Rashi explains that "in her mouth" can refer to speech. By picking specifically the olive leaf, the dove was making a statement that she would rather have her food as bitter as an olive but from the hand of G*d, than as sweet as honey but from the hand of mortal men.[65] While the dove is a symbol of peace, in harmony with all creation, the olive is a symbol of freedom and direct connection with Hashem. True freedom is complete healing, when Hashem's light flows freely within us. The dove was bringing healing to the world by means of the "olive leaf plucked in her mouth." This is supported by the fact that the Hebrew word for 'plucked'– טָרָף/taraf, appears only one additional time in the Bible with the same vowels: "Come and let us return to Hashem, for He has torn (טָרָף), and He will heal us."[66] The olive leaf was from the Garden of Eden, and the dove brought it in order to heal Noach from coughing blood due to the battering physical demands of taking care of the animals in the Ark.[67]

The Dove, the Olive Oil and the Chanukah Miracle

"The dove came in to him toward evening…" What difference does it make that the dove returned toward evening? At nighttime, the Ark would need light, and the dove, therefore, brought not only an olive leaf, but also olives to make oil for lighting.[68] "Just as the dove brought light to the world, so must you, who are compared to a dove, bring olive oil and kindle the light before Me, as it says, 'I command you to bring olive oil'"[69] Noach pressed pure olive oil from the olives he received from the dove, and placed it in a sealed jug that he handed over to his firstborn son, Shem. Shem gave this oil to Avraham, who handed it to Yitzchak, who subsequently gave it to his son Ya'acov. On his way to confront Esav, Ya'acov was left alone,[70] because he had to go back by himself in order to retrieve some small flasks which he had forgotten.[71] The special flask, which Ya'acov risked his life for, was none other than the one containing the oil that Noach had pressed. This flask continued to be passed on through the hands of all Seven Shepherds of Israel, until David received it. When he laid the foundation for the Temple, David hid the flask with prophetic insight, seeing that it would be needed during the time of Chanukah. This is the jug of pure olive oil that the Maccabees found in the Temple defiled by the Greeks. During the rededication of the Temple, it burned miraculously in the Menorah for eight days instead of one. This oil was especially appropriate for the miracle of Chanukah, since it had absorbed each of Israel's seven shepherds' approaches to divine service. Therefore, it was particularly fitting for lighting the seven branches of the Menorah.[72]

Fruit of Redemption

The olive tree, which is the first tree recorded after the destruction of the flood, is the fruit of redemption. Its foliage is evergreen and its oil lights eternally, even during exile through the holy menorah of Chanukah.[73] The bitterness of the olive alludes to a higher realm beyond what can be revealed as sweet in this world. When Hashem created Original Light, He saw that it was too good to be revealed for the people of this world. Therefore, He hid it away for the righteous in the World to Come.[74] We can get a glimpse of this hidden light (*Ohr Haganuz*) every year on Chanukah, when we light the *Chanukiah*, the Chanukah lamp. After the destruction of both Temples, only the Chanukah lights, representing the flames of olive oil burning in the holy Menorah, accompany us throughout our spiritual darkness and light the way to redemption.

The Land of Asher – Flowing with Olives

The land of the tribe of Asher was especially rich with olive orchards, as it is today. Both Ya'acov and Moshe blessed Asher with an abundance of olive oil. The Midrash describes the flag of Asher with a picture of an olive tree.[75] Asher's land encompasses the Galilee, and stretches over the northwestern part of Israel, bordering the Mediterranean Sea to the west. This territory includes Mount Carmel, an especially fertile and bountiful mountain. It produced such large amounts of olive oil in biblical times that Asher became exceedingly wealthy, as the leader in the olive oil trade. The kings of all the neighboring nations would pay a special tribute to Asher in order to have the right to anoint themselves with their oil, as it states:

מֵאָשֵׁר שְׁמֵנָה לַחְמוֹ וְהוּא יִתֵּן מַעֲדַנֵּי מֶלֶךְ: (בראשית מט, כ)

"Out of Asher his bread shall be fat, and he shall give dainties to kings" (Genesis 49:20).

The people of Israel also showered blessings upon the tribe of Asher in gratitude for the oil it provided. Due to the abundant blessing of olives, Asher would crush them with special shoes made of iron and brass in order to allow the oil to run out and flow like rivers to supply olive oil for the entire nation of Israel as it states:

וּלְאָשֵׁר אָמַר בָּרוּךְ מִבָּנִים אָשֵׁר יְהִי רְצוּי אֶחָיו וְטֹבֵל בַּשֶּׁמֶן רַגְלוֹ׃
בַּרְזֶל וּנְחֹשֶׁת מִנְעָלֶךָ... (דברים לג, כד-כה)

"Be Asher blessed by sons: let him be acceptable to his brothers, and let him dip his foot in oil. Your shoes shall be iron and brass..." (*Deuteronomy* 33:24–25).

Growing and Harvesting

The wild olive grows in the groves of Upper Galilee and Carmel. It is a prickly shrub producing small fruits. There are many varieties of cultivated olives, some suitable for oil, and others for fruit. A part cut off from an olive tree may take root and grow into a new tree. Its foliage is dense and when it ages, the fairly tall trunk acquires a unique pattern of twists and protuberances on its bark. This gives a beautifully grained effect, making the wood suitable for small articles and ornaments. The trunk of the adult olive tree is hollow, which renders it unsuitable for manufacturing furniture.

The fruit, which is rich in oil, is usually green at first, but finally turns black. After ripening, the fruit is harvested either by beating the branches with sticks, or by hand picking. The former way, used in biblical times, is quicker, but many branches fall off, diminishing the harvest. The fruit of the fallen branches are to be a gift to the "convert, orphan and widow."[76] The second method was more common during the Talmudic era and was termed מָסִיק/*masik* – 'regular picking,'[77] drawing the fingers down the branches in a milking motion to make the olives fall into the hand. By this method the harvested olives remain whole, whereas the beaten olives are bruised by the beating.

Rabbi Nachman's Teachings on Eating Unripe Fruits

צָרִיךְ לִזָּהֵר מְאֹד, שֶׁלֹּא לֶאֱכֹל פְּרִי, שֶׁלֹּא נִתְבַּשְּׁלָה כָּל צָרְכָּהּ. וּכְמוֹ שֶׁאָסוּר
לָקֹץ אִילָן בְּלֹא זְמַנּוֹ, כְּמוֹ שֶׁאָמְרוּ רַבּוֹתֵינוּ, זִכְרוֹנָם לִבְרָכָה (בָּבָא - בַּתְרָא
כו), כֵּן אָסוּר לִתְלֹשׁ פְּרִי קֹדֶם בִּשּׁוּלָהּ וְכֵן אָסוּר לְאָכְלָהּ. וְהָאוֹכֵל פְּרִי קֹדֶם
גְּמַר בִּשּׁוּלָהּ יְכוֹלָה לְהַזִּיק לוֹ מְאֹד לְנִשְׁמָתוֹ, כִּי יוּכַל לְאַבֵּד נַפְשׁוֹ עַל - יְדֵי
- זֶה. כִּי הַפְּרִי כָּל זְמַן שֶׁהִיא צְרִיכָה לְהִתְגַּדֵּל, יֵשׁ לָהּ כֹּחַ הַמּוֹשֵׁךְ, כִּי הִיא
צְרִיכָה חִיּוּת לְהִתְגַּדֵּל, וְעַל - כֵּן בְּוַדַּאי יֵשׁ לָהּ כֹּחַ הַמּוֹשֵׁךְ, שֶׁמּוֹשֶׁכֶת יְנִיקָתָהּ
וְחִיּוּתָהּ וּכְשֶׁתּוֹלְשִׁין אוֹתָהּ קֹדֶם זְמַנָּהּ, קֹדֶם שֶׁנִּתְבַּשְּׁלָה עֲדַיִן כָּל צָרְכָּהּ,
עֲדַיִן יֵשׁ לָהּ כֹּחַ הַמּוֹשֵׁךְ, כִּי כְּשֶׁמִּתְבַּשֶּׁלֶת כָּל צָרְכָּהּ, שׁוּב פָּסַק מִמֶּנָּה כֹּחַ
הַמּוֹשֵׁךְ, כִּי אֵינָהּ צְרִיכָה עוֹד לִמְשֹׁךְ חִיּוּת אֲבָל כְּשֶׁצְּרִיכָה לְהִתְבַּשֵּׁל עוֹד,
עֲדַיִן יֵשׁ לָהּ הַכֹּחַ הַמּוֹשֵׁךְ.

וְעַל - כֵּן זֶה הָאוֹכְלָהּ קֹדֶם גְּמַר בִּשּׁוּלָהּ, תּוּכַל הַפְּרִי לִמְשֹׁךְ לְעַצְמָהּ
חִיּוּת הַנֶּפֶשׁ שֶׁל זֶה הָאָדָם, מֵאַחַר שֶׁעֲדַיִן יֵשׁ לְהַפְּרִי כֹּחַ הַמּוֹשֵׁךְ כַּנַּ"ל,
עַל - כֵּן תּוּכַל הַפְּרִי לְהַמְשִׁיךְ לְעַצְמָהּ חִיּוּת נַפְשׁוֹ, וְיוּכַל לְאַבֵּד נַפְשׁוֹ.

וְעִם כָּל זֶה, אִם מְבֹרָךְ הַבְּרָכָה שֶׁל הַפְּרִי בְּכַוָּנָה וּבְיִרְאַת - שָׁמַיִם, אֲזַי יוּכַל
לְהִנָּצֵל מִזֶּה, וְגַם אִם הוּא חָזָק בְּיוֹתֵר בַּעֲבוֹדַת ה', יוּכַל גַּם - כֵּן לְהוֹצִיא עוֹד
חִיּוּת מֵהַפְּרִי וְלִמְצֹא שָׁם אֲבֵדוֹת. כִּי יֵשׁ דְּבָרִים אֲבוּדִים, וְיֵשׁ בָּזֶה דְּבָרִים
נִפְלָאִים, סוֹדוֹת נִסְתָּרִים וְנוֹרָאִים מְאֹד, רָזִין עִלָּאִין. וְהָעִקָּר, שֶׁהָאָדָם צָרִיךְ
לִזָּהֵר מְזֶה מְאֹד, הַיְנוּ שֶׁלֹּא לֶאֱכֹל פְּרִי, קֹדֶם שֶׁנִּתְבַּשְּׁלָה כָּל צָרְכָּהּ:

וְדַע, כִּי גַם כְּשֶׁמְּבַשְּׁלִין הַפֵּרוֹת בְּבֵיתוֹ אֵינוֹ מוֹעִיל לָזֶה, אֲבָל אִם הַפֵּרוֹת
שֶׁלֹּא נִתְבַּשְּׁלוּ כָּל צָרְכָּן עַל הָאִילָן, הֵם מֻנָּחִים אֵיזֶה זְמָן, עַד שֶׁנַּעֲשִׂין
מְבֻשָּׁלִין מֵאֲלֵיהֶן בְּתָלוּשׁ, זֶה מוֹעִיל, וּמֻתָּר לְאָכְלָן. וְזֶה דּוֹמֶה כְּמוֹ הָאָדָם
שֶׁהוּא יָגֵעַ וְהוּא מְרַחֵף רְחִיפוֹת הַרְבֵּה בְּפִיו (שְׁקוֹרִין סָאפִּין), עַד אֲשֶׁר יָנוּחַ,
כְּמוֹ - כֵּן אֵלּוּ הַפֵּרוֹת שֶׁנִּתְלְשׁוּ, קֹדֶם שֶׁנִּתְבַּשְּׁלוּ כָּל צָרְכָּן, צָרִיךְ לְהַמְתִּין עַד
שֶׁיָּנוּחוּ מֵרְחִיפָתָן, וְאָז יֵשׁ הֶתֵּר לְאָכְלָן. וְהַדְּבָרִים סְתוּמִים:
(לִקּוּטֵי מוֹהֲרַ"ן - מַהֲדוּרָא בָּתְרָא סִימָן פח)

We must be very careful not to eat any fruit which has not completely ripened, just as it is forbidden to cut down a tree before
its time, as our rabbis of blessed memory taught.[78] Likewise, it is
forbidden to pick a fruit before it is ripe, and it is also forbidden
to eat it. Eating a fruit before it has fully ripened can severely
damage a person's soul. It may even cause him to lose his soul.

The reason is that as long as the fruit still needs to grow, it has the power of drawing [out the nutrients of the tree]; for it needs this life force in order to grow. When it is picked before its time, before it has completely ripened, it still has the power of drawing. Only when it has fully ripened does this power of drawing end, as it no longer needs to draw any further vitality.

Therefore, when a person eats a fruit before it has fully ripened, then the fruit can draw to itself the vitality of the soul of this person. Still, if he blesses the blessing over the fruit with focused intention and awe of Heaven, then he can be saved from this. Likewise, if he is very strong in his divine service, he may also be able to extract further vitality from the fruit and find there lost matters that exist. This includes wondrous matters, very amazing hidden secrets – upper secrets. The main thing is that a person needs to be very careful with this, not to eat a fruit before it is fully ripe.

Know that even if he cooks the fruits, it doesn't help. However, it does help to allow the fruits, which have not completely ripened on the tree, to ripen completely by themselves after being picked. This is similar to a person who is exhausted from exertion and is gasping and heaving until he rests. Likewise, it is necessary to wait until these fruits have rested from their exhaustion, since they were picked before being completely ripe. Only then is it permitted to eat them. These matters are concealed (Rabbi Nachman, *Likutei Moharan*, Second Edition, 88).

Explanation: Rabbi Nachman explains that is extremely damaging to eat unripe fruits, because they are meant to draw further nourishment from their mother tree. If the fruits are picked before they reach full term and before they have completed extracting all the nourishment needed from the tree, then they will attempt to extract this nourishment from the person eating them. This is especially true because a human being is compared to a tree.[79] Therefore, if we eat these unripe fruits, instead of receiving nourishment from them, the fruits will extract nourishment from us. Still, it is permitted to eat fruits which were picked before their time and left to ripen, because after a rest period their power of drawing will settle and they will no longer damage the person who eats them. In addition, reciting the blessing over the fruit with great focused intention (kavanah) can counteract the negative effect of unripe fruit. Likewise, a person who keeps the mitzvot very carefully may be able to extract lost hidden sparks even from these unripe fruits.

Based on the teachings of Rabbi Nachman it seems that black olives are healthier than green, since most often the green olives are actually unripe olives, which when left on the tree will eventually turn black. However, the color of an olive is not always related to its state of maturity. Although many olives start off green and turn black when fully ripe, some olives remain green even when fully ripe, while others start off black and remain black.

Women, Olive Oil and Wisdom

וַיִּשְׁלַח יוֹאָב תְּקוֹעָה וַיִּקַּח מִשָּׁם אִשָּׁה חֲכָמָה... (שמואל ב, יד, ב)

"Yoav sent to Tekoa and took from there a wise woman..."
(II *Samuel* 14:2).

When King David's general, Yoav, wanted to effect the reconciliation between David and his son Avshalom, he sent a messenger to Tekoa to fetch a wise woman from there. This wise woman would play out a cleverly devised script, pleading with the king to save her own son, and then draw a parallel to the king's relationship with Avshalom.[80] The fact that "Yoav sent to Tekoa" indicates that this particular place was conducive to finding a wise woman.[81] The Talmud explains that Yoav was seeking a wise woman from Tekoa, because the abundant olive oil consumed there made it a place of wisdom.[82] Tekoa, which was possibly a town in the upper Galilee, within the territory of the tribe of Asher,[83] was the source of the best quality olive oil fitting to be used in the Temple for lighting the Menorah. The light of wisdom emanates from the Menorah to the sanctuary and from there to the entire world. Since the Menorah was on the south side of the Tabernacle,[84] the south, including the south of the Land of Israel, is linked with wisdom, as our Sages teach: "One who wants to grow wise should go south..."[85] This is a support for the second opinion regarding the location of the biblical Tekoa, south of Jerusalem, near the current settlement bearing that name.[86]

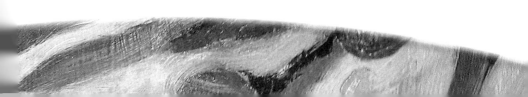

Defining the Quality of Olive Oil

The Oil of the Land

There are numerous kinds of olive oil on the market. It's hard to choose wisely between the concern for health and the need to limit extra expense. Local produce is always preferred, especially if you live in Israel. For those who live in the Diaspora, it is recommended to connect with the Land of Israel by partaking of its produce, especially when it comes to the seven holy species of Israel. Produce grown in the Holy Land conveys its holiness to the highest degree. Yet, it is not simple to choose between the several different kinds of olive oil available.

The Process of Olive Oil Production

What is the difference between refined and cold-pressed olive oil? Is extra virgin olive oil really worth its price? The less the olive oil is handled the better quality and health benefits it retains. Most vegetable oils are generally extracted through petroleum-based chemical solvents. They are, therefore, highly refined in order to remove their impurities. Along with the impurities, refining removes taste, color and nutrients. On the other hand, extra virgin olive oil is essentially 'freshly squeezed' olives, with its natural color, taste, nutrients and vitamins.

Cold-Pressed versus Refined

Producing cold-pressed olive oil today is similar to the ancient method from biblical times. The olives are hand harvested and taken to the mill after a day or two to be crushed into a mash by giant stones weighing several tons. The olive mash is then spread onto thin mats. These mats are placed into a machine press which applies several hundred pounds of pressure. If no heat is applied in the pressing, the oil is 'cold-pressed.' Oil extracted in this way is called 'virgin' olive oil, because it is pure, unrefined and unprocessed. The term virgin olive oil indicates that the oil is extracted 24–48 hours after harvest, avoiding heat, light and air during processing and storage. These precautions protect heat-sensitive phyto-chemicals and help prevent the formation of unhealthy free fatty acids (FFA) that irritate the skin. The amount of FFA present defines the degree of virginity of the oil. The term 'extra virgin olive oil' is used to emphasize that the oil is pressed cold immediately after harvest.

כָּתִית מְעוּלָה/*katit me'uleh* – **Extra virgin** olive oil from the first cold-pressing of the olives is the highest quality of olive oil. Since it is less processed, it has a cloudy look and contains higher levels of antioxidants, particularly vitamin E. כָּתִית/*katit* – **Virgin** olive oil is the next best choice. It, too, is cold-pressed, but is from the second pressing. **Olive oil** or 'pure' olive oil is made from low quality virgin olive oils which must be refined using chemical processes in order to make these oils fit for consumption. The resulting refined olive oil is largely colorless and tasteless. Therefore, a percentage of quality virgin olive oil is blended into this olive oil to provide color and taste. **Olive pomace oil** is residue oil extracted by chemical solvents from

prior pressed olive mash. It needs to be highly-refined in order to remove chemical impurities. Like 'pure' olive oil, refined olive pomace oil is enriched with virgin olive oil. Since it is cheaper, it is widely used in restaurants. **Lampante oil** is olive oil not suitable as food, but is used for oil-burning lamps. Lampante oil is mostly used in the industrial market.

The Olive Oil in the Temple

It is interesting to note that the biblical lamp oil – the olive oil used for the Menorah in the Temple – had to be of the highest quality, even superior to today's extra virgin olive oil. The Torah instructs the children of Israel "to bring clear olive oil beaten for light, to set up the lamp continually."[87] Rashi explains the word כָּתִית/*katit* – 'beaten' (used today to refer to virgin olive oil) as follows: "He pounds the olives in a mortar, but must not grind them in a mill, so that there may be no sediment."[88] He further explains the continued processing of olive oil: "After he has thus extracted the first drop of oil, he may bring the olives into the mill and grind them. The second oil [obtained by grinding] is unfit for use in the candelabrum but is permissible for meal offerings..."[89] For this reason, even today, when lighting the *Chanukiah*, it is recommended to use the very best olive oil. Using the highest quality olive oil for the lights of Chanukah is a *segulah* (spiritual remedy) for begetting righteous children, as it states, "...your children [shall be] like olive plants round about your table."[90] Rabbanit Yamima Mizrachi further explains that although it is permissible to use any kind of oil for the Chanukah candelabra, the Chanukiah that we have today is in commemoration of the Menorah in the Temple, which used only the purest olive oil. Therefore, if we want all the spiritual remedies of the Menorah in the Temple – righteous children, good memory, wisdom, good vision, spiritual and physical health, it is important to use the very best quality olive oil for the Chanukah lights.[91]

Free Fatty Acids and Acidity (FFA)

We often hear about the importance of low acidity in extra virgin olive oil. The lower the percentage of free fatty acid (FFA), the higher the quality of the olive oil. Olive oil contains oleic acid, also known as monounsaturated omega-9 fatty acid. This oleic acid has many health benefits such as decreasing the LDL cholesterol and preventing malignant diseases, especially colon and breast cancer.[92] Therefore, it can be confusing to learn that olive oil with the lowest acidity is the healthiest. We need to understand that oleic acid can be found in two forms: bound and unbound. Bound oleic acid is when the three fatty acid chains of oleic acid are connected to a glycerol backbone. (Imagine your ribs connected to your spine.)Unbound oleic acid occurs when the oleic acid chain is no longer connected to the glycerol backbone. (Imagine that your ribs are no longer connected to your spine. What a mess!) Bound oleic acid provides the desired health benefits. Unbound oleic acid is actually bad for you. Low acidity olive oil contains bound oleic acid. Olive oil with high acidity has the unbound form of oleic acid. When the fatty acid chains in oleic acid become detached from the glycerol backbone, they float around freely, therefore, they are known as free fatty acids. Free fatty acids (FFA) lower the pH of the olive oil, making it very acidic. Oil extracted carelessly or from poor quality olives suffers from a very significant breakdown of the oleic acid into free fatty acids. High free fatty acidity in the oil may be caused by fruit fly infestation, fungal diseases, damage during olive harvest, delays between harvesting and pressing, and careless extraction methods. Thus, the free fatty acidity is a direct measure of the quality of the oil, and reflects the care taken from blossoming and fruit until the olive oil bottles appear on the market. In summary, it is important to buy low acidity olive oil, because high acidity olive oil contains toxic free fatty acids instead of the healthy bound form of oleic acid.[93] Extra virgin olive oil has the lowest acidity of unrefined olive oils.

Definition of the Different Grades of Olive Oil Available

	Extra virgin olive oil	Virgin olive oil	Pure olive oil or just olive oil	Olive pomace oil	Refined olive oil	Lampante (Lamp Oil)
Extracting Process	Cold-pressed	Cold-pressed	Mixed refined and cold-pressed	Refined and blended with virgin oil	Refined	Refined
Oleic Acidity (FFA)	<0.8 %	<1.5%	<2.%	<1.0%	0.3%	3.3 %
Flavor	Superior	Good	Lacking	Neutral	Lacking	Sharp
Odor	Superior	Good	Lacking	Neutral	Lacking	Sharp

Olive Oil's Heat Resistance

It is healthiest to minimize fried food, and consume all oils raw, since heating oil to a certain temperature during cooking may alter its molecular level, causing it to release free radicals and possible harmful trans-fats. Nevertheless, because it is highly monounsaturated, olive oil is resistant to the negative effects of heating such as oxidation and

hydrogenation. It has one of the highest smoking points, making it more suitable for stir-fry than most other oils such as unrefined sunflower and safflower oil. The latter have a smoking point of 225° F (107° C), whereas unrefined olive oil has a smoking point of 320° F (160° C).

Olives Cause Forgetfulness, While Olive Oil Improves Memory

Our Sages had a tradition that olives cause forgetfulness, while olive oil strengthens and sharpens the memory. Rabbi Yochanan said, "Just as olives make a person forget the learning of seventy years, so does olive oil bring back the learning of seventy years."[94] This is why the Land of Israel is not praised for the olives themselves, but only for what is produced from them: the oil,[95] which brings back the learning.[96] Rabbeinu Bachaya explains that olives cause forgetfulness because the olive tree, unlike other trees, does not have a heart. [Its trunk doesn't have the regular distinct pattern of rings]. Therefore, olives close the heart, and make a person forget his learning.[97] Olive oil is designated for wisdom and intelligence, because it gives light, which is similar to the intellect. The olive containing the light-giving oil has the opposite quality. It is material, causing the light of the oil to be suppressed by the body of olive. Therefore, eating olives without their oil makes us forget our learning. However, eating olive oil brings wisdom, for it is complete light.[98]

There are those who say that only raw olives cause forgetfulness, but not pickled or cooked olives. Others say that in all these forms olives cause forgetfulness. It has become a custom to only eat olives with a drop of olive oil sprinkled on them, thereby preventing the olives from causing forgetfulness.[99]

Overcoming the Forgetfulness of the Olive

The holy Arizal teaches that when we meditate with the proper intention (kavanah) while eating olives, we can rectify them to strengthen our memory rather than causing forgetfulness. The proper kavanah for eating olives is to visualize the three letters of Hashem's name — *yud, vav* and *heh* — and for each letter the following names of Hashem: *Elokim, Kel* and *Matz*patz*,[100] which together have the numerical value of 417, equal to that of זַיִת/*zayit* – the Hebrew word for olive.

י/*Yud*	ה/*Hey*	ו/*Vav*
אלקים/*Elokim*	א-ל/*Kel*	מצ-פץ/*Matz*patz* (י-ה-ו-ה)
86	31	300

According to the את-בש/*atbash* system of numerical transformation where the first letter of the alphabet is interchanged with the last, the second with the next to the last etc., the name Matz*patz equals the four-lettered name of Hashem *yud,-hey-vav-hey*. Matz*patz consists of the following Hebrew letter interchanges: *mem* with *yud, tzadi* with *heh* and *peh* with *vav*. The Hebrew word for oil – שֶׁמֶן/*shemen*, equals in atbash the letters ב-י-ט/*beit-yud-tet*, (*shin* equals *beit, mem* equals *yud, nun* equals *tet*). Together *beit, yud* and *tet* have the numerical value of 21, which is also the numerical value of the three letters of Hashem's name: *yud, heh* and *vav*.[101]

⁘ A Taste of Kabbalah – The Secret of Rectified Sexuality and Memory

וארץ הפסיק הענין ליסוד ומלכות שמחוברים יחד. וזית שמן יסוד, כי זית
משכח ושמן מזכיר. והתחלת רע הוא בשכחה כמו שנאמר והיה אם שכח
תשכח וגו', והשורש הוא באבר היסוד כמו שאמרנו במקום אחר דבעוון
מלא אפילו חסיד שבחסידים כו' זהו העטיו של נחש דנגזר מיתה שהוא
העדר קיום באיש ובו הוא כח ההולדה דקיום במין ועל ידי פרי הבטן הוא
הממתקת היסוד ומכחם הזכרון... דהממתקת היסוד בחכמה. לתתא ט' הוא
יסוד ומתתא לעילא ט' הוא חכמה... כל המקרא לשיעורין פי' כטעם נודע
בשערים בעלה. השיעורין הוא קו המדה דהשגת השם יתברך בלב ורוב
שיעורים בזיתים, כי בו הוא סוד קו המידה ורוב שיעור ההשגה הוא כפי
נקיונו ביסוד: (פרי צדיק קונטרס עת האוכל - אות יג)

The [word] אֶרֶץ/*eretz* – land [interspersed between the first
five species and the second two] made a break before *Yesod*
and *Malchut,* which are connected. The olive oil is *Yesod,* for
the olive causes forgetfulness, while the oil strengthens the
memory. The beginning of evil is through forgetting, as it states,
"...it shall be if you surely forget."[102] The root [of forgetfulness]
is in the limb of the *Yesod,* as it states in another place. Even
the most pious of the pious cannot be appointed a guardian
over sexual morality.[103] This is the bite of the snake, which
caused the decree of death, including the loss of self-perpet-
uation and of the power of procreation which establishes the
species. By means of the fruit of the womb, humanity rectifies
Yesod and causes remembrance... The rectification of *Yesod*
is in *Chochmah,* which is the ninth sefirah from below, and
Yesod is the ninth sefirah from above... All Scriptural mention
of שִׁעוּרִים/*shiurim* – measures, is according to the meaning
of "her husband is known in the שְׁעָרִים/*she'arim* – gates."[104]
The שַׁעַר/*sha'ar* – gate/measure is the outline for grasping
Hashem in the heart, and most of the measures are through

olives, for it is the secret of the outline of measure. Most measure and comprehension is according to its purity in *Yesod*. (Rav Tzadok HaKohen of Lublin, *P'ri Tzadik, Et HaOchel* 13).

Explanation: The verse describing the Seven Fruits of Israel is broken up into two parts, with the word אֶרֶץ/*eretz* – 'land.' separating between them.[105] The first five fruits are referred to the way they grow. The second part of the verse mentions only their derivatives: "olive oil and honey." Rav Tzadok explains that the reason for this division is that two species mentioned after the word 'land,' olive oil (associated with *Yesod*), and date honey (associated with *Malchut*) are connected. This is why all Jewish kings, including King Mashiach, are anointed with the pure olive oil of *Yesod*.[106]

Moreover, olives and dates are connected with the Land of Israel, which is called *Malchut*,[107] because these were fruits the Israelites did not have in Egypt. They are written separately because the Land of Israel is distinguished through them. When the Jews complained in the desert, they mentioned fig, grape and pomegranate, but not olive and date.[108] This is a proof that they didn't have those in Egypt.[109]

Olive oil is connected with wisdom. *Yesod* – the ninth sefirah – is rectified specifically by the sefirah of *Chochmah* (wisdom), which is also the ninth sefirah, when counting from the lowest sefirah of *Malchut*. This connection between *Yesod* and *Chochmah* explains the reason why an olive size is the standard measure in Jewish law. Due to this connection, *Yesod* is the gate of understanding and gives the outline and parameter through which everything can be measured and grasped. The purity of *Yesod* determines our ability to comprehend Hashem. This also explains why wisdom-giving olive oil, rather than plain olives, is associated with rectified *Yesod*. Olives, on the other hand, cause us "to surely forget Hashem"[110] which is the beginning of all evil.

This evil stems from inappropriate sexuality, connected with fallen *Yesod*. Even the most pious person is not immune to sexual temptation.[111] We are all affected by the negative inclination originating with the primordial serpent that caused death in the world and further sought the absence of people. By initiating the desire for illicit sexuality, the serpent attempted to cause the breakdown of *Yesod* and prevent holy procreation, namely the fulfillment of the first mitzvah, "be fruitful and multiply," the 'foundation' of the Torah. Bearing children and raising a Jewish family rectifies *Yesod* and causes remembrance of Hashem to be passed down from generation to generation, leading to the *Malchut* of the son of David, Mashiach, the anointed one.[112]

הרואה זיתים בחלום זוטרי פרי ורבי וקאי עסקיה כזיתים והני מילי פרי אבל אילני הויין ליה בנים מרובין שנאמר בָּנֶיךָ כִּשְׁתִלֵי זֵיתִים וגו' איכא דאמרי הרואה זית בחלום שם טוב יוצא לו שנאמר זַיִת רַעֲנָן יְפֵה פְרִי תֹאַר קָרָא הָשֵׁם שְׁמֵךְ הרואה שמן זית בחלום יצפה למאור תורה שנאמר וְיִקְחוּ אֵלֶיךָ שֶׁמֶן זַיִת זָךְ...

He who sees olives in a dream, if they are small his business will become fruitful and multiply like olives. This is if he sees the fruit, but if he sees [olive] trees he will have many children, as it states: "Your children are like olive plants, surrounding your table."[113] *Some say: One who sees an olive in his dream, will acquire a good name, as it is written, "A succulent olive, beautiful exquisite fruit, has Hashem called your name."*[114] *He who sees olive oil in a dream, should anticipate the light of the Torah, as it states, "That they bring you pure olive oil beaten for the light"*[115] *(Babylonian Talmud, Berachot 57a).*

Olive Recipes

General Tip about Storing and Using Olive Oil

Olive oil, like other oils, can easily go rancid when exposed to air, light, or high temperatures.[116] To get the most health benefit and flavor from your olive oil, keep it in a cool dark place, tightly sealed. To further protect the olive oil from the damaging effect of light, store the oil in dark glass bottles or other opaque containers. Try to minimize frying but add olive oil generously to foods after cooking.

FLAVORED OLIVE OIL
Useful and decorative

1. You can make your own flavored/medicated olive oil by filling a glass jar with your favorite herb such as sage, rosemary, thyme or any desired mixture.

2. Pour extra virgin olive oil all the way to the top of the jar, making it airtight to prevent fungus from forming.

3. Leave the herbs steeped in the oil for ten days to two weeks so the oil will absorb the herbal flavor.

Beware of adding fresh herbs and vegetables with high water content to the oil, as this may promote the growth of fungus and bacteria, especially if the herbs are not completely covered by the oil.

If you are using vegetables with high water content in your oil such as garlic, lemon peel, fresh peppers and fresh herbs, keep your flavored oil in the refrigerator and use it within a week.

If you dry the herbs in the sun or in a food dehydrator you may leave whole sprigs of thyme, rosemary, dried peppers, etc. to decorate the inside of the bottle without needing refrigeration.

GARLIC OIL

Fill a decorative 1-liter bottle with extra virgin olive oil.

Add a clean head of garlic (whole if desired), and leave it to marinate for a few days. Strain off the garlic.

This oil is also helpful to cure your children's and friends' ear-aches: Dip a cotton ball in the garlic oil, insert it in the affected ear and leave it overnight.

Flavored olive oils and dressings make great gifts. They can also be included in your *mishloach manot* (Purim gifts).

OLIVE OIL WITH ZA'ATAR (HYSSOP MIXTURE)

An easy dip to complement your bread and salads

  ½ cup extra virgin olive oil
  ¼ cup za'atar mixture

Mix the olive oil and za'atar mixture well with a spoon and pour into a nice glass jar, which you can keep on your dinner table, ready to sprinkle over your whole wheat bread, grains and vegetables.

Instead of serving butter, fill a small condiment dish with extra virgin olive oil and za'atar for use on grains, bread and potatoes, or drizzle it over sautéed vegetables before serving.

MEDITERRANEAN SALAD DRESSING
Use extra virgin olive oil in all your salad dressings

¼ cup fresh lemon juice
¼ cup extra virgin olive oil
2 tablespoons techina
3–4 cloves of crushed garlic
2 teaspoons tamari soy sauce
½ teaspoon sea salt
freshly ground black pepper to taste

Combine all ingredients in a bowl and whisk until well blended. Techina is the secret ingredient which helps keep the oil and lemon juice from separating.

Using fresh lemon juice is much healthier and makes a big difference in taste for those who are sensitive.
Store unused dressing in covered container in the refrigerator for up to one week for ultimate freshness.

Variation
Substitute the lemon juice with apple cider, balsamic or wine vinegar.

PESTO

Green garden goodness

- 2 cups fresh basil, parsley or cilantro
- 4–8 cloves of garlic according to taste
- ¼ cup extra virgin olive oil
- 1 tablespoon sea salt
- ½ cup of whole pine nuts which may be substituted with sunflower seeds (optional)

Process everything in the food processor with the S-blade for about four to five minutes.

The exact amounts are not important, but if you add more olive oil, the pesto will be more liquid. Experiment with how much salt and garlic suits your taste.

OLIVE BEAN DIP

An inexpensive protein-filled dish

1 cup of your favorite beans
¼-½ cup of chopped olives
¼ cup extra virgin olive oil
4 cloves of garlic
A handful of fresh sprigs of dill
½-1 teaspoon paprika
½ teaspoon basil
Pepper to taste

1. Cook the beans until soft.

2. Place the beans in the food processor with the remaining ingredients except the olives.

3. Purée with the S-blade.

4. Add the chopped olives.

5. Chop the dill and add to the mixture.

6. Adjust the seasoning and serve as a dip.

GARLIC FLAVORED OLIVE DIP

A great parve alternative to garlic butter

> One head of finely crushed garlic
> ⅓ cup finely crushed green olives
> ⅓–½ cup of extra virgin olive oil
> A handful of fresh parsley sprigs
> (You may substitute 1 tablespoon dried parsley)

1. Cover the garlic cloves with the olive oil and process in food processor.
2. Chop the parsley and add to the mixture.
3. Add the remaining ingredients.

Don't add salt as cured olives are very salty.

GREEN OLIVE DIP
A flavorful dip for your Shabbat table

> 1 can of pitted green olives (560 g/1.4 lb.)
> 4 cloves of garlic
> ¼ cup extra virgin olive oil
> ¼ cup fresh parsley
> ¼ cup wild greens (lamb's quarters, chickweeds, mallow leaves)

1. Rinse olives in water to remove some of their extra saltiness.
2. Place remaining ingredients in food processor.
3. Purée with the S-blade.
4. Season with freshly ground black pepper to taste and serve as a dip.

Variation

Exchange the parsley with cilantro, basil or a mixture of all of them. Exchange wild greens with any greens like Swiss chard or spinach.

OLIVE WALNUT SPREAD
A protein rich filling spread for your vegetarian Shabbat guests

> 1 can of pitted green olives
> 4 cloves of garlic
> ½–1 cup walnuts
> ¼ cup extra virgin olive oil

Purée in food processor and serve as a dip.
The amounts do not have to be exact. Depending on your preference you can add more or less walnuts.

FLAVORFUL MASHED POTATOES
A very simple popular side dish

> 6 cooked potatoes
> ¼ cup extra virgin olive oil
> 8–10 cloves of garlic
> ¼ cup extra virgin olive oil
> 1–2 chopped onions
> Sea salt and pepper to taste

1. Sauté onions in olive oil, add the garlic.

2. Purée cooked potatoes and extra virgin olive oil together

3. Add roasted garlic, sautéd onions and seasoning.

Children and adults alike will enjoy these exceptionally delicious garlic mashed potatoes.

CURED OLIVES

Transforming the bitterness of olives

Olives are too bitter to be eaten straight off the tree and must be processed to reduce their inherent bitterness, which can be cured either through water, brine, dry salt or lye. Commercially processed olives are treated with a lye solution to remove their bitterness; they are then packed in a white salt solution and canned.

By preparing your own olives you can choose healthy sea salt and avoid commercial preservatives. While brine-cured olives take the longest time, it is the least time-consuming method in the long run and the healthiest way to remove the bitterness from the olives. When olives soak in a concentrated salt solution for several months, they go through a natural fermentation process, which produces live lactic-acid bacteria supportive of digestive health, immune function, and general well-being.

When it comes to curing your own olives in brine it is helpful to get into the habit of planning ahead, understanding that the olives you begin to cure between Sukkot and Chanukah may not be fully ready for Tu b'Shevat, yet they will finally be perfectly cured by Shavuot (Pentecost).

BLACK OLIVES IN BRINE
A healthy pro-biotic alternative to canned olives

3 cups fully ripe black olives of similar size

For the initial brine solutions:
4 cups water
¼ cup sea salt

For the final brine solution:
4 cups water
¼ cup sea salt
½ cup wine or good natural vinegar
A handful of bay leaves
3 tablespoons olive oil
Coriander, citrus rind, black pepper corns, chilies, oregano, rosemary, sage, or garlic according to taste

1. Pick the fully ripe black olives from the tree. You can hand pick them into a container or use the ancient method of spreading a cloth on the ground below the olive tree to be picked and beat the branches with a stick until all the olives fall into the cloth, which you can then fold together to carry the olives to your home.

2. Check the olives for scars which may indicate the entrance of olive fly larvae burrows. Tiny dots on an olive are acceptable, but a telltale beige scar means there is a visitor lurking within your olive. Discard any olives with blemishes.

3. Sort the olives according to size. Similar-sized olives should be placed in the same jar to ensure even curing.

4. Place the olives in containers – stoneware, earthenware and glass jars are suitable. It is preferable to get hold of pickling jars with rubber rings. Otherwise you may use any clean,

optionally sterilized jar with a lid. (How to sterilize your jars: Wash them well first, and then immerse the jars and their lids in a large pot filled with boiling water. Allow the water to simmer for a few minutes before lifting the jars out carefully, letting them dry on clean paper towels).

5. Place the olives in the jars (keeping the different sizes olives in separate jars). Fill the jars about two-thirds. Then cover the olives with the initial brine solution. Place a rock or another heavy object the size of your fist on the olives in the jar. This keeps the olives underwater. Seal the jars with the lids, and store in a cool, dark place.

6. Allow the olives to soak in brine for three to six months. Don't change the brine more than once a month. Do not re-rinse the olives, as the natural yeasts on the olives can become a 'starter' to get the next batch of brine going in the curing process.

7. Add half a cup of good quality, natural vinegar to the final brine solution and feel free to experiment with herbs and spices. Try adding a handful of bay leaves, and improvise with coriander, citrus rind, black pepper, chilies, oregano, rosemary, sage, garlic, etc. In order to expose the olives' natural taste, take care to not overdo on the spices. Add a tablespoon of olive oil to the top of each jar before sealing. The olives should keep for more than a year if properly stored.

WATER CURED PICKLED OLIVES (Simplified version)
Suitable for impatient cooks

Pick olives and check for bugs carefully. Soak and change water daily for seven days. Then pickle the olives in a mixture of saltwater (salty enough to make an egg float), several cloves of whole garlic, bay leaves, whole peppers, dill etc. It is also possible to use part lemon juice and part saltwater. Leave the olives in the pickling mixture for three to six months.

MOROCCAN INSPIRED COOKED OLIVES
A favorite Shabbat Appetizer

1 can pitted green olives
1 whole head of chopped garlic
4–5 tablespoons extra virgin olive oil
2 cans of organic crushed tomatoes (total 600 g or 1½ lb.)
½ teaspoon sweet paprika
½ teaspoon basil or other green spices to taste

1. Sauté garlic in olive oil for five minutes until slightly browned.

2. Add the olives and continue sautéing for approximately five more minutes.

3. Add the crushed tomatoes with spices and simmer on low heat for about half an hour.

4. Serve warm or cold.

BLACK OLIVE GREEN BEAN SALAD
Flavorful and festive

½ kg (1 lb.) topped and tailed string beans
½ cup black olive rings
½ cup extra virgin olive oil
¼ cup slivered almonds
3 tablespoons finely chopped parsley
¼ cup lemon juice
1 tablespoon tamari soy sauce
1 teaspoon cumin
½ teaspoon sea salt

1. Steam or cook the string beans with a little water for 10-15 minutes until *al dente* soft.

2. Drain the beans and toss with the olive oil, herbs and spices while beans are still slightly warm.

3. Add the lemon juice and additional ingredients.

Anti-Inflammatory Health Benefits of Olives

In traditional herbal medicine, preparations from olives and olive leaves have often been used in treatment of inflammatory problems, including allergy-related inflammation.[117] New research explains how olives provide us with anti-inflammatory benefits, especially during circumstances involving allergy. Olive extracts have been shown to function as antihistamines at a cellular level. By blocking the histamine receptors, called H1 receptors, olive extracts may help to lessen a cell's histamine response. Because histamine can get overproduced in allergy-related conditions and in the inflammatory process, it's likely that olives' anti-inflammatory benefits involve this antihistamine pathway. Olives may also have a special role to play as part of an overall anti-allergenic diet. [118]

... וְהָיָה פִרְיוֹ לְמַאֲכָל וְעָלֵהוּ לִתְרוּפָה: (יחזקאל מז, יב)

"...and its fruit shall be for food and its leaf for medicine"
(*Ezekiel* 47:12).

OLIVE LEAF TEA
A healing pleasant drink

2 handfuls olive leaves
8 cups water

1. Boil the water,

2. Place olive leaves (alone or mixed with other herbs/teas) in a tea
    cozy or directly into the boiling water.

3. Immediately reduce heat to a high simmer and let tea brew for
    approximately 15 minutes until the water boils down to half its
    original volume.

4. Stir tea occasionally, strain to drink and/or refrigerate.

Tea should be a medium amber color with a slightly bitter taste.

To combat a specific ailment, sip twice this amount of olive leaf tea
over a three-day period.

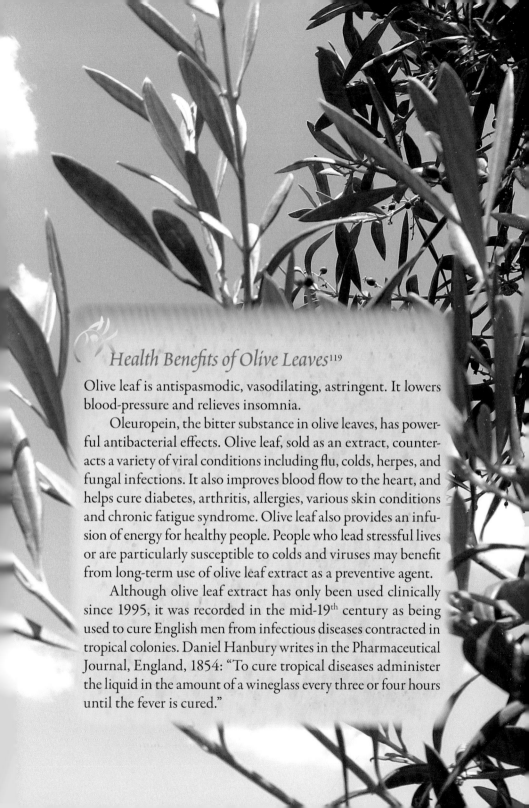

Health Benefits of Olive Leaves[119]

Olive leaf is antispasmodic, vasodilating, astringent. It lowers blood-pressure and relieves insomnia.

Oleuropein, the bitter substance in olive leaves, has powerful antibacterial effects. Olive leaf, sold as an extract, counteracts a variety of viral conditions including flu, colds, herpes, and fungal infections. It also improves blood flow to the heart, and helps cure diabetes, arthritis, allergies, various skin conditions and chronic fatigue syndrome. Olive leaf also provides an infusion of energy for healthy people. People who lead stressful lives or are particularly susceptible to colds and viruses may benefit from long-term use of olive leaf extract as a preventive agent.

Although olive leaf extract has only been used clinically since 1995, it was recorded in the mid-19th century as being used to cure English men from infectious diseases contracted in tropical colonies. Daniel Hanbury writes in the Pharmaceutical Journal, England, 1854: "To cure tropical diseases administer the liquid in the amount of a wineglass every three or four hours until the fever is cured."

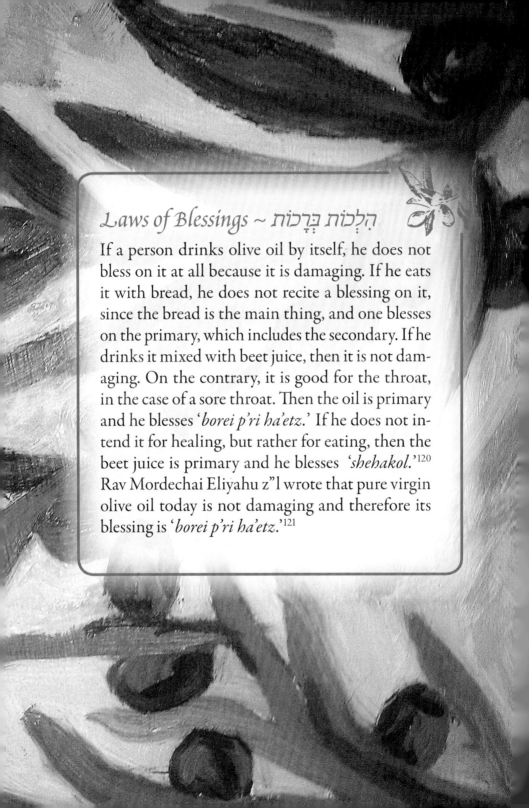

Laws of Blessings ~ הִלְכוֹת בְּרָכוֹת

If a person drinks olive oil by itself, he does not bless on it at all because it is damaging. If he eats it with bread, he does not recite a blessing on it, since the bread is the main thing, and one blesses on the primary, which includes the secondary. If he drinks it mixed with beet juice, then it is not damaging. On the contrary, it is good for the throat, in the case of a sore throat. Then the oil is primary and he blesses *'borei p'ri ha'etz.'* If he does not intend it for healing, but rather for eating, then the beet juice is primary and he blesses *'shehakol.'*[120] Rav Mordechai Eliyahu z"l wrote that pure virgin olive oil today is not damaging and therefore its blessing is *'borei p'ri ha'etz.'*[121]

I'm Oliver Bliss. I strive toward holiness in everything I do. I want to be pious not only in learning and prayer but also whenever I walk on the street, as it states: "In all your ways know Him, and He will direct your paths."[122] While I'm careful never to look at a woman other than my beautiful wife and daughters, I am still a friendly guy. With my gaze looking down, I have no problem speaking with women as long as it is for a higher purpose. I connect easily with people, and care deeply about everyone. I naturally find creative ways to reach out and bring lost children back to the Land and the Law. Besides my rigorous schedule of Torah learning, somehow I find time to read the newspaper! (Don't ask me how). We can learn a lot about G*d's way by keeping up with the news. This also helps me to pray for exactly what is needed in the world. I hope to be part of making this world a better place and I have started my own grassroots movement for Jewish environmental awareness. I'm also quite health-conscious and work on sanctifying myself through eating and drinking, as the Bible teaches: "A Tzadik (righteous person) eats to satisfy his soul."[123] I try not to eat more than what my body needs and to exercise self-control by leaving over a small portion on my plate. This is only one of the measures I take in order to become a "Tzadik [who] is the foundation of the world."[124]

Endnotes

1. Genesis 49:26. This fits into the attribute of *Yesod,* as a strong foundation must include the outermost bounds of the land. Moreover, this Torah verse refers to Ya'acov's blessing of Yosef, the shepherd of *Yesod.* The entire Torah verse reads: "The blessings of your father are potent above the blessings of my parents **to the utmost bound** of the everlasting hills; they shall be on the head of Yosef, and on the crown of the head of him that was separated from his brothers."

2. Olive – זַיִת/*zayit*, olives –זֵיתִים/*zeitim*, oil – שֶׁמֶן/*shemen* and olive tree – עֵץ שֶׁמֶן/*etz shemen* are mentioned 109 times in the Bible.
    Olive – זַיִת/*zayit* is mentioned in the Bible in the singular form 28 times, 10 times in the Pentateuch and 18 times in the rest of the Bible: Genesis 8:11; Exodus 23:11, 27:20, 29:21, 30:24; Leviticus 24:2; Deuteronomy 8:8, 24:20, 28:40; Judges 9:8, 9:9, 15:5; I Samuel 8:14; II Samuel 12:9; II Kings 18:32; Isaiah 17:6, 24:13; Jeremiah 11:16; Ezekiel 16:59, 22:8; Hosea 14:7; Micah 6:15; Habakkuk 3:17; Haggai 2:19; Psalms 52:10, 128:3; Job 15:33; Nehemiah 8:15.
    Olives – זֵיתִים/*zeitim* are mentioned in the Bible in the plural form 14 times, twice in the Pentateuch and 12 times in the rest of the Bible: Deuteronomy 6:11, 28:40; Joshua 24:13; I Samuel 8:14; II Samuel 15:30; II Kings 5:26; Amos 4:9; Zechariah 4:3, 4:11,4:12, 14:4; Nehemiah 5:11, 9:25; I Chronicles 27:28.
    Oil – שֶׁמֶן/*shemen*, most likely in reference to olive oil, is mentioned in the Bible 61 times, 34 times, in the Pentateuch and 27 times in the rest of the Bible: Genesis 28:18, 35:14, 49:20; Exodus 25:6, 27:20, 29:7, 29:23, 30:25 (twice), 30:31, 31:11, 35:14, 35:15, 37:29, 39:37, 29:38, 40:9; Leviticus 2:1, 2:6, 2:15, 5:11, 8:2, 8:10, 8:26, 10:7, 14:10, 14:21, 21:10, 21:12, 24:2; Numbers 4:16, 5:15, 15:4; Deuteronomy 8:8; I Samuel 16:1; II Samuel 14:2; I Kings 5:25, 17:12; II Kings 20:13; Isaiah 5:1, 10:27, 28:15, 61:3; Ezekiel 34:14; Hosea 2:7; Amos 6:6 (in plural); Micah 6:7, 6:15; Habakkuk 1:16; Haggai 2:12; Psalms 45:8, 141:5; Proverbs 27:9; Job 29:6; Nehemiah 9:25; Song of Songs 1:3 (twice), 4:10; Ecclesiastes 10:1; I Chronicles 4:40.
    Olive tree – עֵץ שֶׁמֶן/*etz shemen* [Oil-Tree] is mentioned six times in the Bible: I Kings 6:23, 6:31, 6:32, 6:33; Isaiah 41:19; Nehemiah 8:15.

3. I Chronicles 29:11.

4. Rav Yitzchak Ginsburgh, *Parshat Eikev: The Seven Species*
    <http://www.inner.org/parshah/deuteronomy/eikev/seven-species-eikev-5769.php#_ednref11> retrieved August 23, 2013.

5. The vitamin and mineral content of olive oil is based on USDA,
    Basic report: 04053, Oil, olive, salad or cooking. The percentage of
    Recommended Daily Dietary Allowance is based on
    <http://www.nutrition-and-you.com/olive-oil.html> retrieved June 23, 2013.

6. The vitamin and mineral content of olives is based on USDA, *Basic
    Report: 09193, Olives, ripe, canned (small to extra large).* The percentage
    of Recommended Daily Dietary Allowance is based on *Olives, ripe,
    canned, (small to extra large)* <http://www.nutrition-and-you.com/olives.
    html> retrieved June 23, 2013.

7. Michael Tierra, *Planetary Herbology,* p. 174.

8. Rashi, Psalms 128:3.

9. Tzonou A, Hsieh CC, Polychronopoulou A, Kaprinis G, Toupadaki
    N, Trichopoulou A, Karakatsani A, Trichopoulos D: *Diet and ovarian
    cancer: a case-control study in Greece.* Int J Cancer 1993, 55:411–414.

10. Rabbi Binyamin Moshe Kohn Shauli, *Nature's Wealth,* p. 131.

11. Rabbi Binyamin Moshe Kohn Shauli, *Nature's Wealth,* p. 132.

12. Rabbi Binyamin Moshe Kohn Shauli, *Nature's Wealth,* p. 130.
    Relying *only* on olive oil may cut your risk of coronary heart disease
    almost in half. See Kontogianni MD, Panagiotakos DB, Chrysohoou
    C, Pitsavos C, Zampelas A, Stefanadis C. *The Impact of Olive Oil
    Consumption Pattern on the Risk of Acute Coronary Syndromes: The
    CARDIO2000 Case-Control Study.* Clin Cardiol. 2007 Mar;30(3):125–9.
    Keys A, Menotti A, Karvonen MJ, Aravanis C, Blackburn H, Buzina
    R, Djordjevic BS, Dontas AS, Fidanza F, Keys MH, et al. *The Diet and
    15-Year Death Rate in the Seven Countries Study.* Am J Epidemiol. 1986
    Dec;124(6):903–15.
    Bendinelli B, Masala G, Saieva C, Salvini S, Calonico C, Sacerdote C,
    Agnoli C, Grioni S, Frasca G, Mattiello A, Chiodini P, Tumino R, Vineis
    P, Palli D, Panico S. *Fruit, Vegetables, and Olive Oil and Risk of Coronary
    Heart Disease in Italian Women: the EPICOR Study.* Am J Clin Nutr.
    2011 Feb;93(2):275–83.

13. Rabbi Binyamin Moshe Kohn Shauli, *Nature's Wealth,* p. 130.

14. Samieri C, Féart C, Proust-Lima C, Peuchant E, Tzourio C, Stapf C,

Berr C, Barberger-Gateau P. *Olive oil Consumption, Plasma Oleic Acid, and Stroke Incidence: the Three-City Study.* Neurology. 2011 Aug 2;77(5):418–25. This study examined the association between olive oil intake and stroke incidence in 7625 people aged 65 and older in France. Compared with participants who did not use olive oil, those with intensive use had a 41% lower risk of stroke.

15.   Casaburi I, Puoci F, Chimento A, Sirianni R, Ruggiero C, Avena P, Pezzi V. *Potential of Olive Oil Phenols as Chemopreventive and Therapeutic Agents Against Cancer: A review of in Vitro Studies.* Mol Nutr Food Res. 2013 Jan;57(1):71–83.

16.   Stoneham M, Goldacre M, Seagroatt V, Gill L. *Olive Oil, Diet and Colorectal Cancer: An Ecological Study and a Hypothesis.* J Epidemiol Community Health. 2000 Oct;54(10):756–60. This study shows new evidence of olive oil's protective effect on colonic mucosa, and positive signs that olive oil indeed prevents the commencement of rectum and bowel cancer.

17.   R Bartolí, F Fernández-Bañares, E Navarro, E Castellà, J Mañé,M Alvarez, C Pastor, E Cabré, M A Gassull, *Effect of Olive Oil on Early and Late Events of Colon Carcinogenesis in Rats: Modulation of Arachidonic Acid Metabolism and Local Prostaglandin E2 Synthesis, Gut* 2000;46:191–199.

18.   Chedraui P, Pérez-López FR. *Nutrition and Health during Mid-Life: Searching for Solutions and Meeting Challenges for the Aging Population.* Climacteric. 2013 Aug;16 Suppl 1:85–95.

19.   Martín-Peláez S, Covas MI, Fitó M, Kušar A, Pravst I. *Health Effects of Olive Oil Polyphenols: Recent Advances and Possibilities for the Use of Health Claims.* Mol Nutr Food Res. 2013 May;57(5):760–71.

20.   Puel C, Mardon J, Agalias A, Davicco MJ, Lebecque P, Mazur A, Horcajada MN, Skaltsounis AL, Coxam V. *Major Phenolic Compounds in Olive Oil Modulate Bone Loss in an Ovariectomy/Inflammation Experimental Model.* J Agric Food Chem. 2008 Oct 22;56(20):9417–22.

21.   Rav Yitzchak Ginsburgh, *Body, Mind, and Soul,* pp. 83–84.

22.   Rashi, Deuteronomy 33:24.

23.   Rashi, I Chronicles 7:31.

24.   Rona C, Vailati F, Berardesca E. *The Cosmetic Treatment of Wrinkles.* J Cosmet Dermatol. 2004 Jan;3(1):26–34. This study indicates that components of olive oil may act as anti-wrinkle agents.

25.   Touitou E, Godin B, Karl Y, Bujanover S, Becker Y. *Oleic Acid, a Skin Penetration Enhancer, Affects Langerhans Cells and Corneocytes.* J Control Release. 2002 Apr 23;80(1–3):1–7.

26. Verallo-Rowell VM, Dillague KM, Syah-Tjundawan BS. *Novel Antibacterial and Emollient Effects of Coconut and Virgin Olive Oils in Adult Atopic Dermatitis.* Dermatitis. 2008 Nov–Dec;19(6):308–15.

27. Rambam, *Mishneh Torah, Hilchot Deot* 4:13.

28. Nisim Krispil, *Medicinal Herbs of the Rambam,* p. 109; Rabbi Binyamin Moshe Kohn Shauli, *Nature's Wealth,* p. 131.

29. Michael Tierra, *Planetary Herbology,* p. 174.

30. Rambam, *Mishneh Torah, Hilchot Deot* 4:13.

31. Rabbi Binyamin Moshe Kohn Shauli, *Nature's Wealth,* p. 132.

32. Nisim Krispil, *Medicinal Herbs of the Rambam,* p. 109.

33. Soriguer F, Moreno F, Rojo-Martínez G, García-Fuentes E, Tinahones F, Gómez-Zumaquero JM, Cuesta-Muñoz AL, Cardona F, Morcillo S. *Monounsaturated n-9 Fatty Acids and Adipocyte Lipolysis in Rats.* Br J Nutr. 2003 Dec;90(6):1015–22.

34. Nisim Krispil, *Medicinal Herbs of the Rambam,* p. 109.

35. Rabbi Binyamin Moshe Kohn Shauli, *Nature's Wealth,* p. 131.

36. Nisim Krispil, *Medicinal Herbs of the Rambam,* p. 109.

37. Rabbi Binyamin Moshe Kohn Shauli, *Nature's Wealth,* p. 133.

38. Nisim Krispil, *Medicinal Herbs of the Rambam,* p. 109.

39. Rabbi Binyamin Moshe Kohn Shauli, *Nature's Wealth,* p. 131.

40. Assaf Ben Bichiyahu, Tiberias, Israel (5th–6th century), known as the 'Jewish Hippocrates.'

41. Rabbi Binyamin Moshe Kohn Shauli, *Nature's Wealth,* p. 132.

42. Based on *Midrash Tanchuma, Parashat Tetzaveh* 6.

43. Jeremiah 11:16.

44. Radak, Jeremiah 11:16.

45. Leviticus 20:26.

46. Deuteronomy 28:1; *Midrash Deuteronomy Rabbah* 7:3.

47. See Psalm 52:10, quoted in full at the beginning of the *Olive* section.

48. *Babylonian Talmud, Menachot* 53b.

49. Rashi, Psalms 128:3.

50. *Rabbeinu Bachaya,* Psalms 128:3.

51. Zechariah 4:2–3.

52. Rabbeinu Bachaya, Numbers 8:2.

53. *Midrash Tanchuma, Parashat B'ha'alotcha* 4:5.

54.   Isaiah 42:6.

55.   Zechariah 4:6.

56.   See for example, Exodus 29:7, 40:9; Leviticus 8:10, 21:10.

57.   See for example, I Samuel 9:16 –the anointing of King Saul; I Samuel 16:12 – the anointing of King David; I Kings 1:29 – the anointing of King Solomon; II Kings 9:6 – The anointing of King Yehu.

58.   Judges 9:8.

59.   Job 8:7.

60.   *Midrash Deuteronomy Rabbah* 7:3.

61.   Rabbi Natan of Breslau, Rabbi Natan Sternhartz (1780–1845), לקוטי הלכות/*Likutei Halachot, the Laws of Blessings on the Fruits, halacha* 3–4.

62.   See Rambam, *Hilchot Shevu'ot* 4:1.

63.   Based on Proverbs 13:25.

64.   Based on Rabbi Natan of Breslau, *Likutei Halachot, Orach Chaim, Hilchot Birchot Hapeirot* 3–4, translated by Dov Grant.

65.   Rashi, Genesis 8:11, based on *Babylonian Talmud, Eruvin* 18b.

66.   Hosea 6:1.

67.   Rabbi Yehoshua Zambrowsky, Warsaw (1874–1939), עטרת יהושע/*Ateret Yehoshua on Parashat Noach.*

68.   *Kli Yakar*, Genesis 8:11.

69.   Exodus 27:20, *Midrash Tanchuma, Tetzaveh* 5:5.

70.   Genesis 32:25.

71.   Rashi, Genesis 32:25, based on *Babylonian Talmud, Chulin* 91a.

72.   The *Imrei Noam*, Rabbi Meir Horowitz of Dzikow (1819–1877), cited by *P'ri Mayim Chaim*, David Hertzberg, Jerusalem 2003, cited by Rabbi Abba Wagensberg, Noah's Rainbow Menorah <http:// www.thirdtemple.com/parashas/rainbow-menorah.html> retrieved May 27, 2013.

73.   Ramban, Numbers 8:2.

74.   Rashi, Genesis 1:4.

75.   *Midrash Numbers Rabbah* 2:7.

76.   Deuteronomy 24:20.

77.   *Mishnah, Tractate Challah* 3:9.

78.   Rabbi Yosef said: "I will not cut them down, because Rav has said that it is forbidden to cut down a date tree that bears a *kav* [1.3 kg] of dates," and Rabbi Chanina said: "My son Shichat only died because he cut down a date tree before its time [i.e., before the tree was dead]. You, Sir, can cut them down if you like" (*Babylonian Talmud, Baba Batra* 26a).

79. Deuteronomy 20:19.

80. For the full story see II *Samuel*, 14:2–14.

81. Rabbi Shemuel Edeles, the MaHaRShA, *Chidushei MaHaRShA* on *Menachot*, 85b.

82. *Babylonian Talmud, Menachot*, 85b.

83. Radak, II Samuel 14:2.

84. Exodus 26:35.

85. *Babylonian Talmud, Baba Batra* 25b.

86. Tekoa is mentioned together with Bethlehem in for example II Chronicles 11:5–6,

87. Exodus 27:20.

88. Rashi, *ad. loc.*

89. Rashi, *ad. loc.*

90. Psalms 128:3.

91. Based on the *Chida*, Rabbi Chaim Yosef David Azulai, Jerusalem (1724–1806); The teachings of Rabbanit Yamima Mizrachi, *Spiritual Remedies for the Holiday of Chanukah*, edited by Yikrat Friedman, Kislev 25, 5772, 102/21/12.

92. Fistonić I, Situm M, Bulat V, Harapin M, Fistonić N, Verbanac D. *Olive oil biophenols and women's health.* Med Glas (Zenica). 2012 Feb;9(1):1–9.

93. An example of the toxic effect of FFA is found in Boden G, *Effects of Free Fatty Acids (FFA) on Glucose Metabolism: Significance for Insulin Resistance and Type 2 diabetes*, Exp Clin Endocrinol Diabetes. 2003 May;111(3):121–4.

94. *Babylonian Talmud, Horayot* 13b.

95. Deuteronomy 8:8 "… a land of wheat, and barley, and vines, and fig trees, and pomegranates; a land of olive **oil** and honey."

96. Rabbi Samuel Edeles, the MaHaRShA, *Chidushei MaHaRShA* on *Horayot* 13b.

97. Rabbeinu Bachaya, Genesis, 34:1.

98. Maharal, *Chidushei Aggadot,* part 4, p. 61.

99. HaGaon Rav Yisrael Va'aletz, Budapest-Israel (1887–1973), ספר הזיכרון/*The Book of Memory*.

100. Rav Tzvi Elimelech Shapira of Dinov, Poland (1783–1841), בני יששכר/*B'nei Yissaschar, The Articles of the Month of Kislev and Tevet* 4:15; Arizal, *P'ri Etz Chaim, the Gate of Shabbat*, chapter 13.

101. Arizal, *Sefer HaLikutim, Parashat Ekev*, chapter 8.

102. Deuteronomy 8:19.

103. *Jerusalem Talmud, Ketubot* 7a.

104. Proverbs 31:23.

105. Deuteronomy 8:8, quoted in full in our introduction.

106. See for example, I Samuel 10:1; I Kings 1:39; Psalms 89:21.

107. Arizal, *Sha'ar HaPesukim, Parashat Matot.*

108. Numbers 20:5.

109. *Meshech Chachmah*, Rabbi Meir Simcha of Dvinsk, Lithuania (1843–1926), Deuteronomy 8:8.

110. Deuteronomy 8:19.

111. *Jerusalem Talmud, Ketubot* 7a.

112. Based on Rav Tzadok HaKohen of Lublin, *P'ri Tzadik, Et HaOchel* 13.

113. Psalms 128:3.

114. Jeremiah 11:16.

115. Exodus 27:20

116. Kalua CM, Bedgood DR Jr, Bishop AG, Prenzler PD. *Discrimination of Storage Conditions and Freshness in Virgin Olive Oil.* J Agric Food Chem. 2006 Sep 20;54(19):7144–51.

117. Rosignoli P, Fuccelli R, Fabiani R, Servili M, Morozzi G. *Effect of Olive Oil Phenols on the Production of Inflammatory Mediators in Freshly Isolated Human Monocytes.* J Nutr Biochem. 2013 2013 Aug;24(8):1513–9.

118. Yamada P, Zarrouk M, Kawasaki K, Isoda H. *Inhibitory Effect of Various Tunisian Olive oils on Chemical Mediator Release and Cytokine Production by Basophilic Cells.* J Ethnopharmacol. 2008 Mar 5;116(2):279–87.

119. The health benefits of olive leaves mentioned here are adapted from the writings of James R. Privitera, M.D *Olive Leaf Extract A New/Old Healing Bonanza for Mankind* <http://curezone.com/foods/oliveleaf.asp> retrieved May 27, 2013.

120. *Shulchan Aruch, Orach Chaim*, 204:4.

121. Rabbi A.A. Mandelbaum, וְזֹאת הַבְּרָכָה/*V'zot Habracha* (*Dorshei Yechudecha* Research Institute, Jerusalem 2001), p. 378.

122. Proverbs 3:6.

123. Proverbs 13:25.

124. Proverbs 10:25.

Phoenix Dactylifera ~ דְּבַשׁ

Dates

מַלְכוּת ~ Malchut – Royalty / Kingdom

Date Honey~(תְּמָרִים) דְּבַשׁ *Phoenix Dactylifera*
Malchut ~ מַלְכוּת (Royalty / Kingdom)

זֹאת קוֹמָתֵךְ דָּמְתָה לְתָמָר וְשָׁדַיִךְ לְאַשְׁכֹּלוֹת: (שיר השירים ז, ח)

"This, your stature is like a date palm, and your breasts are like clusters [of grapes]" (Song of Songs 7:8).

המלכות נקראת תמר, בסוד זאת קומתך דמתה לתמר...
(אריז"ל, ספר הליקוטים - שופטים - פרק ד)

Malchut is called a date palm, in the secret of:
"This, your stature is like a date palm..."
(Arizal, Sefer HaLikutim, The Book of Judges, chapter 4).

Attribute: *Malchut* – Royalty/Kingdom

Character trait: The ability to refine speech (expression)[1]

Holiday: Sukkot, when we shake the *lulav* – the closed frond of the date palm

Weekday: יוֹם שַׁבָּת/*Yom Shabbat* – Seventh day of the week (Saturday)

World: יְצִירָה/*Yetzirah* – Formation (hard inedible pit)

Body parts: The mouth, female sexual organ and feet

Shepherd: דָּוִד/David

Prophetess: אֶסְתֵּר/Esther

Numerical value: 306, equivalent to the word אִשָּׁה/*isha* – 'woman'[2]

Mentioned in the Bible 36 times[3]

Greek/Latin Name: 'Phoenix' means purple or red (fruit), and 'dactylifera' refers to the finger-like appearance of the fruit bunch.

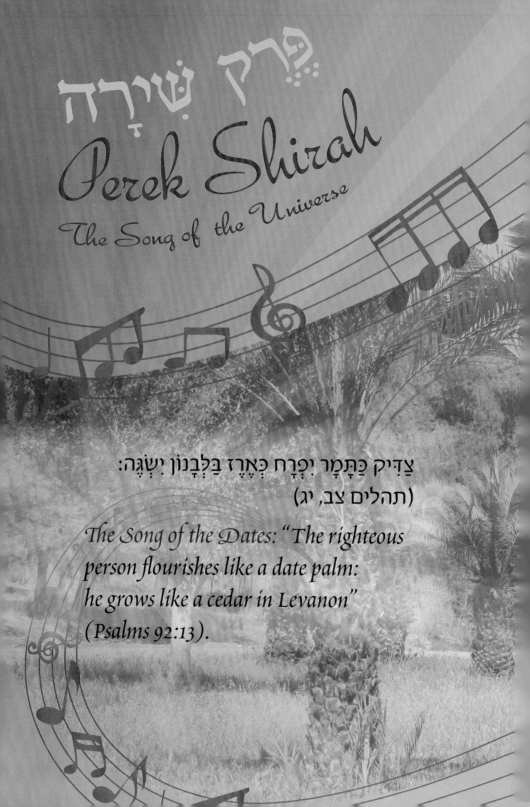

פֶּרֶק שִׁירָה

Perek Shirah

The Song of the Universe

צַדִּיק כַּתָּמָר יִפְרָח כְּאֶרֶז בַּלְּבָנוֹן יִשְׂגֶּה:
(תהלים צב, יג)

*The Song of the Dates: "The righteous
person flourishes like a date palm:
he grows like a cedar in Levanon"
(Psalms 92:13).*

The date palm teaches that spiritual growth comes with investment, effort and persistence that grant true achievements. Just as the date palm and the cedar are the tallest of all the trees, likewise the righteous rise and keep growing until they reach their highest potential.[4]

Nutrition Facts and Information about Dates

Mineral Content of Dates[5]

Dates are an excellent source of potassium and copper.[6] They are rich in iron, magnesium, manganese and selenium.[7] Dates also contain phosphorous, calcium, boron, cobalt, fluorine and zinc.[8]

Vitamin Content of Dates

Dates are a good source of niacin and vitamin B6. They also contain vitamin A,[9] thiamin, and small amounts of riboflavin and folate.[10]

Dietary Fiber and Antioxidants

Dates are high in dietary fiber (8.0 g/100 g), primarily insoluble dietary fiber. They are also a good source of antioxidants, mainly carotenoids and phenolics.[11]

Oriental Medicine

According to Chinese medicine, dates are included among the tonic and nutritive foods because of their sweet flavor.[12] Dates are also building and softening. Their sweet flavor is composed of the elements of earth and water. Dates are nourishing and counteracts general debility, weakness, symptoms of aging, lack of semen and impotence. They are contraindicated for kapha (water) disorders, including obesity, mucous diseases and diabetes.[13]

Dates Nutritional Facts/100 g

Minerals		RDA
Calcium	64 mg	6.5%
Iron	0.90 mg	11%
Magnesium	54 mg	13%
Phosphorus	62 mg	9%
Potassium	696 mg	16%
Sodium	1 mg	0%
Zinc	0.44 mg	4%
Copper	0.362 mg	40%
Manganese	0.296 mg	13%
Vitamins		**RDA**
C	0.0 mg	0%
B1 (Thiamin)	0.050 mg	4%
B2 (Riboflavin)	0.060 mg	4.5%
B3 (Niacin)	1.610 mg	10%
B6	0.249 mg	11.7%
B9 (Folate)	15 μg	4%
A	149 IU	5%
K	2.7 μg	2%
E	Not listed	Not listed

Dates correspond to Malchut. The attribute of *Malchut* is to receive, channel and unify. The tall, cylinder-shaped date palm, likewise, channels the sweetness from the depths of the earth and makes it accessible for human consumption through its delicious fruits. The sticky dates, moreover, can unify the remaining ingredients in any raw-food dessert.

Kingdom from Tamar

When the people of Israel rise to royalty, they are compared to the tall date palm.[14] Perhaps this is why the beginning of the Kingdom of Israel emanates from a woman called Tamar, which means date. Tamar became the first mother of Kingdom through her union with Yehuda, the ancestor of King David. The word תָּמָר/*Tamar* also means 'replacement' and includes the Hebrew word מַר/*mar* – which means 'bitter.'

The Crown of Sweetness

It is possible that the energy of the Tamar, with its incredible sweetness, has the ability to replace and transform the bitterness of our exile by 'sweetening the judgments in their root.' This Chassidic concept entails relating to a difficult situation from a higher perspective, where it becomes part of the greater good.[15] We still await the coming of King Mashiach, the final bough of the Davidic dynasty,[16] who will reveal the sweetness at the root of all judgment and suffering. How suitable that dates are termed 'the crown of sweets.'

Dates, Kingdom and Unity

The role of the king is to unify his people. The date palm symbolizes unity, since it has only one trunk. Moreover, the stickiness of dates can serve as a unifier when mixed with other substances. According to Jewish mysticism, *Malchut* has no quality of its own.[17] It is a

transparent vehicle for reflecting the Divine flow in the lower world. The stately, tall and straight date palm, with its strong roots gleaning nourishment from deep within the poor desert soil, reflects the concept of *Malchut*: The channel that connects heaven and earth, allowing everything from above to manifest below. An old saying describes the date palm as growing with 'its feet in the water and its head in the fire.'

Malchut: The Internal Channel from Mouth to Feet

While the other sefirot have mainly one organ associated with them, there are various organs associated with *Malchut*, such as the mouth, the feet and the reproductive organs.[18] Perhaps this is because *Malchut* is an internal channel that passes through the human body from the mouth to the feet, through the uterus in the front, and the end of the digestive system in the rear. Therefore, *Malchut* also corresponds to the digestive system.[19] Dates have the ability to balance and stabilize digestion by treating both constipation and diarrhea. Modern research confirms the Talmud's teaching that dates regulate the digestive tract and heal intestinal illnesses.[20] Liberal use of dates is highly beneficial in the treatment of constipation, as its roughage stimulates sluggish bowels.[21] In order to get the greatest benefit from their laxative effect, it is recommended to soak the dates for 12 hours in water. Due to their high potassium content, dates also alleviate diarrhea by replacing lost potassium.

Heal Cancer, 'The Other Side of Malchut'

Cancer has been termed 'the other side of *Malchut*,' because cancer cells reproduce in an anarchistic way. Therefore, it makes sense that dates associated with *Malchut* are beneficial for curing cancer. Dates contain selenium, which may help prevent cancer.[22] They also contain glucan which has been found to exhibit potent anti-tumor activity.[23] The USDA nutritional guidelines recommend an intake of

20–35 grams of dietary fiber daily,[24] of which dates are an excellent source.[25] Bedouin Arabs, who eat them on a regular basis, have an extremely low incidence of cancer and heart disease.[26] The Hebrew word for cancer – סַרְטָן/*sartan* consists of the words *sar tan* (from the word טִינָה/*tina*), which means 'remove grudge.' Perhaps, since dates help elimination, their spiritual energy may also have the ability to cure cancer, by helping to eliminate negative emotions such as holding on to a grudge.

Alleviate Alcoholic Intoxication

Malchut entails self-control, which is the opposite of losing inhibitions through indulging in alcoholic beverages. This fits in with the fact that dates constitute an excellent remedy for alcoholic intoxication. Drinking water in which fresh dates have been soaked overnight will bring quick relief from alcoholic intoxication.

The Medicine of Moshe

Just as Kingdom has nothing on its own,[27] Moshe Rabbeinu (our teacher), in his humility, made himself into a transparent vessel for Divinity. *Malchut* unifies all the attributes reflected within it. Like the date palm, which symbolizes unity, Moshe Rabbeinu unified the people of Israel in his capacity as their first king.[28] About Moshe it states, "He was a king in Yeshurun, when the heads of the people and the tribes of Israel were gathered together."[29] Moreover, Moshe Rabbeinu nourished the Jewish people with the same nourishing quality of the date.[30] He brought the sweet and nutritive manna to the children of Israel.[31] Therefore, it is not surprising that the date is attributed specifically to Moshe Rabbeinu through the Hebrew acronym תרופת משה רבינו/*Terufat Moshe Rabbeinu* – The Medicine of Moshe our Teacher. The first letter in each of these Hebrew words together spell out תמר/*Tamar* – date. Indeed, dates have been proven as highly nutritious and medicinally beneficial for curing a number of human diseases.[32]

Healing Properties

In traditional medicinal practices, dates are considered as tonic and aphrodisiac.[33] Date fruit extracts have been reported to possess anti-ulcer, anti-cancer,[34] antidiarrheal,[35] hepatoprotective, antimutagenic, antioxidant,[36] aphrodiasiac,[37] anti-inflamatory, antimicrobial,[38] antigenotoxic,[39] antihyperlipidemic and nephroprotective activities.[40] Infusion, decoction, syrup or paste of dates is administered for a sore throat, cold and bronchial catarrh. It is also taken to relieve fever. The seed powder, too, is used in some traditional medicines. A gum that exudes from the wounded trunk is employed in India for treating diarrhea and genito-urinary ailments. The roots are used to relieve toothaches.[41]

Rambam classifies dates among the foods which should be eaten in moderation.[42] A person who is unable to control his appetite for dates may get headaches and hemorrhoids. Fresh dates are the most harmful in this respect. However, Rambam teaches that dates are beneficial for sexual performance and stamina.[43] They are excellent for men who suffer from impotence and infertility.[44] A handful of dates soaked in fresh goat's milk overnight, and then ground in the same milk with a pinch of cardamom and honey, becomes a very useful tonic for increasing sexual endurance.

The Talmud highlights the importance of eating dates in moderation through the following anecdote: Rabbi Ula was astonished about how cheap dates were in Babylon. He wondered why the Babylonian Jews did not learn more Torah, since they didn't need to work hard for their sustenance. After having bought three baskets of dates for only one dinar, and having eaten his fill, Ula suffered diarrhea the entire night. He then became impressed with the Jews of Babylon, who were able to learn Torah although they were sustained by this 'deadly poison.'[45] Dates can be very nutritious and healthy, as long as we don't eat too many of them. More than a handful of dates at one time is harmful for most people.

Dates for Women

Malchut corresponds to the female reproductive organs. When you cut open a date and remove the pit, the cavity actually resembles the shape of the vagina. The date pit itself, likewise, has the shape of the vagina. Date palm seeds contain the feminine hormone estrone.[46] Dates also contain certain stimulants that strengthen the muscles of the uterus and facilitate dilatation during delivery.[47] Dieticians

recommend dates as the best food for breastfeeding women. The approximately 80% sugar content of dates makes it an ideal high-energy food for nursing mothers. Dates enrich the breast milk to make the child healthy and resistant to disease. Rabbi Nachman teaches that dates remove worry.[48] They may also contain elements that assist in alleviating depression,[49] possibly relieving postpartum depression.

Energy Tonic

Dates with goat's milk sustained the desert people for thousands of years. They are easily digested and supply extra energy. According to the Talmud, dates warm and strengthen.[50] They have a valuable tonic effect on all age groups. The minerals and vitamins of dates help treat anemia and general debility.[51]

Breaking Fasts with Dates

Mohammed used to break his fast with fresh dates. If fresh dates were not available, he would eat dried dates.[52] Throughout the world, Muslims break the daily fast of Ramadan with dates, just as Muhammad did nearly 1,400 years ago. Eating two or three dates quickly restores blood sugar and prevents overeating after fasting, since hunger is caused more by low blood sugar than by an empty stomach. It is unhealthy to eat large quantities of food on an empty stomach immediately after fasting. Therefore, eating a few dates first helps the body start its digestive process and provides energy to digest the rest of the meal. Breaking a fast with dates is a wise decision, because fasting empties the stomach of food. Thus the liver doesn't have sufficient energy to transfer to the various organs. Sweets are the fastest foods to reach the liver. When one eats ripe dates, the liver accepts them, benefits from them and then transfers the benefit to the rest of the organs of the body. After this process, the body is ready to accept and digest additional food.[53]

A Metaphor for the Sweetness of Torah

In the Torah verse that describes the Seven Species of Israel, dates are called honey. This nomenclature connects dates to Torah, for Torah is compared to honey, as it states, "...sweeter than honey."[54] Therefore, forty years before the Jewish people were exiled to Babylon, they planted date palms there, so that the sweet taste of the dates would accustom their tongue to Torah.[55] Ula explains that the reason Israel was exiled specifically to Babylon was in order that they should eat dates and be busy in Torah.[56]

A traditional Jewish practice, since medieval times, is to drizzle honey on the letters of the Hebrew *'Alef Bet'* written on a slate. When being initiated into Torah learning, young children lick off the honey so that the taste of Torah will always seem as sweet as honey. In addition to being sweet, honey is also sticky, which teaches us the concept of *deveikut* – cleaving to the Torah. Even after the initial sweetness wears off, we will continue to be attached to Torah.

The sticky surface of dates attracts dust and impurities from the air. Therefore, it is advisable to select dates carefully and wash them thoroughly before use. Metaphorically, we need to carefully select authentic Torah and reject the various pseudo-Kabbalistic New Age teachings that flood the world today. Even those Torah scholars, who are able to filter out the nuggets of kosher sweetness, must ensure to rinse them well from their external impurities.

Dates – Mother's Perfect Dessert

ואמר רב חנא בגדתאה תמרי משחנן משבען משלשלן מאשרן ולא
מפנקן אמר רב אכל תמרים אל יורה מיתיבי תמרים שחרית וערבית
יפות במנחה רעות בצהרים אין כמותן ומבטלות שלשה דברים מחשבה
רעה וחולי מעים ותחתוניות מי אמרינן דלא מעלו עלוי מעלו ולפי שעתא
טרדא מידי דהוה אחמרא דאמר מר השותה רביעית יין אל יורה ואיבעית
אימא לא קשיא הא מקמי נהמא הא לבתר נהמא דאמר אביי אמרה לי
אם תמרי מקמי נהמא כי נרגא לדיקולא בתר נהמא כי עברא לדשא:
(תלמוד בבלי מסכת כתובות י, ע"ב)

Rabbi Chana of Bagdad said: "Dates are warming, satisfying, laxative, strengthening, without being pampering." Rav said: "If one has eaten dates, he should not give a legal decision." An objection was raised. "Dates are wholesome morning and evening, in the afternoon they are bad, at noon they are incomparable,[57] and they remove three things: Evil thought, intestinal disorders and hemorrhoids. Do we say that they are no good?" They are indeed good; [they cause] only momentarily unsteadiness. It is analogous to wine, for the Master [Shemuel] said: "He who has drunk one-fourth [of a log] of wine shall not give a legal decision."[58] If you wish, you may say, "There is no difficulty – this is before eating bread, and that is after bread,"[59] for Abaye said: "Mother told me: 'Dates before bread are as an axe to the palm tree, after bread a bar to the door'"[60] (Babylonian Talmud, Ketubot 10b).

Explanation: Dried dates are filling and warming because they contain 270 calories per 100 grams. Their natural sugars are digested quickly. Dates are laxative because of their high fiber content.[61]

One should not give any legal decision after eating dates because they are intoxicating.[62] Eating large amounts of dates may produce an elevated level of blood sugar, which can cause blurriness and drowsiness, similar to the effects of drinking alcohol.[63]

Since dates quickly give a feeling of being full, it is not recom-

mended to eat a large amount of dates before meals, because they
will ruin the appetite. However, after the meal, "there is nothing like
them" because they are satisfying.[64] Therefore, it is not good to eat
them in the afternoon after a nap before dinner, but rather in the
morning and evening after the meal, when their laxative property
facilitates proper bowel movement. At noon after being satisfied with
a good meal, they are better than in the evening, because during the
day when one is out in the field, it is easier to relieve oneself.[65] The
reason dates alleviate hemorrhoids is due to their laxative properties, since hemorrhoids are often caused by straining during bowel
movement. It is also possible that dates contain specific attributes
that counteract this ailment.

Dates nullify evil thought, because satisfaction without a heavy
stomach causes a general relaxed feeling of wellbeing.[66] They make
the heart happy, especially at noon, the time of light and rejoicing.
After a meal, dates strengthen the body, the same way that a bar
strengthens a door.[67]

Male and Female

Only one plant – the date palm – was known in ancient Babylonia
to have male and female trees. In order to produce dates, the female
date palm is pollinated with flowers from the male palm.[68] This fits
with the concept of *Malchut*, which unifies the male and female
aspects manifested in the female. *Malchut* corresponds to the unity
of male and female within the female that bears fruit.

The Midrash tells of a female date palm called Temarah, who
bore no fruit. A male date palm passed by and saw her. The female
date palm desired this male date palm in her heart and looked out
from Jericho for him to impregnate her. Just as date palms have
desire, likewise the righteous have desire for Hashem, as it states, "I
have surely hoped for Hashem."[69]

Why is the righteous person compared to a date palm? The
date palm, when cut, does not return for a long period; so with the
righteous person; when he disappears from the world, no one re-

places him until a certain time. Just as the date has male and female trees, likewise, the righteous person is both male and female. The male is the righteous man and the female the righteous woman, like Avraham and Sarah.[70]

The Date Palm of Devorah

The prophetess Devorah chose to sit under the shade of the date palm when she judged the Jewish people.

וְהִיא יוֹשֶׁבֶת תַּחַת תֹּמֶר דְּבוֹרָה בֵּין הָרָמָה וּבֵין בֵּית אֵל בְּהַר אֶפְרָיִם וַיַּעֲלוּ
אֵלֶיהָ בְּנֵי יִשְׂרָאֵל לַמִּשְׁפָּט: (שופטים ד, ה)

"She dwelt under the date palm of Devorah between Rama and Beit E-l in Mount Efraim. The children of Israel came up to her for judgment" (Judges 4:5).

Devorah placed her seat of judgment under a date palm, also called the Devorah palm, so that the Israelites could turn to her for judgment of their various disputes. Devorah decided to litigate under the open branches of the date palm outside her house, to ensure that all matters would be settled in public, and to prevent suspicion about unfair treatment and corruption.

Dates of Unification

כתמר מה תמר זה אין לו אלא לב אחד אף ישראל אין להם אלא לב אחד
לאביהם שבשמים: (תלמוד בבלי מסכת סוכה מה, ע״ב)

*Just as a date only has one heart, also Israel only has one heart
to their Father in heaven (Babylonian Talmud, Sukkah 45b).*

The date palm has no branches; its leaves grow directly out of its
trunk. In this way it gives the image of unity. This is a metaphor for
the unification Devorah caused Israel to achieve. In addition, it is
upright and tall, alluding to Israel walking upright with G*d, our
Father above. The date branches, which are really its leaves, grow
from the inside of the tree, from its heart.

Devorah chose to judge outside, in public, in the heart of the
city, under the date palm, in order to avoid being alone with any man
(יחוד/*yichud*).[71] This way, she also averted suspicion and gossip about
having any possible intimate contact with male litigants. Avoiding
seclusion with other men teaches us about Devorah's devotion and
one-heartedness to her husband. She sat under the date palm to
ensure that no other man would interfere in her holy union with
her husband.

Malchut corresponds to female sexuality. Therefore, the date
palm of Devorah represents purity and rectification in intimate
relations. The relationship between husband and wife reflects the
relationship between the congregation of Israel and Hashem. Since
Devorah had only one heart for her husband, she had the ability to
unite all Israel to have one heart for Hashem.

Effective Remedy for a Weak Heart

Dates are beneficial for heart conditions.[72] Soak dates overnight in
water. In the morning, remove their seeds and crush them in the
water in which they were soaked. Eat this date-mush at least twice
a week.

Eternal Fertility

Malchut represents female fertility. The oldest seed ever to take root is a 2,000 year-old-date palm seed from Israel named Methuselah.[73] It was discovered at the Masada excavations in the 1970s, conducted by Hebrew University archaeologist Ehud Netzer. The ancient seeds from which Methuselah sprouted were found in a jar into which the inhabitants of Masada threw their date pits. For the past two millennia, since the Great Revolt of the Jews against the Romans in 66–73 CE, the seed lay dormant, until January 25, 2005, when the desert agriculture expert, Elaine Soloway of Kibbutz Ketura, successfully germinated it. She chose the day of Tu b'Shevat to plant the seeds, one of which began to sprout about two months later.[74] When the seedling was transferred to a larger pot, fragments of the seed's shell clinging to the plant's roots were discovered. The fragments were sent to the University of Zurich, where researchers dated them to be around 2,000 years ago.[75]

If it is a female plant, and the sapling continues to flourish, it will be possible to renew a species of date that grew in the Kingdom of Judea in ancient times, but disappeared in the centuries following the revolt at Masada. This could be an exciting alternative to today's date palms growing in Israel, which were imported during the 1950s and 1960s from modern cultivated Iraqi, Moroccan and Egyptian varieties.[76]

Growing and Harvesting

The Middle East has been growing date palms for centuries. The average date palm is about 18–20 feet tall and yields about 38 pounds of dates per year. Israeli date palms are now yielding 400 pounds per year and some are short enough to be harvested from the ground or a short ladder.

אָמַרְתִּי אֶעֱלֶה בְתָמָר אֹחֲזָה בְּסַנְסִנָּיו... (שיר השירים ז, ט)

"I said, I will go up into the date palm: I will take hold of its boughs..." (Song of Songs 7:9).

I want to climb up on the date palm, to ascend unto it like a ladder. I want to hold on to its boughs. One holds on to its branches in order to gather its fruits.[77]

The Righteous are Compared to the Date Palm

צַדִּיק כַּתָּמָר יִפְרָח כְּאֶרֶז בַּלְּבָנוֹן יִשְׂגֶּה: (תהילים צב, יג)

"The righteous shall flourish like the date palm: he shall grow like a cedar in Levanon" (Psalms 92:13).

The righteous person is compared to the date palm, which is straight, tall and strong, pleasant, tenacious and fruitful.[78] Its wide shade symbolizes that the reward of the righteous extends far. Just as the heart of the date palm is directed above, likewise the heart of the righteous is directed to Hashem.[79]

Why is the tzadik compared both to the date palm and the cedar? If it would have only compared him to the cedar, I might have thought that a righteous person does not produce fruits in the same way as the cedar does not bear fruits. Therefore, it states: "date palm." If it would have only stated "date palm," I might have thought that just as the trunk of the date palm does not replace itself; neither does the trunk of the righteous person replace itself. Therefore, it also states: "cedar."[80]

Just as the date palm has no waste, there is no waste in Israel. The fruit of the date palm is for eating; its heart (lulav)[81] is used for prayer and praise, its branches for shade (*sechach*), its fiber for ropes, its twigs for a sieve and its rafts as beams for the house. So too, every person in Israel is needed. Some are knowledgeable in Bible, some in Mishnah, others in Talmud and homiletic understanding of the Torah (*Aggadah*). There are also unlearned people, who still perform mitzvot, and give charity.[82]

Versatile Uses of Date Plant Material

The date palm is the most versatile of all indigenous plants, and virtually every part of the tree is utilized to make functional items ranging from rope and baskets to bee-keeping hives, fishing boats and traditional dwellings. It is said that there are as many uses of the date palm as there are days in a year.

Date pits are soaked and ground up for animal feed. Their oil is suitable for use in soap and cosmetic products. They can also be processed chemically as a source of oxalic acid. The pits are burned to make charcoal for silversmiths and can be strung in necklaces. Date pits are also ground and used like coffee beans, or as an additive to coffee. According to traditional Egyptian belief, swallowing a few date pits will prevent childbearing for many years.

Date palm leaves are used for making huts and fences. During the holiday of Sukkot, the leaves are selected for the *sechach* (the roof of the Sukkah – booth) and its heart for the lulav. Mature leaves are also made into mats, screens, baskets and fans. Processed leaves can be used for insulating boards. Dried leaf petioles are a source of cellulose pulp, used for walking sticks, brooms, fishing floats and fuel. Leaf sheaths are prized for their scent, and fiber from them is also used for rope, coarse cloth and large hats.

Stripped fruit clusters are used as brooms. In Pakistan, gooey, thick syrup made from the ripe fruits is used as a coating for leather bags and pipes to prevent leaking.

Date palm wood is used for posts and rafters for huts because it is lighter than coconut wood and more durable. It is also used in construction, for example, of bridges and aqueducts. Leftover wood is burnt for fuel. During Talmudic times in Babylon, date palm wood was even used to make tables and lamps.[83]

Date palm sap is used to make palm syrup, and numerous edible products are produced from this syrup.

❊ A Taste of Kabbalah – G*d the Healer and Date Palms

...כָּל הַמַּחֲלָה אֲשֶׁר שַׂמְתִּי בְמִצְרַיִם לֹא אָשִׂים עָלֶיךָ כִּי אֲנִי הַשֵּׁם
רֹפְאֶךָ: וַיָּבֹאוּ אֵילִמָה וְשָׁם שְׁתֵּים עֶשְׂרֵה עֵינֹת מַיִם וְשִׁבְעִים תְּמָרִים...
(שמות טו, כו-כז)

*"...I will bring none of these diseases upon you, which I have
brought upon Mitzrayim, for I am Hashem your healer. And
they came to Elim where there were twelve springs of water, and
seventy date palms..."* (Exodus 15:26–27).

ושבעים תמרים הם ע' מלאכים הסובבים כסא הכבוד וממונים על
ע' אומות שבעולם כל אחד ואחד ממונה על אומתו... ולא עוד אלא
בתמרים יש שבעים מינים דכתיב ושבעים תמרים ולא היו דומים זה לזה
ופעולות זה אינו דומה לזה וטעם זה אינו דומה לזה ע"כ... ונרמז לך בזה
כי מי"ב עינות אלה שהם ד' מחנות שכינה שואבים בה שבעים תמרים
הם המלאכים הסובבים כסא הכבוד המשילום בתמרים על שם הקומה,
והנה דוגמתם יצאו מיעקב י"ב שבטים הנחלקים לד' מחנות ומהם היו
שבעים נפש... (רבנו בחיי, שמות טו, כז)

The seventy date palms correspond to the seventy angels that
surround the Throne of Glory, and are in charge of the seventy
nations of the world, each in charge of one specific nation. Likewise, there are seventy different kinds of date palms with individual tastes and properties. The verse alludes to the fact that
the seventy date palms drew their sustenance from the twelve
springs, which represent the four camps of the Shechinah. The
angels who surround the Throne of Glory are compared to
date palms because of their tall stature (קוֹמָה/*komah*). They are
likened to the twelve tribes, descended from Ya'acov, who were
divided into four camps.[84] The seventy souls of Israel derived
from these [twelve tribes] (*Rabbeinu Bachaya*, Exodus 15:27).

Explanation: G*d's promise to be our healer is mentioned in the same breath as the description of the seventy date palms growing by the twelve springs of Elim. What is the connection between "I am Hashem your healer" and the "seventy date palms"?

Perhaps we can learn from this juxtaposition that Hashem's healing energy is manifested through these seventy date palms. The twelve springs from which the seventy date palms are nourished represent the twelve tribes of Israel, who in return are nourished by G*d. The place, Elim, is a contraction of *Elokim,* meaning G*d. Seventy is a significant number. It represents the seventy facets of the Torah.[85] The seventy souls that went down to Egypt also correspond to the seventy nations of the world. Just as the seventy date palms were nourished by the twelve springs, so will the seventy nations receive their nourishment from the people of Israel, when the tribes of Israel learn to live in unity and harmony with Hashem, and one another. Then, Israel can become true vessels for Hashem's boundless healing.

הרואה תמרים בחלום תמו עונותיו שנאמר
תַּם עֲוֺנֵךְ בַּת צִיּוֹן...

He who sees dates in a dream, his transgressions have ceased, as it says, "Your transgression has ceased,[86] daughter of Tzion"[87] (Babylonian Talmud, Berachot 57a).

Date Recipes

Alternative to Refined Sugar

Refined sugar contains no fiber, vitamins or minerals. In order to neutralize refined carbohydrates, and metabolize this incomplete food, the body must borrow nutrients from healthy cells, depleting the body of vital vitamins and minerals. Many readily available alternatives to refined sugar offer the potential benefit of additional antioxidant activity.[88] Date honey or syrup is an ideal alternative to processed sugar in most cooking and baking. The natural fiber in dates prevents the insulin rush created by refined sugar, which lowers the blood sugar rapidly, and causes a significant drop in energy and endurance. It is possible to sweeten most dishes with date syrup. I have used dates and date syrup in smoothies, ice creams, jams, and as a sweetener in baked goods, from muffins to oatmeal cookies and apple crisps.

Because there is an uncertainty whether the after-blessing for desserts made with mashed dates is '*borei nefashot*,' or '*M'ein Shalosh*,' it is recommended to eat three to four dates or other fruits from the Seven Species (depending on the size of the fruits, altogether the volume of a matchbox), together with a kezayit of additional food that requires the after-blessing of '*borei nefashot*,' with any of the date-dessert recipes in this section. See *Laws of Blessings* in this section, pages 378–380.

PRESERVING DATES
It's good to always have dates on hand for a quick energy snack

You can store dried dates in a cool, dry place from six months to a year.

Tightly wrapped fresh dates will keep for up to two weeks in the refrigerator.

HOME MADE DATE SYRUP

A great sweetener for pancakes and baked goods

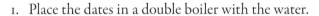

> 1 cup pitted dates
> 2 cups water

1. Place the dates in a double boiler with the water.
2. Bring it to just before boiling and simmer for half an hour.
3. Whisk into syrup in a blender, add water if needed to form the desired consistency.
4. Keep your natural syrup in the fridge, since it doesn't contain preservatives. When stored in the refrigerator it will keep for a few months.

HOME MADE DATE SUGAR

An alternative to refined white sugar

1. Arrange sliced dates on a baking sheet and bake at 450 F° (232 C°) for 10–15 minutes, or until very dry and hard as rocks.
2. Grind or process in a food processor to make sugar.

COCONUT DATE BITS

A simple, healthy and heavenly Shabbat dessert

> 12–16 dates
> Half a fresh coconut, cut into small, finger-sized pieces

1. Open the dates, remove the pits and check for bugs.

2. Insert the coconut bits inside the dates in place of the pits.

3. Arrange on a platter with fresh strawberries in the center, inside half of a coconut shell (optional).

DREAM OF DATE BALLS

These are always a hit, even with kids who are used to junk food

2 cups mashed or chopped pitted dates (500 g)
½ cup rolled oats
½ cup coconut
1 cup almonds, sunflower, flax or sesame seeds,
or any mixture of nuts and seeds of your choice
½–1 cup fresh apples or mushy fruits of your choice
2 tablespoons grated ginger
Shredded coconut for rolling
Water as needed

1. Cut apples or other fruits into quarters.
2. Place in food processor with remaining ingredients except shredded coconut.
3. Process with the S-blade, adding enough water to make a sticky mass.
4. Shape into balls, and roll in shredded coconut or sesame seeds. Enjoy!

You can be creative with your energy balls and throw almost anything in them that you have on hand. The fresh ginger really adds a delicious flavor. When I don't have time to roll the mixture into individual balls, I just make one large cylinder-shaped roll, which I cut into slices before serving it.

DATE ENERGY BALLS

It's hard to believe that these date balls are sugar free

2 cups chopped pitted dates
½ cup nuts (very coarsely ground)
½ cup techina
6 tablespoons carob powder
2 tablespoons fresh grated ginger (optional)
Juice of one ripe orange or lemon (optional)
Shredded coconut for rolling

1. Mix everything by hand rather than in the food processor. (The date mass will become caramel like, and the coarsely ground nuts will add delicious texture).

2. Shape into balls and roll in shredded coconut.

CAROB ALMOND DATE BALLS

A great energy burst for children as well as adults

1½ cup almonds
½ cup hazelnuts
½ cup coconut chunks (fresh, if possible; otherwise, shredded)
½ cup ground sesame seeds
¼ cup ground flax seeds
15 pitted dates
1 tablespoon honey
4 tablespoons carob powder

1. Process everything in the food processor until smooth.
2. Shape into cylinders and roll in shredded coconut.
3. Slice before serving or shape into balls rolled in coconut.
4. Place in a sealed container in the freezer.
5. Remove from freezer about 15 minutes before serving.

These date balls will keep longer than people can wait to eat them.

RAW FRUIT PIE WITH NUTTY DATE CRUST
A an unbelievable raw-food treat with the most amazing crust

Crust
2 cups walnuts
1½ cups dates

1. Choose dates that are firm and not too mushy.

2. Process your crust in two batches. Combine half the dates and half the walnuts in each batch.

3. Process about 40 seconds until well mixed and ground, but not smooth. The texture needs to be as coarse as possible while ground enough to hold together when pressed.

4. Press evenly into a 23 cm (9 inch) tart pan.

5. Set in the refrigerator for one hour.

Filling
3 sliced apples, peaches, apricots or whatever fruit you have around
Juice of 1 lemon
¼ teaspoon cinnamon, with a dash of ground clove and or allspice
2 tablespoons honey

1. Spread apple mixture evenly over crust.

2. Cover with a thin layer of honey.

3. Serve right away, or keep in freezer or refrigerator until needed.

Filling Variation

1 cup puréed apricots
¼ cup apple juice concentrate or fruit syrup
2 sliced apples or other fruit
Shredded coconut for topping

1. Spread a thin layer of sliced apples or other fruit on crust.
2. Process apricots with apple juice concentrate until smooth.
3. Spread evenly over the apples.
4. Sprinkle shredded coconut on top.

GUILT-FREE CHOCOLATE MOUSSE PIE WITH NUTTY CRUST

Elegant, exquisite and hard to resist

Crust

1 cup cashews or other nuts

(I use half almonds and half sunflower seeds)

Half a fresh coconut or 1 cup dried shredded coconut

1 cup dates

1 tablespoon coconut or almond oil

Pure vanilla extract (optional)

Process the crust ingredients in the food processor with the S-blade until well-mixed. The texture needs to be as coarse as possible while ground enough to hold together when pressed. Press evenly into a 23 cm (9 inch) tart pan. Place in the freezer for half an hour. You can experiment with different natural date crusts using a variety of nuts and spices such as ginger, cardamom and cinnamon. You may substitute part of the dates with honey or maple syrup. You can make the crust more or less sweet according to the ratio of nuts to sweetener. Enjoy. It's all good!

Mousse

2 cups nuts (cashews, walnuts, almonds, sunflower seeds etc.
or a mixture of any nuts)

12–15 pitted dates

(You may substitute part of the dates with soaked raisins,
honey or maple syrup).

2 tablespoons cocoa or cacao powder

1 tablespoon coconut oil

A pinch of salt

Water according to need

1. Process the nuts in the food processor with the S-blade.

2. Add the remaining ingredients except for the water.

3. Add the water very gradually until desired consistency is
    reached. (The mousse needs to be neither hard nor too moist).

4. Spread the mousse on top of the nut crust and place in the
    freezer.

5. Remove from freezer about 15 minutes before serving.

6. Decorate with organic strawberries or other colorful fruit.

ALMOND CHOCOLATE FILLED DATES
Absolutely fabulous, flavorful and festive, worth the extra effort

20 large pitted dates
40 whole almonds

Almond-Chocolate Filling
⅓ cup ground almonds
⅓ cup cocoa or cacao powder
2 tablespoons honey or date syrup
1 tablespoon shredded coconut
1 teaspoon pure vanilla extract
½ teaspoon cinnamon
¼ cup techina

1. Process the almonds in the food processor with the S-blade until minced.

2. Add remaining ingredients and process until everything is well-combined.

3. Assemble the dates by taking a heaping teaspoon of the almond-chocolate filling and wrapping it around an almond.

4. Fill a date cavity with the almond covered by the almond-chocolate filling.

5. Press an almond in the center of the almond chocolate-filled date.

6. Repeat steps 3–5 in order to assemble the rest of the dates.

POMEGRANATE PALM HEARTS SALAD

An attractive salad with complementary colors of green, white and ruby red

1½ cup sliced hearts of palm
3 cups torn fresh spinach or other greens
1 bunch (about ½ cup) arugula
1 coarsely grated carrot
1 red pepper sliced in long strips
2 stalks chopped celery
A handful of chopped black olives
½ cup of pomegranate arils
½ cup sunflower sprouts
(you may substitute alfalfa or other sprouts)
⅓ cup olive oil
2 tablespoons apple cider vinegar
¼ teaspoon garlic granules
¼ teaspoon sea salt
¼ teaspoon freshly ground black pepper

1. Toss the vegetables together with olive oil.

2. Add spices and mix well.

3. Add vinegar.

4. Sprinkle pomegranate arils and sprouts on top.

Laws of Blessings ~ הִלְכוֹת בְּרָכוֹת

Jews have been eating hearts of palm for probably 2000 years. The Talmud discusses their correct blessing.[89] Rav Yehuda said that the blessing should be '*borei p'ri ha'adamah*' like any other vegetable, whereas Shemuel held that it should be '*shehakol*' since palm trees are not planted with the intention to eat their hearts, which eventually harden. Based on this statement, it became the accepted halachic ruling to recite '*shehakol*' on palm hearts.[90] However, today, contemporary producers of palm hearts cultivate plantations of particular palm species for the sake of the hearts just like any other crop. Therefore, it seems that the correct blessing before eating palm hearts should be '*borei p'ri ha'adamah*' and not '*shehakol*' (It would not be '*borei p'ri ha'etz*' because one is eating the stem, not the fruit).[91]

The Blessings for Mashed Dates and Desserts made with Dates

The blessing, on dates which have been mashed by hand and made into a dough by removing their pits, is not changed, and we bless on them: '*borei p'ri ha'etz*,' and the after-blessing '*M'ein Shalosh*.'[92] This is also the case if we make a fruit marmalade from them, on which we bless '*borei p'ri ha'etz*.'

There is an opinion to bless 'shehakol,' and it is good *lechatchila*[93] to bless 'shehakol.' However, if we blessed 'borei p'ri ha'etz' we are covered (*yotze*), because [the fruits] are the main ingredient (*ikar*).[94]

Even if the fruit is completely mashed, as long as its substance remains, we still bless 'borei p'ri ha'etz.' This is the case with mashed vegetables such as mashed potatoes: their original *bracha* (blessing) remains.

It is not clear whether the opinion brought by the Rama to bless 'shehakol.' contradicts the ruling of Rav Yosef Karo and refers to mashed dates in general, or whether it refers specifically to fruit jam that has lost its original form completely. In any case, the halacha is according to Rav Yosef Karo, that as long as the substance of the fruit/vegetable still exists, the original blessing remains. However, when the produce has lost its original form completely to the extent that it is no longer recognized, then we bless *lechatchila* 'shehakol' as the Rama teaches that this blessing covers everything 'bedieved.' However, regarding the after-blessing, 'borei nefashot' does not cover the Seven Species, even if fruit has lost its form completely. Therefore, if fruits from the Seven Species have been completely puréed, it is best to eat them together with something else that requires the after-blessing of 'borei *nefashot,'* in order to eliminate any doubt. If these are not available, it seems that we could still recite the *'M'ein Shalosh'* after-blessing. This is because the Seven Species, even when they have lost their original form completely, can still be considered fruits covered by their original blessing.[95]

Rabbi Mandelbaum helps us to distinguish between the mashed produce that has lost its form completely and the fruits/vegetables whose substance still remain. If the produce is mashed by hand or with a hand tool such as a fork, then even if its exterior form is completely lost, its interior form and substance still remains and it, therefore, retains its original blessing. However, if the fruits/vegetables are mashed in a blender or in a food processor for a long time, then even the interior form is lost.[96] Therefore, the blessing *'shehakol'* applies to all my recipes which are processed in the food processor for a long time or cooked with water. The blessing *'borei p'ri ha'etz'* covers my date energy balls which are mixed by hand. The date nut crusts in this section would also require the *'borei p'ri ha'etz'* blessing since they are only processed briefly in the food processer and their consistencies remain coarse.

I am Queen Tamar, a tall, slender woman dedicated to my people. While holding my head up high and walking upright, I run my corporation with wisdom and kindness. My motto is: "Love and truth preserve the king; and his throne is upheld by kindness."[97] I'm in charge of *The Global Philanthropic Corporation* (GPC), which ensures that the basic needs of every man, woman and child in the entire world are fulfilled, as well as their emotional and spiritual yearnings. Perhaps the success of the corporation is due to the fact that various kinds of people gravitate toward me because I can forget myself and identify with all of them. Affluent donors from the four corners of the earth continually contribute to the GPC, and I delegate the responsibilities of providing food, medical care and education to my very proficient international staff. My administrator sets up online meetings enabling every staff member to receive my gentle instructions and encouragement. So far, we have fed six million people and built 22,000 schools and adult education centers. I do not have to think about myself and my own needs. Channeling so much goodness in the world brings me fulfillment and happiness. I don't even need much sleep, as the wise King Solomon teaches, "She perceives that her merchandise is good; her candle does not go out by night."[98] Yet, I don't take credit for any of these accomplishments. I'm just an emissary of the Only One, allowing Him to act through me.

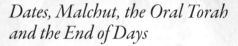

*Dates, Malchut, the Oral Torah
and the End of Days*

Just as he who climbs the date palm without being careful may fall and die, likewise, anyone who comes against Israel will receive what he deserves from their hands in the end (*Midrash Genesis Rabbah* 41:1).

The Hebrew word for dates, תָּמָר/*tamar,* is related to the word תֹּם/*tom,* which means 'finish,' 'cease,' 'complete,' or 'end.' For this reason we partake of dates during the Rosh Hashana Seder,[99] while reciting: "May it be your will that our foes cease (יִתַּמּוּ/*yitamu*) to harass us!" The date is called 'end' because it is the last of the Seven Species, and it seems that it has the power to make the soul seek the End of Days.

One reason why Israel was exiled to Babylon was in order to "eat dates and be involved with Torah."[100] The Oral Torah was specifically established in Babylon, because "Honey makes the tongue accustomed to Torah."[101]

Dates correspond to the mouth, represented by the Oral Torah, since *Malchut* is the channel for everything to pass through. Everything in the physical reality includes an inner spiritual dimension. On the physical level, dates loosen the bowels. The corresponding spiritual attribute is the power of the soul to eliminate all kinds of waste and impurity from the environment. For this reason, dates flourish in lowlands. They grew in Babylon, which is low like a pit, where all waste collects. Preceding the End of Days, when the world descends to its lowest point and is filled with refuse, the spiritual energy of the dates is needed to eliminate both the physical and spiritual contamination of the earth.

"The righteous person will flourish like a date palm,"[102] specifically from the lowest place. The date palm has the power to bring about a good ending through the righteous. The righteous date palm will help us reveal that bitter darkness leads to a good and sweet end. Just as the date palm extracts the few drops of water from the dry desert soil, so will the righteous person find merit for the Jewish people during their spiritual decline prior to the End of Days, Amen![103]

Endnotes

1. "בסוד הדיבור שהיא מלכות – The secret of speech is *Malchut*"
   (Arizal, *Sefer HaLikutim, Parashat Emor,* chapter 23).

2. Genesis 2:23.

3. Date –תָּמָר/*tamar*, dates – תְּמָרִים/*temarim*, date palm – תֹּמֶר/*tomer,*
   תִּמֹרָה/*timorah* and date palms תִּמֹרִים/*timorim*, and honey – דְּבַשׁ/*devash*
   when referring to dates are mentioned 36 times in the Bible.
   Date –תָּמָר/*tamar* is mentioned in the Bible in the singular form nine times,
   once in the Pentateuch and eight times in the rest of the Bible: Genesis
   14:7; Judges 20:33; Ezekiel 47:19, 48:28; Joel 1:12; Psalms 12:13; Song of
   Songs 7:8, 7:9; II Chronicles 20:2.
   Dates – תְּמָרִים/*temarim* are mentioned in the Bible in the plural form
   eight times, four times in the Pentateuch and four times in the rest of the
   Bible: Exodus 15:27; Leviticus 23:40; Numbers:33:9; Deuteronomy 34:3;
   Judges 1:16, 3:13; Nehemiah 8:15; II Chronicles 28:15.
   Date palm – תֹּמֶר/*tomer,* תִּמֹרָה/*timorah* is mentioned five times in the
   singular form in the Bible: Judges 4:5; Jeremiah 10:5; Ezekiel 41:18, 41:19
   (twice).
   Date palms תִּמֹרִים/*timorim* are mentioned 10 times in the plural form
   in the Bible: Ezekiel 40:16, 40:26, 40:31, 40:34, 40:37, 41:18, 41:20, 41:25,
   41:26; II Chronicles 3:5. There are two women in the Bible named Tamar.
   The first, who became the mother of the Messianic lineage, is mentioned
   six times in chapter 38 of Genesis, once in The Scroll of Ruth and once in
   I Chronicles. The second, the daughter of King David, who was violated
   by her half-brother Amnon, is mentioned 14 times in chapters 13 and 14
   in II Samuel and once in I Chronicles.
   Honey – דְּבַשׁ/*devash* is mentioned 53 times in the Bible, only four of
   which clearly refer to date honey: Deuteronomy 8:8; II Kings 18:32;
   Jeremiah 41:8; II Chronicles 31:5.

4. Based on Rav Mordechai Weinberg, Album *Perek Shirah,* quoting Rabbi
   Chaim Kanievsky, *Perek b'Shir.*

5. The mineral and vitamin content of dates is based on USDA,
   Basic Report: 09421, *Dates, medjool,* compared with additional scientific

sources quoted below. The percentage of Recommended Daily Dietary Allowance is based on *Dates, medjool,* <http://www.nutrition-and-you.com/dates.html> retrieved June 25, 2013.

6. Dates contain almost twice the amount of potassium as bananas. Compare with USDA National Nutrient Database for Standard Reference where bananas are listed as containing 358 mg per 100 g. *Basic Report*: 09049, *Bananas, raw.*

7. See also Al-Farsi MA, Lee CY, *Nutritional and Functional Properties of Dates.* Crit Rev Food Sci Nutr. 2008 Nov;48(10):877–87. This article claims that "10 minerals were reported, the major being selenium, copper, potassium and magnesium." This differs slightly from the USDA National Nutrient Database, in which selenium is not measured and calcium is one of the major minerals, followed by phosphorus, and only a small amount of copper is listed.

8. Al-Shahib W, Marshall RJ, *The Fruit of the Date Palm: Its Possible Use as the Best Food for the Future?* Int J Food Sci Nutr. 2003 Jul;54(4):247–59. This is compatible with USDA National Nutrient Database. However, USDA does not measure boron, cobalt and fluorine.

9. Contrary to USDA National Nutrient Database, which lists dates as containing no vitamin C, Al-Farsi writes: "Vitamins B-complex and C are the major vitamins in dates" (Al-Farsi MA, Lee CY, *Nutritional and Functional Properties of Dates*).

10. "Dates contain at least six vitamins including a small amount of vitamin C, and vitamins B(1) thiamine, B(2) riboflavin, nicotinic acid (niacin) and vitamin A." (Al-Shahib W, Marshall RJ, *The Fruit of the Date Palm: Its Possible Use as the Best Food for the Future?*)

11. Al-Farsi MA, Lee CY, *Nutritional and Functional Properties of Dates.*

12. Michael Tierra, *Planetary Herbology*, p. 34.

13. Michael Tierra, *Planetary Herbology*, p. 41.

14. Based on Song of Songs 7:8, quoted above.

15. Rabbi Kalonymus Kalman HaLevi Epstein, Kraków, Poland (circa 1753–1823), מאור ושמש/*Maor V'Shemesh, Parashat Vayetze.*

16. Isaiah 1:1–4.

17. See the *Introduction*, p. 18, endnote mark 27, Arizal, *Sefer HaLikutim, Parashat Terumah*, chapter 26.

18. Rav Yitzchak Ginsburgh, *Basics in Kabbalah, The Ten Sefirot: Divine Emanations* <http://www.inner.org/sefirot/sefmalcu.htm> retrieved August 21, 2013.

19. Rav Yitzchak Ginsburgh, *Body, Mind, and Soul*, p. 96.

20. *Babylonian Talmud, Ketubot*, 10b; ChihCheng T. Chao Robert R. Krueger,

The Date Palm (Phoenix dactylifera L.): Overview of Biology, Uses, and Cultivation, Department of Botany and Plant Sciences, Am. J. Bot. September 1, 2011 98:1389–1414.

21. Rabbi Binyamin Moshe Kohn Shauli, *Nature's Wealth,* p. 266.

22. Al-Shahib W, Marshall RJ, *The Fruit of the Date Palm: Its possible Use as the Best Food for the Future?*

23. Ishurd O, Zgheel F, Kermagi A, Flefla M, Elmabruk M. *Antitumor Activity of Beta-D-Glucan from Libyan Dates.* J Med Food. 2004 Summer; 7(2):252–5).

24. *Harvard, School of Public Health, Powerful Ideas for a Healthier World* <http://www.hsph.harvard.edu/nutritionsource/fiber-table/> retrieved June 3, 2013.

25. Al-Farsi MA, Lee CY, *Nutritional and Functional Properties of Dates.*

26. Zohary D, Hopf M, *Date Palm Phoenix Dactylifera. Domestication of Plants in the Old World.* Oxford University Press, 2nd ed., 1993.

27. See the *Introduction*, p. 18, endnote mark 27, Arizal, *Sefer HaLikutim, Parashat Terumah*, chapter 26.

28. Ibn Ezra, Deuteronomy 33:5.

29. Deuteronomy 33:5.

30. Numbers 11:12.

31. *Babylonian Talmud, Ta'anit* 9a.

32. Vayalil PK. *Date fruits (Phoenix Dactylifera Linn): An Emerging Medicinal Food.* Crit Rev Food Sci Nutr. 2012;52(3):249–71.

33. Zohary D, Hopf M, *Date Palm Phoenix Dactylifera. Domestication of Plants in the Old World.* Oxford University Press, 2nd ed., 1993.

34. Ishurda O, John FK. *The Anti-Cancer Activity of Polysaccharide Prepared from Libyan Dates (Phoenix Dactylifera L.).* Carbohydrate Polymers 2005;9:31–5.

35. Abdulla Y, Al-Taher. *Possible Anti-Diarrhoeal Effect of the Date Palm (Phoenix Dactylifera L) Spathe Aqueous Extract in Rats.* Scientific Journal of King Faisal University (Basic and Applied Sciences) 2008;9:131–7.

36. Vayalil PK. *Antioxidant and Antimutagenic Properties of Aqueous Extract of Date Fruit (Phoenix dactylifera L. Arecaceae)* J Agric Food Chem 2002;50:610–7; Doha MA, Al-Okbi SY. *In Vivo Evaluation of Antioxidant and Anti-Inflammatory Activity of Different Extracts of Date Fruits in Adjuvant Arthritis.* Polish Journal of Food and Nutrition Sciences 2004;13:397–402.

37. El-Desoky GE, Ragab AA, Ismail SA, Kamal AE. *Effect of Palm-Pollen Grains (Phoenix Dactylifera) on Sexhormones, Proteins, Lipids and Liver Functions.* J Agric Sci Mansoura Univ 1995;20:4249–68.

38. Sabah AAJ, Mazen AN. *In Vitro Evaluation of the Antiviral Activity of an Extract of Date Palm (Phoenix Dactylifera L.) Pits on a Pseudomonas Phage.* eCAM 2007;15:1–6.

39. Al-Kharage, Rokaya. *Protective Effects of Phoenix Dactylifera (date palm) Against Cisplatin Induced Genotoxicity.* Food Science and Technology Abstracts 1982;4:8C–331 J.

40. A Al-Qarawi AA, Abdel-Rahman H, Mousa HM, BH Ali, El-Mougy SA. *Nephroprotective Action of Phoenix Dactylifera. in Gentamicin-Induced Nephrotoxicity.* Pharmaceutical Biol 2008;4:227–30.

41. ChihCheng T. Chao Robert R. Krueger, *The Date Palm (Phoenix Dactylifera L.): Overview of Biology, Uses, and Cultivation.* HortScience August 2007 vol. 42 no. 5 1077–1082.

42. Rambam, *Mishneh Torah, Hilchot Deot* 4:10.

43. Nisim Krispil, *Medicinal Herbs of the Rambam,* p. 215.

44. Rabbi Binyamin Moshe Kohn Shauli, *Nature's Wealth,* p. 266.

45. *Babylonian Talmud, Pesachim* 88a.

46. Bennett RD, Ko S, Heftmann E. *Isolation of Estrone and Cholesterol from the Date Palm, Phoenix Dactylifera L.* Phytochemistry, Volume 5, Issue 2, March 1966, pp. 231–235, 1016/S0031-9422(00)85122-5.

47. Al-Kuran O, Al-Mehaisen L, Bawadi H, Beitawi S, Amarin Z. *The Effect of Late Pregnancy Consumption of Date Fruit on Labour and Delivery.* J Obstet Gynaecol. 2011;31(1):29–31. This study concluded that the consumption of dates during the last four weeks before labor significantly reduced the need for induction of labor, and was conducive to easier delivery.

48. Rabbi Nachman, הַמִּדוֹת סֵפֶר/*Sefer Hamidot, on Depression*, 35.

49. Rabbi Binyamin Moshe Kohn Shauli, *Nature's Wealth,* p. 266.

50. *Babylonian Talmud, Ketubot* 10b.

51. Rabbi Binyamin Moshe Kohn Shauli, *Nature's Wealth,* p. 266.

52. Al-Tirmidhi 3/79 and others, Saheeh, *Al-Irwa'*, no. 922.

53. Imam Ibn Qayyim Al Jauziyah (Muslim Scholar, 1292–1350), *Healing With the Medicine of the Prophet* (Al-Tibb al-Nabawi,) English translation by Juail Abdual Rub, New Color Edition, Darussalam, 2010.

54. Psalms 19:11; *Sifrei, Parashat Ekev* 12; Rav Tzadok HaKohen of Lublin, *P'ri Tzadik, Et HaOchel* 13.

55. *Jerusalem Talmud, Ta'anit* 25a.

56. *Babylonian Talmud, Pesachim* 88a.

57. That is, very good. Dates are good, or very good, after the meals in the morning, noon and evening. They are not good in the afternoon after a rest (Rashi, *ad. loc.*).

58. A *log* is a liquid measure equal to 0.3 liter (a little more than one cup).

59. There is no contradiction; dates are good after a meal. The passage which declares them bad (unhealthy) speaks of a case where one eats dates before a meal.

60. They sustain the body as the bar supports a door (Rashi, *ad. loc.*).

61. Rabbi Adin Even Yisrael (Steinshaltz), *Babylonian Talmud, Ketubot* 10b.

62. Rashi, *Babylonian Talmud, Ketubot* 10b.

63. Rabbi Adin Even Yisrael, *Babylonian Talmud, Ketubot* 10b.

64. Rabbi Adin Even Yisrael, *Babylonian Talmud, Ketubot* 10b.

65. Rashi, *Babylonian Talmud, Ketubot* 10b.

66. Rabbi Adin Even Yisrael, *Babylonian Talmud, Ketubot* 10b.

67. Rashi, *Babylonian Talmud, Ketubot* 10b.

68. *Babylonian Talmud, Pesachim* 56a.

69. Psalms 40:2, based on *Midrash Genesis Rabbah* 41:1; *Midrash Numbers Rabbah* 3:1.

70. *Zohar,* part 1, p. 82a.

71. *Babylonian Talmud, Megillah* 14a.

72. Rabbi Binyamin Moshe Kohn Shauli, *Nature's Wealth,* p. 266; Pujari RR, Vyawahare NS, Kagathara VG. *Evaluation of Antioxidant and Neuroprotective Effect of Date Palm (Phoenix Dactylifera L.) Against Bilateral Common Carotid Artery Occlusion in Rats.* Indian J Exp Biol. 2011 Aug;49(8):627–33.

73. The Biblical Metushelach became a symbol of longevity, as he lived 969 years, longer than any other man, see Genesis 5:27.

74. The 15th of the Jewish month of *Shevat* at the end of winter season celebrates the New Year for the Tree (*Mishnah, Tractate Rosh Hashana* 1:1).

75. The fragments were discovered by a team led by Sarah Sallon, BSC, MBBS, MRCP (UK), Director and founder of The Louis Borick Natural Medicine Research Centre, Hadassah Medical Center, Jerusalem.

76. Based on *National Geographic News*, November 22, 2005.

77. *Da'at Mikra*, Song of Songs 7:9.

78. Psalms 92:13, with the commentary of Ibn Ezra, *Metzudat David* and Malbim.

79. *Midrash Genesis Rabbah* 41:1.

80. *Babylonian Talmud, Baba Batra* 80b.

81. One of the four ceremonial plant species used during the Jewish holiday of Sukkot.

82. Based on *Midrash Genesis Rabbah* 41:1; *Midrash Numbers Rabbah* 3:1.

83. *Midrash Numbers Rabbah* 3:1.

84. The tribes of Yehuda, Shimon and Gad in the east, Reuven, Yissaschar and Zevulun in the south, Dan, Asher, and Naftali in the north, Efraim, Menashe and Binyamin in the west.

85. *Midrash Bamidbar Rabbah* 13:15.

86. The Hebrew word for date, תָּמָר/*tamar*, is a contraction of the words, תָּמוּ הָמוֹרִים/*tamu hamorim*, which means 'the sinners have ceased.'

87. Lamentations 4:22.

88. Phillips KM, Carlsen MH, Blomhoff R. *Journal of the American Dietetic Association, Total Antioxidant Content of Alternatives to Refined Sugar,* J Am Diet Assoc. 2009 Jan;109(1):64–71.

89. *Babylonian Talmud, Berachot* 36a.

90. *Shulchan Aruch, Orach Chaim* 204:1.

91. Rabbi Yirmiyohu Kaganoff, *Shlita* < http://rabbikaganoff.com/archives/1527> retrieved December 21, 2012.

92. *Shulchan Aruch, Orach Chaim,* 202:7. The *Magen Avraham* (202:18) quotes the *Rokei'ach* as ruling, in line with the Rambam, that one recites '*borei p'ri ha'etz*' over cooked, crushed dates. The *Magen Avraham* also points out that the *Shulchan Aruch* states explicitly in 204:11 that even over fruit crushed up very finely one recites the blessing '*borei p'ri ha'etz,*' and the Rama does not object.

93. The ideal halachic practice is called *lechatchila*, whereas the less preferred, after-the-fact practice is called *bedieved*.

94. The *Rama, Shulchan Aruch, Orach Chaim,* 202:7.

95. *Mishnah Berurah, Orach Chaim* 202: 40–42.

96. Rabbi A.A. Mandelbaum , *V'zot Habracha*, p. 237.

97. Proverbs 20:28.

98. Proverbs 31:18.

99. Jewish New Year Ritual.

100. *Babylonian Talmud, Pesachim* 88a.

101. *Jerusalem Talmud, Ta'anit* 25a.

102. Psalms 92:13.

103. This section is based on Rav Tzadok HaKohen of Lublin, *P'ri Tzadik, Et HaOchel* 13.

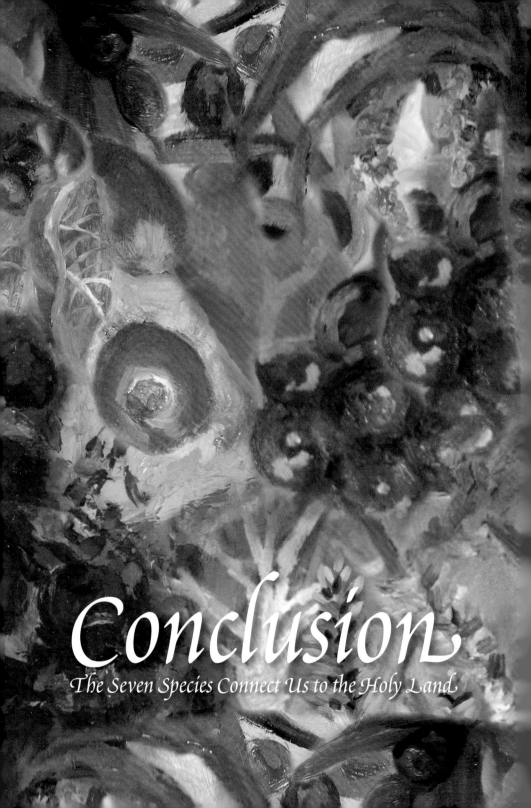

Conclusion

The Seven Species Connect Us to the Holy Land

The Seven Species Connect us to the Holy Land

*A*fter eating a meal of one of the Seven Species, we recite the three-fold after-blessing ('*M'ein Shalosh*') thanking Hashem for the "precious good and spacious Land…," no matter where the fruits were actually grown. Even Italian olives or Californian raisins require this after-blessing, while after eating a Jaffa orange, for example, we only recite the short '*borei nefashot*' even if the orange is imported from Israel. Why do only the Seven Species require the long benediction where we thank Hashem for the Land of Israel?

The Holy Land is specifically praised for these seven holy fruits due to their spiritual genetics that inherently connect them to the Land of Israel. Therefore, these Seven Species have the special ability to arouse the children of Israel's inherent connection with their Holy Land. Moreover, every time we recite the threefold after-blessing, we have the opportunity to rectify the sin of the *meraglim*/spies who found fruits of the Seven Species in the Land of Israel, but nevertheless were not grateful to Hashem for the gift of the Land.[1] Today, when it is possible to grow the same wonderful fruits outside of the Land, Diaspora Jewry may be tempted to walk in the footsteps of the spies and mistakenly think that we do not need the Land of Israel. Therefore, when partaking of the Seven Species grown abroad, we thank Hashem for the Holy Land to remind ourselves that we must always recognize the blessings of the Land of Israel even when enjoying the goodness of Californian grape juice. The fact that we are required to thank Hashem for the Land of Israel, even when we eat fruits grown abroad, reminds Diaspora Jewry on a daily basis that they have no true homeland except the Land of Israel.

The Fruits of the Entire World Receive their Blessings from the Land of Israel

There is a slight difference between the after-blessing for the Seven Species grown in Israel and those grown abroad. We end the blessing for the fruits grown in Israel by thanking Hashem "for the land and for **her** fruits,"[2] rather than the general: "For the land and for **the** fruits" recited over the Seven Species grown outside of Israel.[3]

There is a Talmudic principle that it is inappropriate to bundle blessings together and end a bracha with two praises. Rather we must thank Hashem separately for each goodness that He bestows upon us. It is, therefore, unusual that we conclude the '*M'ein Shalosh*' blessing by seemingly thanking Hashem for two things: for the Land, and for the fruits. However, these two praises are actually one: "Thank You Hashem for the Land that gives us the fruits."

If this is so, how does reciting the '*M'ein Shalosh*' after-blessing then include thanking Hashem for the fruits grown outside of the Land of Israel? It seems that by reciting this benediction, we only thank Hashem for the Land of Israel and the fruits that it produces.

In truth, all blessings everywhere in the world come from the Land of Israel. As a result, all fruits in the world are blessed through the Land of Israel. Therefore, when we thank Hashem for the Seven Fruits of Israel, we recognize that the Land of Israel bestows its blessing on the fruits everywhere in the world. Consequently, we thank Hashem for the Land that produces the fruit, the Land of Israel, that causes the fruits in the entire world to grow.[4]

Absorbing the Torah of the Land by Eating its Fruits

Living in the Holy Land provides a unique ability for understanding its Torah. Since Tu b'Shevat is the day of actualizing our potential for *chidushei* Torah (original Torah insights), it is a special mitzvah then to eat from the fruits of *Eretz Yisrael* (Land of Israel). Partaking in the fruits of the Land nourishes us with the *shefah* (abundance) of understanding the Torah's wisdom that pours into Eretz Yisrael, where the Shechinah dwells. Taking pleasure in her fruits saturates us with the spiritual Torah of the Land.

Whereas it was necessary for the Israelites, during their journey in the wilderness, to eat manna in order to become purified and worthy to receive the Torah, there was no need for the manna to fall in Eretz Yisrael. This is because the holiness of her fruits provides sufficient purification and capability for understanding Torah in the deepest way.

Inheriting the Land in order to Partake of her Fruits

After thanking Hashem for the "precious, good and spacious land," we add in the threefold blessing recited after eating any of the Seven Species or products made from them, "which You have graciously given as a heritage to our ancestors [in order] to eat of her fruit and be satiated with her goodness..." – שֶׁרָצִיתָ וְהִנְחַלְתָּ לַאֲבוֹתֵינוּ לֶאֱכֹל מִפִּרְיָה וְלִשְׂבּוֹעַ מִטּוּבָהּ/*sheratzita v'hinchalta la'avoteinu le'echol mipiriya v'lisboa mituvah*. Several Rabbis suggested removing this sentence, because it may sound as if Hashem grants us the land only for the sake of eating her fruits. However, the *Bach* responds that the purpose of inheriting the Land of Israel is indeed to partake of her fruits, because the goodness of the fruits of the Land emanates from the purity of the Shechinah. When we eat the fruits of Israel, we are nourished by the holiness of Eretz Yisrael inherent in these fruits that receive their sustenance from the Shechinah.[5]

Appendix 1 – *Tu b'Shevat Gleanings*

Tu b'Shevat – Celebrating the Fruits of the Land of Israel

The Seven Species of the Land receive their honorable elevation during their celebration on Tu b'Shevat – the New Year of the Tree. On that holiday, we recognize how these holy fruits are vehicles through which our mutual relationship with Hashem is expressed. Hashem bestows His blessings of fruit upon Israel, and the children of Israel praise Hashem for the fruits of the Holy Land. In addition, since the Torah is a "Tree of Life,"[6] the fruits of the Land reflect the unique Torah of Eretz Yisrael. Just as the tree of the field blossoms on Tu b'Shevat due to the rain water it receives that year, likewise the Tree of Life within us, the Torah, flourishes then. The chidushei Torah granted to us on Rosh Hashana in potential, materialize on Tu b'Shevat through the blossoms of the new fruits.

Fruity People and Vegetative Donkeys

In the beginning of Creation fruits were destined for humanity and vegetables for the beasts. "Hashem, G*d, commanded Adam, saying, 'You shall eat from any tree in the Garden...'"[7] Before eating from the forbidden fruit, Adam and Chava were nourished directly by the fruits of the Garden, being free to devote themselves completely to Torah, without having to work for a living. After the sin Adam was told: "You shall eat the herb of the field."[8] Upon hearing this, he began to shed tears crying, "Shall I and my donkey eat out of the same vessel?"[9] What was so devastating about the offer to eat other plants rather than just fruits? The quality of fruit is distinguished from other plants. Fruit trees have the ability to continue to produce fruit for many generations. Even after the fruit has been consumed, there remains vast potential in the tree. Adam was originally on the level of fruits, a vast reservoir of hidden potential. By eating from the forbidden fruit, he dropped closer to the level of the animals. An animal is called a בְּהֵמָה/*behemah*, consisting of the words בָּהּ מָה/ *bah mah* which means, 'In it is something,' in other words what you see is what you get.' Likewise, the entire vegetable and grain is consumed. When told to eat vegetables like a donkey without hidden potential, Adam understood that his capacity for spiritual development was greatly reduced. We yearn for the final redemption, when we will regain the spiritual heights of Adam in the Garden. "In the future...trees will bear fruit every month, and humanity will eat of them and be healed..."[10] Tu b'Shevat is the day of rejoicing over fruit, the most spiritual of foods, and a day of hope for our ultimate return to our true greatness in the Garden.

The Tu b'Shvat Seder

The fruit Seder on Tu b'Shevat connects us to the Garden of Eden, when humanity ate fruits in the presence of the Shechinah. In the past few decades, as we get closer to our final redemption and return to Paradise, the Tu b'Shevat Fruit Seder has become widespread among Jews across the world. It facilitates partaking of the fruits of the Land in a mindful way, enjoying their colors, textures and tastes, while praising Hashem for the fruits with intentional blessings. Originally in the Garden of Eden, humanity was sustained by the sparks of the holy Hebrew letters of the Torah inherent in the fruits.[11] By blessing the fruits during the Tu b'Shevat Seder, and sharing Torah insights about them, we can elevate our relationship to food, and infuse our eating with Torah, transforming our eating once again into the words of Torah. Moreover, eating fruits on Tu b'Shevat in a mindful way gives us the opportunity to rectify all of our past eating during the entire year.[12]

Between the Tu b'Shevat and Pesach Seders

The Tu b'Shevat Seder, which is somewhat similar to the Pesach Seder, was compiled by the students of the Holy Arizal. It is based primarily on the Kabbalistic work, *Chemdat HaYamim,* later published separately under the title *P'ri Etz Hadar.*[13] The Tu b'Shevat Seder involves appreciating the fruits of the tree, particularly the Seven Species native to the Land of Israel.

Although the Pesach Seder is halacha, the Tu b'Shevat Seder is not obligatory. Halachic sources do mention the *minhag* (custom) to enjoy an abundance of different fruits on Tu b'Shevat.[14] Since the order and the content of the Seder do not follow specific Jewish law, there is much room for flexibility and creativity for each of us to conduct the Seder in our own way.

Pesach celebrates the past redemption of the Jewish People from Egypt and anticipates the return to the Land of Israel. However, Tu b'Shevat celebrates the return to the Land – the entryway to the Garden of Eden, and anticipates the redemption of all humanity, when we will eat, this time, fruit from the Tree of Life.

The Sequences of the Seder Corresponding to the Four Worlds

The fruits of the Tu b'Shevat Seder are divided into four categories corresponding to the Four Worlds that link the upper and lower reality.[15] Each sequence of fruits culminates with a cup of wine. As on Pesach, the wine is poured before the text is read and drunk afterwards. The first cup is white wine, symbolizing the refined ethereal upper world of אֲצִילוּת/*Atzilut* – Emanation. This cup is followed by a cup of white wine with a drop of red added, corresponding to the world of בְּרִיאָה/*Beriyah* – Creation. The third cup, with equal red and white wine reflects the world of יְצִירָה/*Yetzirah* – Formation, whereas the fourth cup, filled with red wine, represents the coarse material lower world of עֲשִׂיָּה/*Asiyah* – Action. During the Tu b'Shevat Seder we spiral downward from the highest world of Emanation beyond any physical manifestation, through the worlds of Formation and Creation, ultimately landing in our physical world of Action.

The Different Categories of Fruit and their Corresponding Kabbalistic Worlds

1. There are no fruits that correspond to the world of Emanation, which is totally spiritual beyond physical manifestation. However, for this category, we have chosen the Seven Species by which the Land of Israel is praised, since these fruits take precedence according to the laws of blessings as will be explained.

2. Wholly edible fruits correspond to the world of Creation.

3. Fruits that are wholly edible except for their inner pits correspond to the world of Formation.

4. Fruits that have outer inedible shells correspond to the world of Action.

It is interesting to note that the Seven Species include fruits from each of these worlds.[16]

Practical Guidelines for Conducting a Tu b'Shevat Seder

It is recommended to set aside at least two hours to run a meaningful Tu b'Shevat Seder with enough time to share and discuss Torah about each of the fruits. Set your Tu b'Shevat table with four fruit platters arranged according to the Four Worlds. It is preferable to prepare thirty kinds of fruit corresponding to the Ten Sefirot in each of the three lower worlds. If this is not possible, a minimum of twelve fruits will do. If you are missing one fruit you can substitute another, preferably from the same category. You can invite each of the participants to bring one kind of fruit and prepare Torah insights to share about it. Be creative! You may decorate your table with fragrant flowers, for instance. Include songs and meditations of your choice between each of the sequences. At the end of your Tu b'Shevat Seder, make sure to recite the threefold 'M'ein Shalosh' after-blessings for cake, wine and fruit together with all the participants.

The Tu b'Shevat Haggadah

Just as Pesach is accompanied by the *Haggadah*, the Tu b'Shevat Seder includes texts with verses from the Bible and passages from the Oral Torah describing the fruits. Before each fruit is eaten, a portion of the Written or Oral Torah is recited and discussed. In contrast to the Pesach Haggadah which is a fixed text, you can create your own Tu b'Shevat Seder text, personally selecting the Torah portions of your choice for each fruit. At the end of this section on Tu b'Shevat, you will find a copy of the Midreshet B'erot Bat Ayin Tu b'Shevat Seder Placemat with selected Torah texts according to the four sequences of the Seder. Feel free to copy it and use it for your upcoming Tu b'Shevat Seder. You may also order your own set of Tu b'Shevat Seder Placemats from our office.

Laws and Order of Blessings

Whenever we eat, the blessing on sustaining foods made from the five grains precedes the rest of the blessings.[17] Therefore, we begin the Seder by blessing '*borei minei mezonot*' on the wheat cracker or cake. When blessing on wheat have in mind to include all other grains as well.

The first blessing recited over the fruits of the tree includes all other fruits on the table. When you eat several different kinds of fruits, choose a fruit from the Seven Species to eat first.[18] The order of blessing within these Seven Fruits is according to their proximity to the word 'land' in the Bible verse.[19] Consequently, we bless '*borei p'ri ha'etz*' on the olive and have in mind that this blessing includes the remaining fruits of the tree. Whenever making a blessing, hold the fruit in your right hand. Whenever possible each person should recite her own blessing.[20]

New Fruits from the Land

Contemplating the marvel of the gift of the divine fruits can teach us many lessons about G*d, life and ourselves. Try to include in your Tu b'Shevat Seder as many fruits as possible grown in the Land of Israel, in order to connect yourself to the Holy Land on this day. Make sure the fruits have been grown and tithed according to the Laws of the Land. It is also recommended that you include a fruit you have not eaten yet during that year, in order to recite the special *shehecheyanu* blessing for eating a fruit for the first time in the season.[21]

Tikun via Eating

During the Tu b'Shevat Seder we have the opportunity to rectify the sin of eating from the Tree of Knowledge, the root of all eating disorders and sin, which corrupted the world and imbued us with the *yetzer hara* – our ego. This original sin caused sparks of holiness to fall into the impure husks. Words of Torah, blessings and proper intentions enable us to raise the fallen sparks within the food and return them to their source in the Garden of Eden. Since the exile from the Garden, every fruit includes a part of both the Tree of Knowledge and the Tree of Life, its antidote. Every time we put food in our mouths, especially on Tu b'Shevat, we have the choice whether to continue the sin of Adam and Eve by eating the Fruit of Knowledge or to eat like the righteous and take each bite from the Tree of Life.[22]

Elevating Sparks

It is our G*d-given opportunity to rectify and unify the upper worlds through the power of blessings and prayer. The purpose of reciting *brachot* (blessings) is to affirm that there is one G*d in the world and that everything belongs to Him. Blessing with proper intention purifies and elevates the Divine sparks contained in the food. Learning Torah, praying to G*d, and using the food's energy to perform a mitzvah elevate the sparks contained in the food to the upper worlds, from where they had originally fallen. The sparks of holiness are thereby returned to their source. Whereas, the blessings on mitzvot draw down celestial abundance, blessings over food and other pleasures are meant to rectify the worlds themselves, by elevating them and connecting each one with the world above it. This way, even our lowest world can receive the Holy influence of the highest light.[23]

Tu b'Shevat – An Occasion to Connect with the Land of Israel and Yearn for Redemption

If you seek to heighten the spirituality of your life by deepening your bond with Eretz Yisrael, the holiday of Tu b'Shevat assumes major importance. When blessing and enjoying the fruits during the Tu b'Shevat Seder, keep in mind that the fruits of the Land of Israel herald the redemption as we learn from the prophets: "But you, mountains of Israel shall give forth your branches and yield your fruit to My people, Israel; for soon they will come."[24] Based on this verse, the Talmud reveals that there is no more revealed sign of the End of Days, than when the Land of Israel will produce fruits in abundance.[25]

Midreshet B'erot Bat Ayin
Tu b'Shevat Seder

A land of wheat, and barley, and vine, and fig tree, and pomegranate; a land of olive oil and honey (Deuteronomy 8:8).

אֲצִילוּת – The World of Emanation
Fill the glasses with: **White Wine** יַיִן לָבָן

Wheat חִטָּה But he would feed him with the finest of the wheat; and with honey out of the rock I will satisfy you (Psalms 81:17).

Olive זַיִת But I am like a fresh green olive in the house of G-d. I trust in the love of G-d forever and ever (Psalms 52:10).

Date תָּמָר The righteous person flourishes like the date palm. He grows like a cedar in Levanon (Psalms 92:13).

Grape גֶּפֶן But they shall sit every man under his vine and under his fig tree; and none shall make them afraid, for the mouth of Hashem of hosts has spoken it (Micah 4:4).

Fig תְּאֵנָה He who guards the fig tree shall eat its fruit, and he who watches his master will be honored (Proverbs 27:18).

Pomegranate רִמּוֹן Let us get up early to the vineyards; let us see if the vine has flowered, if the grape blossoms have opened, if the pomegranates are in flower. There I will give you my love (Song of Songs 7:13).

Wine יַיִן ...and on the vine were three shoots; and it was as though it budded, and its blossoms shot forth; and its clusters brought forth ripe grapes (Genesis 40:10).

מדרשת בארות בת עין
סדר ט"ו בשבט

אֶרֶץ חִטָּה וּשְׂעֹרָה וְגֶפֶן וּתְאֵנָה וְרִמּוֹן אֶרֶץ זֵית שֶׁמֶן וּדְבָשׁ: (דברים ח, ח)

עוֹלָם הָאֲצִילוּת
למלא את הכוסות בְּיַיִן לָבָן

חִטָּה וַיַּאֲכִילֵהוּ מֵחֵלֶב חִטָּה וּמִצּוּר דְּבַשׁ אַשְׂבִּיעֶךָ: (תהילים פא, יז)

זֵית וַאֲנִי כְּזַיִת רַעֲנָן בְּבֵית אֱלֹקִים בָּטַחְתִּי בְחֶסֶד אֱלֹקִים עוֹלָם וָעֶד: (תהילים נב, י)

תָּמָר צַדִּיק כַּתָּמָר יִפְרָח כְּאֶרֶז בַּלְּבָנוֹן יִשְׂגֶּה: (תהילים צב, יג)

גֶּפֶן וְיָשְׁבוּ אִישׁ תַּחַת גַּפְנוֹ וְתַחַת תְּאֵנָתוֹ וְאֵין מַחֲרִיד כִּי פִי הָשֵׁם צְבָקאוֹת דִּבֵּר: (מיכה ד, ד)

תְּאֵנָה נֹצֵר תְּאֵנָה יֹאכַל פִּרְיָהּ וְשֹׁמֵר אֲדֹנָיו יְכֻבָּד: (משלי כז, יח)

רִמּוֹן נַשְׁכִּימָה לַכְּרָמִים נִרְאֶה אִם פָּרְחָה הַגֶּפֶן פִּתַּח הַסְּמָדַר הֵנֵצוּ הָרִמּוֹנִים שָׁם אֶתֵּן אֶת דֹּדַי לָךְ: (שיר השירים ז, יג)

יַיִן וּבַגֶּפֶן שְׁלֹשָׁה שָׂרִיגִם וְהִוא כְפֹרַחַת עָלְתָה נִצָּהּ הִבְשִׁילוּ אַשְׁכְּלֹתֶיהָ עֲנָבִים: (בראשית מ, י)

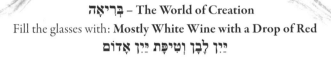

בְּרִיאָה – The World of Creation
Fill the glasses with: **Mostly White Wine with a Drop of Red**
יַיִן לָבָן וְטִיפַת יַיִן אָדוֹם

Etrog אֶתְרוֹג You shall take for yourselves on the first day: the fruit of the hadar tree, branches of date palms, and the boughs of thick leafed trees, and willows of the brook; and you shall rejoice before Hashem your G-d for seven days (Leviticus 23:40).

Apple תַּפּוּחַ Like the apple tree among the trees of the wood, so is my beloved among the sons. I sat down under his shadow with great delight, and his fruit was sweet to my taste (Song of Songs 2:3).

Carob חָרוּב Everyday a heavenly voice goes out from Mount Chorev and declares: "The whole world is fed in the merit of Chanina my son, yet for Chanina my son, one measure of carobs is enough from Friday to Friday." (*Babylonian Talmud, Berachot* 17b).

Pear אַגָּס Among the trees, a crossbreed between the pears, the curstumenian pears, the quinces, and the azarole is permitted. Apples, crab apples, peaches, almonds, jujubes, and the lote, although they resemble one another, a crossbreed between them is prohibited (*Mishnah, Tractate Kelayim* 1:4).

Wine יַיִן He brought me to the house of wine, and his banner over me was love (Song of Songs 2:4).

יְצִירָה – The World of Formation
Fill the glasses with: **Half Red Half White Wine** חֲצִי יַיִן אָדוֹם וְחֲצִי יַיִן לָבָן

Prune שְׁזִיף Do not gaze upon me, for I am black, because the sun has scorched me (Song of Songs 1:6).

Peach אֲפַרְסָק From when must the fruits be tithed? Figs when they begin to ripen; grapes and wild grapes when their kernels can be discerned from their skins; sumac and berries when they turn red; all red fruits when they turn red; pomegranates when they soften; dates when they begin to leaven; peaches when they produce [red] veins; nuts when they make a receptacle. Rabbi Yehuda says, "nuts and almonds from when they grow a peel" (*Mishnah, Tractate Ma'asarot* 1:2).

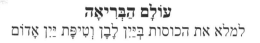

עוֹלָם הַבְּרִיאָה
לְמַלֵּא אֶת הַכּוֹסוֹת בְּיַיִן לָבָן וְטִיפַת יַיִן אָדֹם

אֶתְרוֹג וּלְקַחְתֶּם לָכֶם בַּיּוֹם הָרִאשׁוֹן פְּרִי עֵץ הָדָר כַּפֹּת תְּמָרִים וַעֲנַף עֵץ עָבֹת וְעַרְבֵי נָחַל וּשְׂמַחְתֶּם לִפְנֵי הַשֵּׁם אֱלֹקֵיכֶם שִׁבְעַת יָמִים: (ויקרא כג, מ)

תַּפּוּחַ כְּתַפּוּחַ בַּעֲצֵי הַיַּעַר כֵּן דּוֹדִי בֵּין הַבָּנִים בְּצִלּוֹ חִמַּדְתִּי וְיָשַׁבְתִּי וּפִרְיוֹ מָתוֹק לְחִכִּי: (שיר השירים ב, ג)

חָרוּב אמר רב יהודה אמר רב: בכל יום ויום בת קול יוצאת מהר חורב ואומרת: כל העולם כולו נזונין בשביל חנינא בני, וחנינא בני - די לו בקב חרובין מערב שבת לערב שבת: (תלמוד בבלי מסכת ברכות יז, ע"ב)

אַגָּס וּבָאִילָן, הָאַגָּסִים וְהַקְּרֻסְטּוּמֵלִין, וְהַפְּרִישִׁים וְהָעֻזְרָדִים, אֵינָם כִּלְאַיִם זֶה בָזֶה. הַתַּפּוּחַ וְהַחֶזְרָד, הַפַּרְסְקִים וְהַשְּׁקֵדִין, וְהַשֵּׁיזָפִין וְהָרִימִין, אַף עַל פִּי שֶׁדּוֹמִין זֶה לָזֶה, כִּלְאַיִם זֶה בָזֶה: (משנה מסכת כלאים א, ד)

יַיִן הֱבִיאַנִי אֶל בֵּית הַיַּיִן וְדִגְלוֹ עָלַי אַהֲבָה: (שיר השירים ב, ד)

עוֹלָם הַיְצִירָה
לְמַלֵּא אֶת הַכּוֹסוֹת בְּחֲצִי יַיִן אָדֹם וְחֲצִי יַיִן לָבָן

שְׁזִיף אַל תִּרְאוּנִי שֶׁאֲנִי שְׁחַרְחֹרֶת שֶׁשֱּׁזָפַתְנִי הַשָּׁמֶשׁ בְּנֵי אִמִּי נִחֲרוּ בִי שָׂמֻנִי נֹטֵרָה אֶת הַכְּרָמִים כַּרְמִי שֶׁלִּי לֹא נָטָרְתִּי: (שיר השירים א, ו)

אַפַרְסֵק מֵאֵימָתַי הַפֵּרוֹת חַיָּבוֹת בַּמַּעַשְׂרוֹת, הַתְּאֵנִים מִשֶּׁיַּבְחִילוּ. הָעֲנָבִים וְהָאֲבָשִׁים, מִשֶּׁהִבְאִישׁוּ. הָאוֹג וְהַתּוּתִים, מִשֶּׁיַּאְדִּימוּ. וְכָל הָאָדֻמִּים מִשֶּׁיַּאְדִּימוּ. הָרִמּוֹנִים, מִשֶּׁיִּמַּסּוּ. הַתְּמָרִים, מִשֶּׁיַּטִּילוּ שְׂאוֹר. הָאַפַרְסְקִים, מִשֶּׁיַּטִּילוּ גִידִים. הָאֱגוֹזִים, מִשֶּׁיַּעֲשׂוּ מְגוּרָה. רַבִּי יְהוּדָה אוֹמֵר, הָאֱגוֹזִים וְהַשְּׁקֵדִים, מִשֶּׁיַּעֲשׂוּ קְלִפָּה: (משנה מסכת מעשרות א, ב)

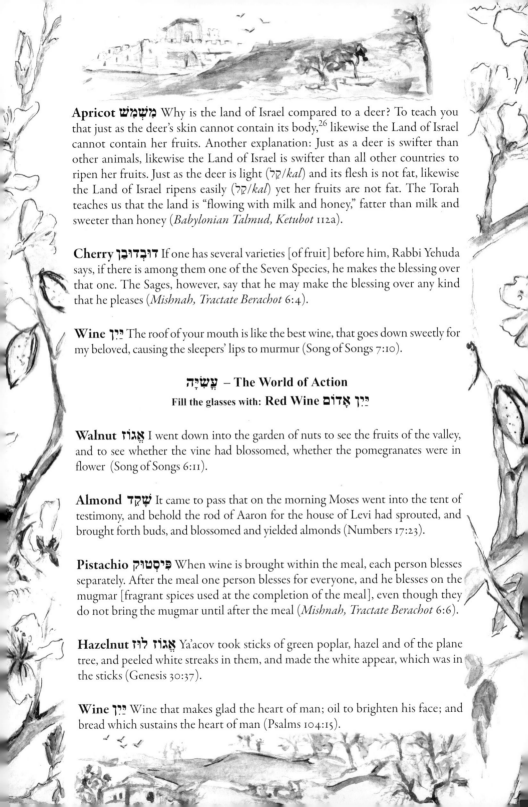

Apricot מִשְׁמֵשׁ Why is the land of Israel compared to a deer? To teach you that just as the deer's skin cannot contain its body,[26] likewise the Land of Israel cannot contain her fruits. Another explanation: Just as a deer is swifter than other animals, likewise the Land of Israel is swifter than all other countries to ripen her fruits. Just as the deer is light (קַל/*kal*) and its flesh is not fat, likewise the Land of Israel ripens easily (קַל/*kal*) yet her fruits are not fat. The Torah teaches us that the land is "flowing with milk and honey," fatter than milk and sweeter than honey (*Babylonian Talmud, Ketubot* 112a).

Cherry דוּבְדְּבָן If one has several varieties [of fruit] before him, Rabbi Yehuda says, if there is among them one of the Seven Species, he makes the blessing over that one. The Sages, however, say that he may make the blessing over any kind that he pleases (*Mishnah, Tractate Berachot* 6:4).

Wine יַיִן The roof of your mouth is like the best wine, that goes down sweetly for my beloved, causing the sleepers' lips to murmur (Song of Songs 7:10).

עֲשִׂיָּה – The World of Action
Fill the glasses with: Red Wine יַיִן אָדוֹם

Walnut אֱגוֹז I went down into the garden of nuts to see the fruits of the valley, and to see whether the vine had blossomed, whether the pomegranates were in flower (Song of Songs 6:11).

Almond שָׁקֵד It came to pass that on the morning Moses went into the tent of testimony, and behold the rod of Aaron for the house of Levi had sprouted, and brought forth buds, and blossomed and yielded almonds (Numbers 17:23).

Pistachio פִּיסְטוּק When wine is brought within the meal, each person blesses separately. After the meal one person blesses for everyone, and he blesses on the mugmar [fragrant spices used at the completion of the meal], even though they do not bring the mugmar until after the meal (*Mishnah, Tractate Berachot* 6:6).

Hazelnut אֱגוֹז לוּז Ya'acov took sticks of green poplar, hazel and of the plane tree, and peeled white streaks in them, and made the white appear, which was in the sticks (Genesis 30:37).

Wine יַיִן Wine that makes glad the heart of man; oil to brighten his face; and bread which sustains the heart of man (Psalms 104:15).

מְשֻׁמָשׁ אמר רב חסדא מאי דכתיב ואתן לך ארץ חמדה נחלת צבי למה ארץ ישראל נמשלה לצבי לומר לך מה צבי זה אין עורו מחזיק בשרו אף ארץ ישראל אינה מחזקת פירותיה דבר אחר מה צבי זה קל מכל החיות אף ארץ ישראל קלה מכל הארצות לבשל את פירותיה אי מה צבי זה קל ואין בשרו שמן אף ארץ ישראל קלה לבשל ואין פירותיה שמנים תלמוד לומר זבת חלב ודבש שמנים מחלב ומתוקים מדבש: (תלמוד בבלי מסכת כתובות קיב, ע"א)

דּוּבְדּוּבָן הָיוּ לְפָנָיו מִינִים הַרְבֵּה, רַבִּי יְהוּדָה אוֹמֵר, אִם יֵשׁ בֵּינֵיהֶם מִמִּין שִׁבְעָה, מְבָרֵךְ עָלָיו. וַחֲכָמִים אוֹמְרִים, מְבָרֵךְ עַל אֵיזֶה מֵהֶם שֶׁיִּרְצֶה: (משנה מסכת ברכות ו, ד)

יַיִן וְחִכֵּךְ כְּיֵין הַטּוֹב הוֹלֵךְ לְדוֹדִי לְמֵישָׁרִים דּוֹבֵב שִׂפְתֵי יְשֵׁנִים: (שיר השירים ז, י)

עוֹלָם הָעֲשִׂיָּה
לְמַלֵּא אֶת הַכּוֹסוֹת בְּיַיִן אָדֹם

אֱגוֹז אֶל גִּנַּת אֱגוֹז יָרַדְתִּי לִרְאוֹת בְּאִבֵּי הַנָּחַל לִרְאוֹת הֲפָרְחָה הַגֶּפֶן הֵנֵצוּ הָרִמֹּנִים: (שיר השירים ו, יא)

שָׁקֵד וַיְהִי מִמָּחֳרָת וַיָּבֹא מֹשֶׁה אֶל אֹהֶל הָעֵדוּת וְהִנֵּה פָּרַח מַטֵּה אַהֲרֹן לְבֵית לֵוִי וַיֹּצֵא פֶרַח וַיָּצֵץ צִיץ וַיִּגְמֹל שְׁקֵדִים: (במדבר יז, כג)

פִּיסְטוּק בָּא לָהֶם יַיִן בְּתוֹךְ הַמָּזוֹן, כָּל אֶחָד וְאֶחָד מְבָרֵךְ לְעַצְמוֹ. לְאַחַר הַמָּזוֹן, אֶחָד מְבָרֵךְ לְכֻלָּם. וְהוּא בְּתוֹךְ הַמָּזוֹן, כָּל אֶחָד וְאֶחָד מְבָרֵךְ לְעַצְמוֹ. לְאַחַר הַמָּזוֹן, אֶחָד מְבָרֵךְ לְכֻלָּם. וְהוּא אוֹמֵר עַל הַמֻּגְמָר, אַף עַל פִּי שֶׁאֵין מְבִיאִין אֶת הַמֻּגְמָר אֶלָּא לְאַחַר הַסְּעֻדָּה: (משנה מסכת ברכות רו, משנה ו)

אֱגוֹז לוּז וַיִּקַּח לוֹ יַעֲקֹב מַקַּל לִבְנֶה לַח וְלוּז וְעַרְמוֹן וַיְפַצֵּל בָּהֵן פְּצָלוֹת לְבָנוֹת מַחְשֹׂף הַלָּבָן אֲשֶׁר עַל הַמַּקְלוֹת: (בראשית ל, לז)

יַיִן וְיַיִן יְשַׂמַּח לְבַב אֱנוֹשׁ לְהַצְהִיל פָּנִים מִשָּׁמֶן וְלֶחֶם לְבַב אֱנוֹשׁ יִסְעָד: (תהילים קד, טו)

Appendix II – *Blessings before Partaking of the Seven Species and their Derivatives*

The following blessing is recited before eating baked bread made from the five grains – wheat, barley, rye, oat and spelt:

בָּרוּךְ אַתָּה הָשֵׁם אֱלֵקֵינוּ מֶלֶךְ הָעוֹלָם הַמּוֹצִיא לֶחֶם מִן הָאָרֶץ:

Baruch ata Hashem Elokeinu melech ha'olam hamotzie lechem min ha'aretz.

Blessed are you, Hashem our G*d, Sovereign of the world, Who brings forth bread from the earth.

The following blessing is recited before eating a cooked or baked dish made primarily from the five grains:

בָּרוּךְ אַתָּה הָשֵׁם אֱלֵקֵינוּ מֶלֶךְ הָעוֹלָם בּוֹרֵא מִינֵי מְזוֹנוֹת:

Baruch ata Hashem Elokeinu melech ha'olam borei minei mezonot.

Blessed are you, Hashem our G*d, Sovereign of the world, Who creates different kinds of sustaining foods.

The following blessing is recited before drinking wine or grape juice:

בָּרוּךְ אַתָּה הָשֵׁם אֱלֵקֵינוּ מֶלֶךְ הָעוֹלָם בּוֹרֵא פְּרִי הַגָּפֶן:

Baruch ata Hashem Elokeinu melech ha'olam borei p'ri hagafen.

Blessed are you, Hashem our G*d, Sovereign of the world, Who creates the fruit of the vine.

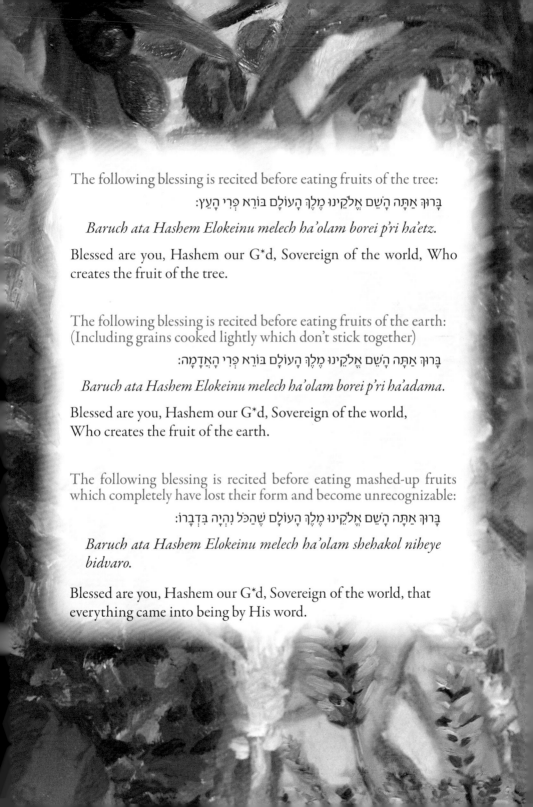

The following blessing is recited before eating fruits of the tree:

בָּרוּךְ אַתָּה הָשֵׁם אֱלֹקֵינוּ מֶלֶךְ הָעוֹלָם בּוֹרֵא פְּרִי הָעֵץ:

Baruch ata Hashem Elokeinu melech ha'olam borei p'ri ha'etz.

Blessed are you, Hashem our G*d, Sovereign of the world, Who creates the fruit of the tree.

The following blessing is recited before eating fruits of the earth:
(Including grains cooked lightly which don't stick together)

בָּרוּךְ אַתָּה הָשֵׁם אֱלֹקֵינוּ מֶלֶךְ הָעוֹלָם בּוֹרֵא פְּרִי הָאֲדָמָה:

Baruch ata Hashem Elokeinu melech ha'olam borei p'ri ha'adama.

Blessed are you, Hashem our G*d, Sovereign of the world,
Who creates the fruit of the earth.

The following blessing is recited before eating mashed-up fruits which completely have lost their form and become unrecognizable:

בָּרוּךְ אַתָּה הָשֵׁם אֱלֹקֵינוּ מֶלֶךְ הָעוֹלָם שֶׁהַכֹּל נִהְיָה בִּדְבָרוֹ:

Baruch ata Hashem Elokeinu melech ha'olam shehakol niheye bidvaro.

Blessed are you, Hashem our G*d, Sovereign of the world, that everything came into being by His word.

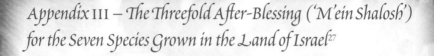

Appendix III – The Threefold After-Blessing ('M'ein Shalosh') for the Seven Species Grown in the Land of Israel[27]

בְּרָכָה אַחֲרוֹנָה מֵעֵין שָׁלוֹשׁ:
בָּרוּךְ אַתָּה הַשֵּׁם אֱלֹקֵינוּ מֶלֶךְ הָעוֹלָם עַל:
עַל הַיַּיִן - עַל הַגֶּפֶן וְעַל פְּרִי הַגֶּפֶן:
עַל פֵּירוֹת מִשִּׁבְעַת הַמִּינִים - עַל הָעֵץ וְעַל פְּרִי הָעֵץ:
עַל מְזוֹנוֹת - עַל הַמִּחְיָה וְעַל הַכַּלְכָּלָה:
עַל מְזוֹנוֹת וַיַּיִן בְּיַחַד - עַל הַמִּחְיָה וְעַל הַכַּלְכָּלָה וְעַל הַגֶּפֶן וְעַל פְּרִי הַגֶּפֶן:
וְעַל תְּנוּבַת הַשָּׂדֶה וְעַל אֶרֶץ חֶמְדָּה טוֹבָה וּרְחָבָה שֶׁרָצִיתָ וְהִנְחַלְתָּ לַאֲבוֹתֵינוּ
לֶאֱכֹל מִפִּרְיָהּ וְלִשְׂבּוֹעַ מִטּוּבָהּ, רַחֵם (נָא) הַשֵּׁם אֱלֹקֵינוּ עַל יִשְׂרָאֵל עַמֶּךְ וְעַל
יְרוּשָׁלַיִם עִירֶךָ וְעַל צִיּוֹן מִשְׁכַּן כְּבוֹדֶךָ וְעַל מִזְבְּחֶךָ וְעַל הֵיכָלֶךָ, וּבְנֵה יְרוּשָׁלַיִם
עִיר הַקֹּדֶשׁ בִּמְהֵרָה בְּיָמֵינוּ וְהַעֲלֵנוּ לְתוֹכָהּ וְשַׂמְּחֵנוּ בְּבִנְיָנָהּ וְנֹאכַל מִפִּרְיָהּ
וְנִשְׂבַּע מִטּוּבָהּ וּנְבָרֶכְךָ עָלֶיהָ בִּקְדֻשָּׁה וּבְטָהֳרָה:
בְּשַׁבָּת:
וּרְצֵה וְהַחֲלִיצֵנוּ בְּיוֹם הַשַּׁבָּת הַזֶּה:
בר"ח:
וְזָכְרֵנוּ לְטוֹבָה בְּיוֹם רֹאשׁ הַחֹדֶשׁ הַזֶּה:
בר"ה:
וְזָכְרֵנוּ לְטוֹבָה בְּיוֹם הַזִּכָּרוֹן הַזֶּה:
ביו"ט:
וְשַׂמְּחֵנוּ (על פי חב"ד וְזָכְרֵנוּ) בְּיוֹם חַג (פְּלוֹנִי) הַזֶּה:
כִּי אַתָּה הַשֵּׁם טוֹב וּמֵטִיב לַכֹּל וְנוֹדֶה לְּךָ עַל הָאָרֶץ וְעַל:
עַל הַיַּיִן - פְּרִי גַפְנָהּ:
בָּרוּךְ אַתָּה הַשֵּׁם עַל הָאָרֶץ וְעַל פְּרִי גַפְנָהּ:
עַל הַפֵּירוֹת - פֵּרוֹתֶיהָ:
בָּרוּךְ אַתָּה הַשֵּׁם עַל הָאָרֶץ וְעַל פֵּרוֹתֶיהָ:
עַל מְזוֹנוֹת - הַמִּחְיָה:
בָּרוּךְ אַתָּה הַשֵּׁם עַל הָאָרֶץ וְעַל הַמִּחְיָה:
עַל מְזוֹנוֹת וַיַּיִן בְּיַחַד - הַמִּחְיָה וְעַל פְּרִי הַגֶּפֶן:
בָּרוּךְ אַתָּה הַשֵּׁם עַל הָאָרֶץ וְעַל הַמִּחְיָה וְעַל הַכַּלְכָּלָה וְעַל פְּרִי גַפְנָהּ:

Blessed are You Hashem our G*d, King of the universe for...

After food prepared from the five kinds of grain: the sustenance and the nourishment,

After wine: the vine and the fruit of the vine,

After the five fruits of the Seven Species: the tree and the fruit of the tree, for the produce of the field, and for the precious, good and spacious Land, which You have graciously given as a heritage to our ancestors, to eat of her fruit and be satiated with her goodness. Have mercy, Hashem our G*d, on Israel Your people, on Jerusalem Your city, and on Tzion the abode of Your glory, on Your altar and on Your Temple. Rebuild Jerusalem the Holy City, speedily in our days, and bring us up to it and make us rejoice in it, and we will bless You in holiness and purity.

On Shabbat: May it please You to strengthen us on this Shabbat day.

On Rosh Chodesh, Festivals and Chol haMoed: Remember us for good on this day of...

On Rosh Chodesh: Rosh Chodesh. *On Rosh Hashana*: Remembrance. *On Pesach*: the Festival of Matzot *On Shavuot*: the Festival of Shavuot. *On Sukkot*: the Festival of Sukkot. *On Shemini Atzeret*: Shemini Atzeret, the Festival.

For You, Hashem, are good and do good to all, and we offer thanks to You for the Land and for...

After food prepared from the five kinds of grain: the sustenance. Blessed are you Hashem, for the Land and for the sustenance.

After wine or grape juice: the fruit of her vine. Blessed are you Hashem, for the Land and for the fruit of her vine.

After the five fruits of the Seven Species: her fruits. Blessed are You Hashem for the Land and for her fruits.

Endnotes

1.   Numbers 13:23–13:32.

2.   See the discussion about the after-blessings for the Seven Species in *Babylonian Talmud, Berachot* 44a: What do we say in this case [over fruit]? Rabbi Chisda said: "For the land and for her fruits." Rabbi Yochanan said: "for the land and for the fruits." Rabbi Amram said: "They are not at variance: the latter is for us [in Babylon], and the former for them [in Israel]."

3.   For the full Hebrew and English text of the '*M'ein Shalosh*' after-blessing with the different versions for fruit grown in Israel and abroad, see *Appendix* III – *The Threefold After-Blessing* ('*M'ein Shalosh*') *for the Seven Species grown in the Land of Israel.*

4.   This section is based on a Torah I heard by Rabbi Salfer, Rosh Yeshiva of Yeshivas Doresh, in Highland Lakes, Florida. Rabbi Salfer quoted his friend Rav Chananya Abisror regarding how the Land of Israel gives the blessings to produce the fruits of the entire world.

5.   Rabbi Yoel Sirkis, Lublin-Kraków (1561–1640), Commentary to the *Arba'ah Turim, Bayit Chadash* (The Bach), *Laws of Remaining Blessings, Shulchan Aruch, Orach Chaim* 208.

6.   Proverbs 3:18.

7.   Genesis 2:16.

8.   Genesis 3:18.

9.   זלגו עיניו דמעות אמר לפניו רבונו של עולם אני וחמורי נאכל באבוס אחד (*Babylonian Talmud, Pesachim* 118a). This section is based on Rav Tzadok HaKohen of Lublin, *P'ri Tzadik, for Tu b'Shevat.*

10.   האילנות ליתן פירותיהן בכל חדש וחדש אדם אוכל מהם ומתרפא (*Midrash Exodus Rabbah* 15:21).

11.   Rav Tzadok HaKohen of Lublin, *Likutei Amerim* 11.

12.   Rav Tzadok HaKohen, *P'ri Tzadik, for Tu b'Shevat* 2.

13.   The book *Pri Etz Hadar* was first published as part of *Chemdat HaYamim*, in Tzefat, 1641.

14.   *Mishnah Berurah* 131:31; *Kitzur Shulchan Aruch* 139:26.

15. See the *Barley* section, the end of *A Taste of Kabbalah – The Seeds of Blessing,* p. 111.

16. The fig, which is totally edible, from the world of Creation; grapes, olives and dates, with their inedible pits from the world of Formation; wheat, barley and pomegranates with their inedible shells, from the world of Action. See the *Fig* section, *A Taste of Kabbalah – Light, Shells, Souls and Fruit,* pp. 206–208, based on Arizal, *Sefer HaLikutim, Parashat Vayetze,* chapter 36.

17. Although only wheat and barley are mentioned among the Seven Species in Deuteronomy 8:8, spelt, rye and oats are included as their subspecies. See the *Introduction* endnote 6, and *Shulchan Aruch, Orach Chaim* 211:6.

18. *Mishnah Berurah* 211:4–5.

19. *Mishnah Berurah* 211:21.

20. *Shulchan Aruch, Orach Chaim* 213:1; *Mishnah Berurah* 213:12.

21. בָּרוּךְ אַתָּה הָשֵׁם אֱלֹקֵינוּ מֶלֶךְ הָעוֹלָם שֶׁהֶחֱיָנוּ וְקִיְּמָנוּ וְהִגִּיעָנוּ לַזְּמַן הַזֶּה/*Baruch Ata Hashem Elokeinu Melech Ha'Olam shehecheyanu, v'kimanu, v'higianu lazman haze* – Blessed are You Hashem our G*d King of the Universe, Who has granted us life, sustained us and enabled us to reach this occasion.

22. Based on Rav Tzadok HaKohen of Lublin, *P'ri Tzadik, for Tub'Shevat.*

23. Based on Rav Chaim Volozhin, *Nefesh HaChaim* 2:3–4 and 14.

24. Ezekiel 36:8.

25. *Babylonian Talmud, Sanhedrin* 98a.

26. Once skinned the body of the deer cannot fit into the skin again.

27. Hebrew Ashkenazi version, English Chabad version.

About the Author

ℛebbetzin Chana Bracha Siegelbaum, a native of Denmark, is founder and director of *Midreshet B'erot Bat Ayin: Holistic Torah for Women on the Land*. She holds a Bachelor of Education in Bible and Jewish Philosophy from Michlala Jerusalem College for Women, and a Master of Art degree in Jewish History from Touro College. Rebbetzin Chana Bracha creates curricula emphasizing women's spiritual empowerment through traditional Torah values. In 2010 she published her first book, *Women at the Crossroads*: *A Woman's Perspective on the Weekly Torah Portion*. In addition to attending her orchard of about fifty fruit trees, the Rebbetzin, a gifted spiritual healer, also practices *EmunaHealing* through Emunah, tefilah and energy work. Chana Bracha has a married son and several grand-daughters, and lives with her husband and younger son on the Land of the Judean Hills, Israel.

About the Artist

Jessica Friedman Vaiselberg was raised in Louisville, KY. She graduated from a visual arts programme at high school in 2002, and studied at Memphis College of Art until 2004 before graduating from University of Louisville in 2006 with a degree in Fine Arts. During her time spent as a student at Midreshet B'erot Bat Ayin, she embarked on a project 'Dessert Flowers,' recently displayed at the Zspace Gallery in Brooklyn Artist Show.  Much of her inspiration comes from the beauty and passion she has experienced in Israel. Jessica married, with three children, lives in Long Island, where she has a home studio, and offers lessons to all ages! Check out her website www.jessicasartstudio.webs.com.

About Midreshet B'erot Bat Ayin

Midreshet B'erot Bat Ayin: Holistic Torah for Women on the Land, was envisaged in 1996 by Rebbetzin Siegelbaum. It is situated in the heart of the Judean Hills in Israel. Here, women of all backgrounds and ages receive nourishment for mind, body and Soul by integrating textual Torah  study (Bible, Jewish Law, Prayer, Jewish Philosophy and Chassidism) with cultivation of the Land of Israel, creative spiritual expression and healthy living.

Glossary

Adar: Hebrew month corresponding to February/March.

Aharon: Aaron

Alef Bet: The Hebrew alphabet consisting of 22 letters.

Asiyah: Realm of Action – the lowest of the Four Worlds, corresponding to our physical world.

Atzilut: Realm of Emanation – the highest of the Four Worlds, beyond physical manifestation.

Avraham: Abraham

Bar Mitzvah: Celebrating a 13-year-old Jewish boy's coming of age and responsibility for his moral and religious duties.

Bedieved: Less preferred halachic practice – after the fact.

Beriyah: Realm of Creation – the second of the Four Worlds.

Bracha/brachot: Blessing/blessings

Chai/Chaim: Life

Challah: Bread offering, today used to describe the Shabbat bread

Chametz: bread, grains and leavened products not consumed on Pesach.

Chanukah: Hanukkah – Festival of Lights, celebrating the miracle of the jug of oil in the Temple which burned for eight days.

Chanukiah: Special candelabra for Chanukah

Chassidic: A branch of Judaism emphasizing spirituality through deep connection and popularization of the inner dimensions of the Torah founded by Rabbi Yiarael Ba'al Shem Tov, (1698–1760) Ukraine. The word Chassid/ic is related to the Hebrew word for loving-kindness and piety.

Chava: Eve

Chayah: The second to the highest, innermost and transcendental level of the soul. Literally, 'the living one.'

Chayot: Highest rank of angels in Judaism

Cheshvan: Hebrew month corresponding to October/November

Chezkiyahu: Hezekiah

Chidush/Chidushei/Chidushim: Original Torah insight(s)

Chitah: Wheat

Chol haMoed: Intermediate days of Pesach and of Sukkot, on which necessary work is permitted.

Cholent: Traditional Shabbat stew left on the hotplate overnight.

Deveikut: Devotion; literally, cleaving to Hashem and His Torah.

Emunah: Faith

Eliyahu: Elijah

Elul: Hebrew month corresponding to August/September

Eretz Yisrael: Land of Israel

Gematria: 'Jewish Numerology' – systems of converting Hebrew letters and words into numerical values.

Geveret: Madame, Mrs. or Miss.

Halacha/halachic: Jewish law/according to Jewish law

Hallel: Prayer of praise consisting of Psalms 113 through 118, Hallel is recited on Pesach, Shavuot, Sukkot, Chanukah and Rosh Chodesh (New Moon).

Haggadah: A booklet telling the story of the Jews leaving Egypt. It contains the order of the Seder and is used by the Seder leader and participants to conduct the rituals of the Seder; literally, 'narrative/story.'

Hashem: G*d; literally, 'The Name'

Havdalah: The ceremony marking the end of Shabbat or a festival, which includes the blessing over wine.

Hester Panim: The hiding of G*d's face.

Kavanah: Intention, during blessings and prayers and while performing mitzvot.

Ketubah: Marriage contract

Kezayit: An olive size, (approximately 28 cc/1 fl. oz.). A Kezayit is the minimum volume of food, which requires an after-blessing when eaten within a certain time period.

Kelipah: Shell, in Kabbalah – spiritual shell that hides G*d's light.

Kiddush: Literally, 'sanctification' – the halachic prayer ritual and blessing recited over wine before the evening meal and day meal on Shabbat and holidays.

Kislev: Hebrew month corresponding to November/December

Kohen/Kohanim: Priest/s; literally, from the word 'to serve'

Kohen Gadol: High Priest

Kollel: Used in 'Jewish Numerology' (gematria) counting the word itself as one when adding the numerical value of each letter of the word.

L'Chaim: Cheers; literally, 'to life!'

Lechem: Bread

Lechatchila: The ideal halachic practice

Log: A liquid measure of 0.3 liter, a little more than one cup.

Lulav: One of the four ceremonial plant species used during the prayers of the Jewish holiday of Sukkot.

Maccabee(s): A family of Kohanim, who organized a successful revolt (168 B.C.) against Hellenism and the Syrian rule over Israel, and rededicated the Temple in Jerusalem. The name Maccabee was originally a title of honor given to Yehuda, son of Mattityahu of the Chasmonean family. Later, the name was extended to include his whole family, specifically Mattityahu and Yehuda's four brothers Yochanan, Shimon, Elazar, and Yonatan. Literally, Maccabee means 'Hammer.'

Mashiach: The Messiah

Menorah: The seven branched candelabra which burned perpetually in the Temple of Jerusalem

Midrash/Midrashic: Homiletic interpretation of the Torah, from the root meaning 'to seek out' or 'to investigate' the deeper level between the lines.

Mishnah: The first compilation of the oral law (Talmud), compiled about year 200 CE. Literally, 'teaching.'

Mishnah Berurah: Ashkenazi commentary on the Shulchan Aruch, written by Rabbi Yisrael Meir Kagan Radun, Poland (1838–1933); literally, 'clear teaching.'

Mitzvah/Mitzvot: Divine commandment/commandments

Moshe: Moses

Nefesh: Lowest soul part (animal soul), connected with the body.

Neshamah: Divine (intellectual soul); literally, 'breath of life.'

Nissan: Hebrew month corresponding to March/April

Nukvah: The lowest of the 'family' of Divine Personae/Faces (Partzufim) according to Lurianic Kabbalah. Nukvah is the 'Daughter,' corresponding to Malchut, associated with the Feminine Shechinah.

Noach: Noah

Omer: Biblical unit of measurement representing one day's ration, roughly equal to two quarts or two liters. The counting of the Omer refers to the forty-nine days between Pesach and Shavuot, counting from the day following Pesach when, in Temple times, an Omer of barley was offered.

Pat: Bread – mainly used for individual size bread, like a pitah which derives from this word. Literally, 'fragment,' or 'morsel.'

Parasha/t: Torah portion – One of the Torah's 54 weekly sections. The entire Torah is read in the synagogue annually, through rotation of a weekly parasha.

Parve: A Hebrew and Yiddish term that describes food without any meat or dairy ingredients.

P'ri: Fruit

Pesach: Passover

Pintele yid: A Yiddish term meaning 'Jewish spark' referring to the essential Jewishness inherent in every Jewish soul.

Revi'it: Liquid measure equal to a small cup (86 cc/2.9 fl. oz.), which requires an after-blessing when drunk over a short time period.

Rivkah: Rebecca

Rosh Chodesh: New Moon Festival

Rosh Hashana: Jewish New Year; literally 'Head of the Year.'

Ruach: Spirit, the next level of soul after nefesh, connected to the emotions; literally, 'wind.'

Ruach Hakodesh: Divine inspiration, a lower level of prophetic spirit; literally Holy Spirit.

Sechach: Roof of Sukkah Booth

Seder: Literally, 'Order,' a ceremonial meal including recital of the Haggadah, (the story of the Exodus from Egypt), and eating symbolic foods. Keeping the Pesach Seder is halachic requirement. The Sephardi tradition includes a Rosh Hashana and Tu b'Shevat Seder.

Seudah/Seudot: Meal/meals

Shechinah: (Divine Feminine Indwelling Presence)

Shemuel: Samuel

Shavuot: Pentecost; literally, 'festival of weeks.' This holiday follows the counting of seven weeks from Pesach.

Shevat: Hebrew month corresponding to January/February

Shulchan Aruch: The Code of Jewish Law kept by all observant Jews, compiled by Rav Yosef Karo in Tzefat during the 16th century.

Sotah: Suspected adulteress

Talmud: Literally, 'instruction.' The authoritative body of Jewish Law and Narrative comprising the Mishnah and the Gemarah (c. 500 CE) – a commentary on the Mishnah. The terms Talmud and Gemarah are often used interchangeably.

Tamuz: Hebrew Month corresponding to June/July

Techina: Sesame butter

Tefilah: Prayer

Tikun: Spiritual rectification

Torah: Literally, 'teaching,' referring strictly to the Five Books of Moses, but extended to include the entire body of Jewish teachings.

Tov/Tovah: Good

Tu b'Shevat: New Year of the Tree, marking the beginning of a new cycle of tithes linked to the renewed growth of the trees. Literally, 'the 15th of the Hebrew month of Shevat.'

Tzadik/Tzadikim: Righteous person/s

Yechidah: The highest, most innermost and transcendental level of the soul; literally, 'the single one.'

Ya'acov: Jacob

Yehoshua: Joshua

Yetzirah: Realm of Formation – the third of the Four Worlds.

Yitzchak: Isaac

Yetzer hara: Negative inclination or impulse, (ego)

Yichud: The prohibition of seclusion between a man and a woman who are not married, with the exception of immediate family members.

Yosef: Joseph

Yoshiahu: Josiah

Za'atar: A common Middle Eastern spice consisting mainly of dried hyssop, sesame seeds and salt.

Index